From Weimar to the Wall

From Weimar to the Wall

MY LIFE IN GERMAN POLITICS

RICHARD VON WEIZSÄCKER

*Former President of
the Federal Republic of Germany*

TRANSLATED FROM THE GERMAN BY RUTH HEIN

BROADWAY BOOKS

NEW YORK

Library of Congress Cataloging-in-Publication Data
Weizsäcker, Richard, Freiherr von, 1920–
   From Weimar to the Wall : my life in German politics / by Richard
von Weizsäcker.
     p.   cm.
   Includes index.
   ISBN 0-7679-0301-3
   1. Weizsäcker, Richard, Freiherr von, 1920– . 2. Presidents—
Germany—Biography. 3. National socialism. 4. Germany—Politics
and government—20th century. I. Title.
DD260.65.W45W442   1999
943.087′092—dc21
[b]   98-50156
                                               CIP

FIRST EDITION

Designed by Claire Naylon Vaccaro

Photo-editing and research, Monica Suder, Mill Valley, CA.

All photos copyright Helmut R. Schulze, except the following: insert pages 1,
2, courtesy Richard von Weizsäcker, page 11, top: copyright dpa; page 12,
bottom: copyright Keystone; page 14, top: copyright Ullstein Bilderdienst;
page 14, bottom: copyright Helmut R. Schulze, courtesy Richard von Weizsäcker.

99 00 01 02 10 9 8 7 6 5 4 3 2 1

Contents

A Prefatory Note

When I mentioned to my daughter that I was writing my memoirs, she suggested I choose a title that did not allude to the waning century. Young people always think the world is starting all over again, and never more so than now at the dawn of a new millennium. They know perfectly well they did not grow to adulthood in a vacuum, without roots. But what they hope for is a new world created and shaped by them. Their attitude is a promising sign of their vitality and energy.

Does this mean that Rilke's exhortation—"Anticipate every parting as if it had already come and gone, like the winter that is just departing"—still holds true? "As if it had already come and gone"—no, that doesn't really apply. Nature's seasons have no clear starting point, any more than the moments of history. The futures of both are already contained in their pasts, and none of us can ignore this connection. That is why we have memory.

And yet history cannot tell us what to do tomorrow, it doesn't come with an instruction manual. Today Jakob Burckhardt's statement that history does not teach us how to be clever for one more day but can make us wise forever may sound strange; the great skeptic did not foresee the direction our century would take. But he would surely urge us not to ignore his statement now as the century is coming to an end—perhaps especially not now.

The twentieth century has exposed the extremes of human existence. The ordeals of the age make it difficult and yet all the more necessary to understand the past that involved us so intimately. Our vision of the past will not keep the younger generation from arriving at its own judgments. If education and the passing on of experiences have any meaning at all, then part of it must be to encourage the young to exercise their intellectual powers freely. Young people must find the confidence to trust their own eyes, feelings, and values. But their ability to form their own opinions will be strengthened by a clear awareness that sizable parts of the past will continue to affect their future. Having a sense of history means having some awareness of events that happened before their lives started.

The words I put down here are not a work of history. They simply describe one life—my own—rooted in and integral to one family. The credo of the Weizsäckers has always included taking an active role in the vital problems of the age. Many times events in my family coincided with historical moments. Since my own life followed a similar path, I cannot possibly make a clear-cut distinction between the personal and the historical as I recall events. I am concerned less with broad analyses than with my own impressions as I remember what actually happened to me.

The course of my life crossed four distinct periods of our century, and I would like to characterize each one briefly from my particular vantage point: the Weimar Republic; Hitler and the Second World War; the partition of Europe and Germany in a polarized world; and reunification.

I was a child during the dramatic years of the Weimar Republic. Since my grandfather had left the German state of Württemberg's government and my father was in the diplomatic service, we lived in Berlin, where I felt protected and sheltered. By the late 1920s Berlin had grown into a European metropolis, and while political restlessness and social tensions were very evident even to us schoolboys, I could not begin to understand the extraordinary cultural creativity at work. Without comprehending the full extent of current events, we spent our time in the schoolyard discussing the latest news with childish passion.

At age twelve I became an avid newspaper reader, devouring the papers twice a day.

I was also twelve when Hitler came to power on January 30, 1933.
Because my father was a diplomat assigned to the League of Nations, I
spent most of the following years abroad and did not return to
Germany until 1938, when I was called up for military service. War
broke out soon after, and I spent the next seven years in uniform.

A particular kind of evil was at work, of a sort we could not
comprehend. The ethical norms I had been raised to uphold no longer
seemed to apply. We stared into the abyss and, consciously or unconsciously, it swallowed us up.

The lives and experiences of today's young people are so very
different from ours and the criteria that help form their attitudes deviate so greatly from that earlier period, they must truly wonder how the
monstrous crimes committed by the National Socialist regime could
have been committed. At the end of the war I was twenty-five—an age
at which I both asked questions and had questions asked of me. I am
especially concerned with discussing this period and all that occurred
then. These events are no less significant to me than the concerns that,
decades later, brought me into public life.

I lived the third of my four lifetimes in the Federal Republic of
Germany as it was constituted before reunification. Even as Germany
was being liberated from Hitler's dictatorship, countless numbers were
exposed to new miseries. For example, the memoirs of Hans
Lehndorff, a physician, describe life in East Prussia in the period 1945–
47 and give a glimpse of the difficulties and desperate conditions prevailing in some sections during the early postwar years.

There was no new Versailles Treaty as after the First World War and no repetition of Weimar. The Bonn Republic, as we called it, became a fixture in West European and transatlantic political culture with its Basic Law, flourishing economy, and the skill with which it structured alliances, especially with countries to the east. As the super-powers replaced the traditional Great Powers that had maintained a precarious system of balances, they became possessed by East-West conflicts and the Cold War in the Atomic Age. These two situations came to dominate Germany's actions and attitudes as well.

Twelve million expellees and refugees entered the country and were absorbed to the best possible degree—an even greater feat than the later "economic miracle" that won the admiration of the world. These developments unfolded while the older generation ran the nation. These men had held on to their memories of Weimar and showed little desire to allow younger people a share in governing the new republic. The older group did not step aside until the late 1960s, when a newly created, democratically equalized society began traveling the road to partnership with the West, finding its objective in German-German reconciliation. While relations with East Germany and other neighbors to the east at first grew out of the citizenry itself and the churches, whose links with the East had never been destroyed, the principal political figures adopted a leading role in this effort. In fact, my first political actions were in the area of East-West relations—the focal points being Poland, the German Democratic Republic (GDR or East Germany), and Berlin—long before I was elected to political office.

As the world continued to revolve under what may be called an atomic stalemate, the Soviet Union gradually became a collaborator on issues of mutual security, though we could not yet foresee the total collapse of the Soviet system. Bipolarity seemed inevitable until Mikhail Gorbachev realized that basic reform was necessary to stabilize his nation and keep it competitive. While the Helsinki Accords had paved the way by fostering liberation and civil rights movements in the nations of the Eastern bloc, suddenly Gorbachev's reforms unleashed an avalanche of new freedoms from dictatorial and state-controlled supremacy. The Berlin Wall was forcibly breached, the Warsaw Pact dissolved, the Cold War ended. And without the necessity of a new constitutional law, Germany was reunited. The European Union now set out on the road that led to Maastricht.

The fourth of my four lifetimes, the decade in which I became the first president of a reunited Germany, has given us the crucial challenge of surviving in our newly won freedom. It is our most glorious and yet hardest task. We have not mastered it yet. It will serve to write *finis* to my recollections.

PART ONE

The

Weimar

Republic

Roots in Württemberg

I was born under the sign of a new order. I first saw the light of day on April 15, 1920, in an attic of the royal palace in Stuttgart. But royalty was not my host; the red flag flew from the rooftop above me.

The revolution that put an end to the First World War had transformed the kingdom of Württemberg into a republic. The actual changeover had come about quite peacefully. During the capture of the palace only one act of force occurred: when the new flag was raised. Otherwise no damage was done to the royal residence.

The good citizens of Württemberg in general are not given to violence—they prefer rational compromise. Even the revolutionaries went about their mission with circumspection and good manners. Their last king, Wilhelm II, gave them no trouble. After the king, with considerable dignity, announced his abdication on November 30, 1918, Wilhelm Keil, the leading Social Democrat, declared publicly that the revolution had not in any way been directed against the person of King Wilhelm but only against the concept of a monarchy— an ideal corrupted by the emperor of the same name ruling from Berlin. The respect, the article continued, the people had always felt for Württemberg's king continued unchanged. Even the leader of the Spartacists—left-wing socialists who wanted a Soviet republic established in Germany—acknowledged that King Wilhelm had behaved in exemplary fashion. Asked to comment on the necessity of abolishing the monarchy, the Spartacist leader explained laconically, "It's only 'cause of the system." At the jubilee of 1916 celebrating the king's being on the throne for twenty-five years, the chairman of the Social

Democrats had even announced that although they were republicans, when the great day came they would vote for King Wilhelm for the presidency. To the end he remained a principled, humane, and effective ruler who did all he could to further his province's development. During his reign Württemberg became "an ideal spot."

But now it was the spring of 1920. My parents and their three children—my older siblings—had spent the winter in The Hague, where my father was naval attaché at the German embassy to the Netherlands. Here his job and salary were abruptly canceled. With my mother about to give birth, the family made hasty preparations to travel home—but how could they? All over Germany uprisings were unleashed by both the left and the right: bloody riots broke out frequently and unexpectedly, the national debt rose to 300 billion marks, and the Kapp Putsch—a right-wing extremist attempt to topple the republican government in March 1920—caused further disruptions. This attempted coup drove the national government headed by Friedrich Ebert into retreat, first to Dresden and then to Stuttgart. Once settled, it called on the working class to protect the republic. The response was a general strike—the trains stopped running.

After great difficulty my parents found a small Dutch freighter plying the Rhine to take my family on board in Nijmegen. Thus began a six-day journey down a river on which there was no other traffic, past abandoned ports, past gunfire in Duisburg, past Allied flags in Cologne and Bonn. Responding to the ominous name of the ship *Kinderdyk*, I came close to being born on board. Fortunately, before that happened, the ship arrived at Mannheim and from there we got to Stuttgart, and so I—like both my parents and three of my four grandparents—came into the world in Württemberg's capital.

My father's family came from the Frankish area of Hohenlohe, which the Elector—later King—Friedrich of Württemberg had annexed, though not without help from the French. For quite some time the people of Hohenlohe continued to think of Württemberg as a foreign country and had little inclination to make common cause with the Swabians there. When my great-great-grandfather set out from the old Hohenlohe residence at Öhringen for Blaubeuren in Württemberg to go to school, his mother implored him not to pick up the "ugly" Swabian dialect and to remain true to the Frankish way of speaking. Nevertheless, eventually the various peoples in Württemberg meshed peaceably.

The subdivided, varied, and often somewhat cramped countryside tends to drive the adventurous out into the wider world, though they never forget their beloved home. Its people are more given to reflection than chatter, more inclined to preservation than revolution. Though their feelings are as strong as anyone's, they prefer to keep them to themselves so as not to intrude on the feelings of others.

Many Stuttgart families hail from the countryside, and even industrialization has not entirely removed the markedly rural outlook. Many factory workers still cultivate little plots of land. The good life means being hardworking and frugal, and many people try to attain more than the basic need, meaning a little house of their own.

Swabian inventors and innovators have given the world the astronomical telescope and gasoline engine, the harmonica and the Volkswagen. Even in earlier times, significant impulses to further the intellectual development and unification of Germany came from Swabia. The names of Kepler and List, Hegel and Schelling, Schiller and Uhland, Hölderlin and Mörike recall this inspiration. Some of them moved away from the narrow confines of home to foreign parts, where on occasion they quickly gained greater fame than they had ever enjoyed at home. Helmut Thielecke, the Rhenish theologian who subsequently moved to Württemberg, used to say that Swabians were too clever for their limited horizons. They found it difficult to feel any great love for anyone who had been foolish enough to move away. When Hegel, then world-renowned, died in Berlin in 1831, all the Stuttgart newspapers, the *Schwäbische Merkur,* did to acknowledge the loss was reprint the official announcement from Berlin's *Allgemeine Preussischen Staatszeitung.* Instead of preparing its own obituary, the local paper merely added three words: "born in Stuttgart." This crucial fact had been omitted in the national publication.

My Weizsäcker ancestors, members of the rural middle class, lived near Öhringen where for generations they were millers with varying degrees of success. The poverty they had overcome drove them to help themselves with a vengeance. Gradually they brought into being a family of ministers and scholars, officials and politicians. The process ran its course without the aid of inherited titles, palaces, or estates. Every generation worked to achieve its own position. What remained crucial was individual qualification according to the rules of emerging bourgeois society, which countered the hereditary aristocracy with a nobility of achievement.

Certainly the driving force behind this bourgeois growth was to be found in industry, in small and mid-sized businesses, in artisanship, in trade, and in manufacturing. To strive for and hold on to independence, individuality, and autonomy, to be obligated to no man—that was the prevailing work ethic. Wanting to be an independent object rather than a subject, to be and remain free, however, meant of necessity creating a bourgeois public sector and accepting responsibility for its success. It was important to broaden one's horizons, to acquire a well-rounded education that could also prove highly useful in one's own career. In line with the ideas of the new humanism, it was essential for people to better themselves with a general education, take part in public affairs, and pursue cultural aims. Even more than the arts, the sciences found strong supporters among the middle classes.

This is how the artisan, business, and educational strata of the bourgeoisie merged, and the Weizsäcker family evolved the same way. The talented son of the last ancestor to work as a miller, my great-grandfather, became the family's first intellectual. Recipient of a stipend from the Hohenlohe sovereign, he became a theologian and canon in Öhringen.

His younger son, Julius, followed in his father's footsteps and took part in the Tübingen ecclesiastical uprising of 1848. The Tübingen collegiate church was founded during the Reformation as a "royal fellowship" for the upcoming theological generation and played a crucial role in the long cultural history of southwestern Germany.

Hegel, Hölderlin, and Schelling emerged from it. Julius Weizsäcker, who accepted the ideal of unity and republicanism for Germany, was influenced by the groundbreaking historian Leopold von Ranke into becoming a historian also and spent his academic career at six universities. He won his chair at Tübingen against the other applicant, Jakob Burckhardt; finally he held a professorship at Friedrich-Wilhelm University in Berlin. Always an independent scholar with a politically aware mind, he was a type not at all uncommon at the time.

The oldest son of the Öhringen canon, Carl Weizsäcker, my great-grandfather, was a theologian in Württemberg. Specializing in ecclesiastical history, his principal work was entitled *Das apostolische Zeitalter der christlichen Kirche* (The Apostolic Age of the Christian Church). Dedicating his undogmatic mind to historical research, his translation of the New Testament—which ran to twelve editions and in which he tried to apply to the Greek original the results of his research—became famous. He was considered unorthodox and independent, both liberal and conservative.

His lively political interests, however, kept him from isolation in an ivory tower. He was named rector of the university of Tübingen and later chancellor, a position that made him the state's representative to the university and thus an ex officio member of the Württemberg parliament. There he spoke quite independently from government viewpoints.

My great-grandfather was also a pioneer in the ecumenical movement. An anecdote survives about his friendship with Bishop Haefele, the Catholic prelate from Rottenburg. The Bishop had returned from the First Vatican Congress in Rome, where the dogma of the Pope's infallibility was established. The Bishop of Rottenburg was the last German bishop to relinquish his deep-seated objection to the dogma. When Weizsäcker met him at the Tübingen railway station, the platform was iced over. Offering the Bishop his arm as support, he remarked, "To prevent downfallibility."

Soon after, my great-grandfather saw himself reflected in the mirror of downfallibility. It was his habit to stop at a Tübingen bakery each day to buy a soft pretzel sold by a small boy for three pfennigs. One day he could find only two pfennigs in his pocket and asked the boy if he would hand over the pretzel for the lesser sum. The boy replied that my great-grandfather could bring the pfennig the following day. But what would happen, my great-grandfather asked, if he should forget? He wouldn't forget, the boy assured him. "But what if I die in the night?" The boy replied, "It really wouldn't be such a great loss."

The theologian's son, my grandfather Karl, took a path that led to politics. After enlisting at age seventeen and fighting in the Franco-Prussian War of 1870–71, he studied law. A member of the judicial bench and the ministry of justice, he took an active and crucial part in the centenary revision of the German civil code. His special contribution was to coordinate the various state ordinances. Subsequently named Cult Minister, as the post was still so elegantly called in Württemberg at the time, he was eventually appointed state foreign minister and in 1906 named Württemberg prime minister, a post he held until the 1918 revolution. He kept his distance from all bureaucracies and parties, and all his life he remained loyal to his king.

I remember my grandfather as short and stout with a quick and sharp tongue, a man both witty and kind. As a young municipal judge he once officiated a divorce action brought by a jealous husband. The judge asked, "Now just look at your wife for a minute—d'you really think someone would wanna run away with *that*?" "Ah, nah," was the reply after some hesitation, and the plaintiff withdrew his suit. Weizsäcker had the reputation of being clever, a skilled diplomat, and temperamental, shifting from sarcasm to politeness, with an emphatic sense of self and a strong judgmental streak, though most of the time he kept his opinions to himself. His friend and colleague Gottlob Egelhaaf believed Weizsäcker carried an "iron fist in a velvet glove."

While studying in Leipzig, he met the daughter of Victor von Meibom, a supreme court judge originally from Hessen. The two young people soon became engaged, and the following day an amusing exchange took place between them. After asking her why she had

accepted his proposal, she replied, "That's not the sorta thing you tell."
She then asked what he would have done if she had turned him down,
and he said that he would have consoled himself with the thought,
"What a silly goose that one is." No, a silly goose my grandmother
certainly was not. She had a keen mind, radiated a quiet, simple
warmth, and had strong feelings about propriety and decency. Do
nothing you can't justify to yourself—that was her rule for herself and
for us. Helpful and strict at the same time, she cared less about the
impression she made on others than about her own standards.

These were unsettling, increasingly difficult times for the prime
minister, with the Reich becoming increasingly isolated within the
community of nations. Given the tension existing between the central
power and the provinces, the latter had little influence on the Reich's
foreign policy, not to mention the Kaiser's provocative actions.

The kingdom of Württemberg still steered a fairly liberal course.
In 1907 Stuttgart was host to an international socialist congress that
included August Bebel, Rosa Luxemburg, Lenin and Trotsky, Jean
Jaurès, and a left-wing revolutionary from Italy named Benito
Mussolini. The conference vote was unanimous in its condemnation of
capitalism and war. The Kaiser in Berlin was outraged that permission
had been given to hold this convention in the Swabian capital: that
sort of thing, he noted, was so typical of the "royal republic of Württemberg."

When the First World War broke out in August 1914 and enthusiasm for the cause was at its height, Karl Weizsäcker told his intimates, "This war will end in a revolution." He, who lost his oldest son
in the early weeks of the war, had little influence on events in the
Reich. He never wavered in recommending moderation, taking all
peace feelers seriously and refusing to pursue expansionist policies. He
was outraged at the dispute, as obstinate as it was senseless, between
the German provinces as to which would take over foreign territory
that had not yet been conquered but was already taken for granted.
His greatest bitterness was devoted to the German U-boat campaign,
whose meager chances and fatal consequences he foresaw clearly. If

Württemberg only had more money, he was apt to say, they could build more lunatic asylums to house all the U-boat idiots.

Eventually the crucially wrong steps were taken, and only a short time later Reich chancellor Theobald von Bethmann Hollweg stepped down and the United States declared war on Germany. At that time the army high command sent two Reich ministers to sound out Weizsäcker to see if he would become Reich chancellor. He declined without a moment's hesitation. It was already much too late, especially as for all practical purposes the Reich government no longer had any power because the military had it all.

The war ended, revolution broke out, and the last royal prime minister of Württemberg—who had been given a hereditary barony by his king in 1916—cheerfully resigned. He promptly cleared out his official chambers to make way for his Social Democratic successor, Wilhelm Blos. Bearing the man no animosity, he could never suppress his penchant for pointed commentary. His name for the incoming family was "the Blossoms."

My Parents and Their Families

The world that now emerged was entirely new. Countless families had been plunged into unhappiness; one of my father's brothers and two of my mother's had died in the war. Now a new, strange, puzzling, and uncertain epoch set in.

Of course the lost war was not the only reason for the fall of the monarchy. During the final decades of the empire, something had been germinating beneath the surface that was often called a revolution. However, in reality it was a transitional phase, when quite thoroughly outdated imperial elements had been kept artificially alive. The monarchs and the privileged hereditary elite were not alone in acting in ways that caused this situation. The established "nobility of achievement," most especially the upper middle class, had also failed. Lacking an adequate understanding of the inexorable changes in a society undergoing industrialization, they had done nothing to further the new conformations. They had become a propertied class whose ideal of free and responsible independence had increasingly given way to a defensive posture. Enmeshed in their preoccupation with prosperity, the "bourgeoisie" had gradually become a partisan political idea. Without its attitude there would be a large piece missing from the concept of the "class society," even if there was not *one* middle class but, according to Max Weber, several middle classes. Not only the monarchy but also the bourgeois epoch as traditionally understood ended with the First World War. Citizenship in the social sense began to evolve.

Though members of my family belonged to the educated middle class, not the propertied middle class, the tensions of the age did not spare them. My mother, Marianne von Graevenitz, was born in 1889

into the Württemberg branch of a Mecklenburg family in existence
since Napoleonic times. Before the war her father was the military
representative of Württemberg in Berlin, where my parents were married in the Church of St. Matthew in 1911. At the end her father
served as adjutant general to the king of Württemberg, with whom he
left the royal castle in Stuttgart on November 9, 1918, moving in the
direction of Bebenhausen. To his contemporaries he was a white
knight; I never had a chance to know him.

His wife, my grandmother on my mother's side, came from a
Swabian family of merchants. A beautiful woman adored and admired
by all her grandchildren, she was a warmhearted grandmother, always
ready for anything. She and my oldest brother carried on a correspondence in verse for over ten years.

As a young girl my mother found it rather difficult to adapt to
society's conventions. All her life she had a lively social conscience, a
strong will, and high standards—especially for herself. The warmhearted sigh of her beloved and sensitive Swabian grandmother Klotz
was in vain: "Submissive and happy all the day—if only my little
Marianne could be that way."

My mother was always appreciative and enjoyed her family, but
she was certainly never submissive. One of her first acts of rebellion
was to object to the verse chosen for her confirmation: "Take joy in the
Lord, He will provide what your heart desires." She longed for challenges, not vague promises. Even as a teenager she did volunteer social
work, looking after foster children and giving piano lessons to two
little girls in an institution for the blind. As for all dances and especially court balls, she thought them repulsive and sulked until her
parents granted her the highly unusual right to refuse all invitations to
such events. When playing cards with her parents she always kept a
more or less visible piece of serious reading matter on her lap under
the table; one of these works was Lily Braun's *Memoiren einer Sozialistin*
(Memoirs of a Socialist). This book, widely read at the time and still
fascinating today, was written by the pacifist daughter of the Prussian
General von Kretschmann and, incidentally, my own wife's great-aunt.

In the prewar empire, which flowered so precipitately and conspicuously, my mother became increasingly aware of the growing abyss between flourishing wealth and growing poverty. In my own childhood I first heard from her the well-worn phrase "Anybody who isn't a socialist at twenty has no heart; he who isn't a conservative at forty has no brains." The saying fairly closely reflected her view of the world, although it made little sense to me in later years. After all, I always thought that a conservative without a highly developed social sense was a bad conservative, just as a socialist can never go far wrong, despite all visionary urges to remedy every instance of injustice, if he respects what is worth preserving. I know my mother would never disagree with that view.

Humane and social impulses guided her from childhood onward, though she never studied political theory or, like Lily Braun, underwent a profound break with her world to become a revolutionary. She concentrated her efforts on more practical acts. For example, during the war she was a ward and surgical nurse in field hospitals. When, after the war, women were first allowed to vote for the Weimar parliament, my mother also occasionally took part in revolutionary rallies, voting somewhat to the left of the conservatives. It's true that when women were asked which way they would vote, the older generation of my family would say, "We won't know until we find out how Grandpapa is going to vote."

My father, Ernst, born in 1882, joined the navy as a cadet in 1900 and remained in the service until shortly after the end of the war. Though the navy symbolized the unity of the empire, which he espoused without reservations, that commitment never made him forget his Swabian nationality for a minute. Nevertheless, Admiral Alfred von Tirpitz's naval policy, supported and promoted by the Kaiser's enthusiasm, had become a challenging expression of Germany's claim to a larger "place in the sun." My father enjoyed the human element; all his life he happily recalled the camaraderie among his crew, which numbered over two hundred. Though the buildup of the navy caused a great deal of friction between nations, the sailors enjoyed a close relationship with their British counterparts and went on long voyages aboard every kind of vessel all the way to the Far East. Delicate watercolors painted by my father recall these adventures. As a young lieutenant he was a guest at the dinner table of the fabled old Dowager Empress of China and observed how the servants, even before all the guests had left, poured the remnants of wine from the glasses back into the bottles—but that was apparently part of the local culture.

He soon had a more immediate experience of Kaiser Wilhelm's influence on the navy. During his training period he was put in charge of a group of cadets; then, as a young lieutenant, he became the trainer for Prince Adalbert, the only one of the sovereign's sons to join the navy. Subsequently, as the so-called flag lieutenant to the fleet commander, he had frequent opportunities to observe the Kaiser. His opinion remained clear enough, though always discreet, and he interpreted His Majesty's dramatic conduct as expressions of an excessive pride that indicated both conceit and insecurity. He also saw that the Kaiser was all too easily swayed whenever conflicting opinions skirmished within the navy's upper echelons.

My father was in the habit of quoting Lloyd George on the outbreak of hostilities: "We all stumbled into the war." On board the flagship *Friedrich der Grosse* he took part in the Battle of Jutland— the only major naval engagement between Great Britain and Germany during the First World War. Measured only by losses, the outcome was in Germany's favor, but the battle failed to break the British naval blockade and did not affect the course of the war itself. In the debate concerning unlimited U-boat warfare my father shared his father's deep concern about this senseless project, which critically jeopardized the further course of the war.

Toward the end of the war he was assigned to the navy staff headquarters as liaison officer, serving under chief of staff Paul von Hindenburg and quartermaster general Erich Ludendorff—the real German decision makers during the latter stages of the First World War. He found Hindenburg a quiet, uncomplicated, even-tempered man who never shifted responsibility onto others and who gave no sign of political leanings. Ludendorff was cut from quite a different cloth. He exhausted his energies in ceaseless plans and decisions and made use of the highest authority of the Supreme Command in all major questions of domestic and foreign policy, though more often than not he was in no position to understand or test the importance or consequences of these decisions. My father participated actively but had no influence in discussions centering on peace efforts. On November 9, 1918, he was in Spa.

He never put any stock in the myth of the stab in the back. While my mother had long ago sensed the deep social roots of the coming revolution, it was the empire's foreign policy that caused my father concern: the arriviste attempt of the incipient empire to usurp a leading role on the world stage against Britain without support on the Continent; and the fatal lack of more sensible moderation in conducting international affairs. The tenor of his thinking and further actions was grounded in these considerations. His immediate first reaction to the Entente's conditions for armistice and peace was, "They'll give rise to the next war; our children will have to fight it." Thus he foresaw the turns our lives would take.

Early Years

But now the first order of business was to make a fresh start in a new and puzzling world. There was no end to our worries that Germany would be divided into two parts, north and south. Riots were the order of the day. Rosa Luxemburg and Karl Liebknecht were assassinated by right-radical conspirators, as, subsequently, were Matthias Erzberger and Walther Rathenau.

Following his inclination, my father tried for a position in the foreign service. The job possibilities here were vague and meager at first, and he had a family of six to feed. Then he received an extraordinarily tempting offer from Georg Klingenberg, the Berlin industrialist. Reason, he wrote his parents, argued in favor of a career in business, but his heart drove him to the foreign office. Finally his inner voice won out.

His first assignment led him to the peace and quiet of a neutral country as consul in Basel. The city was marked by its rapid economic and industrial rise, the traditional and current rank of its university—with the names of Jakob Burckhardt, Friedrich Nietzsche, Karl Barth, and Edgar Salin—and especially its aristocratic families—Vischer, Burckhardt once again, Sarasin, and other notable names. Access to them was difficult; a newcomer passed the test only when one of them said something like, "Enfin notre genre" (Finally, one of us).

In spite of numerous incidents caused by a few of the roughly twenty-five thousand German nationals there, it was easy to get along with the Basel authorities. Invariably an amicable tone prevailed in the notes they exchanged with the consulate. When I came to Basel in 1987 during a state visit, the cantonal representatives presented me with a photocopied collection of the well-preserved notes; the gift warmed my heart.

In Basel my parents made two friendships that lasted all their lives. One was with Carl J. Burckhardt, Jakob's nephew, himself an outstanding historian and author of a biography of Cardinal Richelieu, a writer of the first order, and a close friend of the poet Hugo von Hofmannsthal. By profession he was actually a diplomat; later he served as high commissioner of the League of Nations in Danzig (now Gdansk) and president of the International Red Cross in Geneva. He remained a close personal and political friend to my parents through all the years of chaos and crises. I did not meet him until after the Second World War; he was a man with a skeptical mind and an irresistible personality.

The other particularly close relationship developed with Robert and Margret Boehringer, and this friendship included the whole family. At this point too I stumble across my own earliest memories. I can still recall the trusting and submissive respect I felt on December 6, 1923, for the Basel Santa Claus, who was ever benevolent and never unmasked—none other than Robert Boehringer. I was the beneficiary of his calm and kindly strength well into his old age and my middle years. Next to my parents he was the most important adult in my life; his invariably unquestioning support played a crucial role in my development. Though he was a highly successful consultant to the Basel pharmaceutical industry, his principal occupation was that of private scholar. Many experts thought him perhaps an even better archaeologist than his brother Erich, even though the latter had risen to the rank of president of the German Archaeological Institute. Robert was a poet, the most intimate—and, in the end, the closest—friend and heir of Stefan George. When I was eleven years old in Berlin, he took my brothers and sisters as well as me to a studiolike, awesomely high-ceilinged attic apartment. He sat me down next to an old gentleman who put his strong hand on my neck in a way I can feel to this day. Much later I learned that I had met Stefan George on this occasion.

With his Jewish wife, a highly talented lawyer, Robert Boehringer, a native of Swabia, emigrated from Germany to Switzerland as early as 1932, anticipating the coming horror. Settling in Geneva, he worked for the International Red Cross and helped out wherever he could. More than anyone else he stood by my father during the sensitive professional conflicts of the Nazi period and even later during the Nuremberg Tribunal. His support was that of a critical friend who exuded deep trust and understanding. After the war, when Theodor Heuss presided over the Federal Republic, he made sure that Boehringer's German citizenship was restored.

At the end of 1924 my father was transferred to Copenhagen. The Danes' principal problem was their German neighbor, but tensions were overcome with good will and, at least for the minorities on both sides, with considerable success. It seemed to my father that the most important thing from a political point of view was to balance the Entente bloc in the League of Nations, which was such a problem for Germany, with a silent alliance of neutral nations.

Our whole family enjoyed the Danes' humane qualities. Their talent for living was just about unmatched among European peoples.

I learned to read and write in the German Petri school. Of course I had already mastered the rudiments at home, just as throughout my childhood I reaped great educational advantages from the loving and steady intellectual encouragement of my family, especially my mother. Though I hardly ever had actual help with homework—that too was a household rule—my advantage over other six-year-olds in the Copenhagen school became evident when on the first day of classes I recited Schiller's poem "The Glove." In later pedagogic-political discussions it was easy for me to understand the glaring problems caused by the family- and environment-driven inequalities of opportunity.

In Copenhagen I made an anonymous friend. Every day an elderly gentleman rode down the street where I happened to be playing. He impressed me deeply, high on his horse. I greeted him respectfully, and he waved back warmly. The more time passed, the more familiar he became. No word ever passed between us. I was stunned to learn his identity one day: the King of Denmark, who, in the peaceful world of that time, rode out alone every afternoon.

I had a girlfriend as well, whom I adored. She was the youngest daughter of the German head of mission—my father's boss, Ulrich von Hassell, son-in-law of Admiral von Tirpitz, later one of the conspirators and victims of tyranny after the attempt to assassinate Hitler, on July 20, 1944. His daughter Fey, called Li, who like myself was six or seven years old, and I along with our older siblings played elaborate games, especially charades. Li grew into a wonderful woman, married, moved to Italy, and later wrote an impressive book about the harsh years of resistance and her imprisonment by the Gestapo. I am still proud of the friendship she showed me in our early school days.

My father was called back to Berlin shortly to oversee preparations for the Geneva disarmament conference and, soon after, to head the section dealing with the League of Nations in the foreign office— at that time the most important political task in German foreign policy. This assignment marked the beginning of a period of regular travel for him between Geneva and Berlin. He was as persuaded of the necessity of the League of Nations as he was aware of the almost insurmountable task facing the German delegation. The general secretary of the international organization, Sir Eric Drummond, discussing the German position, said to my father, "You are *in* the league, you are not *of* the league." The European victors of the First World War dominated the conference, and progress toward equal rights of security and peace came to a standstill. The hopes Germany had placed in the British for more generous terms were rarely fulfilled; the United Kingdom in general held back precisely where its initiative was most needed—that is, in restraining France. But the worst blow was that the isolationist United States refused to participate in the conference.

From 1927 to 1932 my father and the German delegation worked on models to prevent war and maintain disarmament. He composed memoranda about a European economic community. Of course the big guns of the great Geneva conference were not diplomats but ministers

representing their governments. The interplay of the two clashing ideologies repeatedly sparked friction.

Diplomats must work circumspectly behind the scenes to weave
the necessary web for as long as it takes to achieve a satisfactory result.
But again and again elected officials thwart the diplomats' efforts, insisting on picking the fruit before it is ripe. The stars on the Geneva
stage worked impatiently on scoring points that could be politically
exploited at home. "They thought in terms of speeches," was the way
my father described the relationship between his boss, Gustav Stresemann, and the French foreign minister, Aristide Briand, although he
always had the highest respect for Stresemann's strenuous efforts to
lead Germany out of international isolation. At the time he probably
underestimated the unbearable pressure Stresemann was under, not
only in the Reichstag but more specifically within his own party. The
statesman, already ill, eventually broke under this burden at an all too
early age.

Domestic policy is and remains embedded in and motivated by
foreign affairs. Diplomats may often feel that the parliamentary and
public-relations tone of voice used at home constitutes an amateur
hindrance to their professional work. Nevertheless it is hard for diplomats and the people they represent if they underestimate the very real
and crucial influence of domestic policy on foreign affairs. In Geneva
the absence of this awareness may have played a discernible role, but
not a critical one. It weighed in all the more heavily at a later time,
when the National Socialists seized the reins of domestic policy.

Childhood

Our move from Copenhagen to Berlin in 1927 brought us a private life and, at least for my own childhood, happy years in the bosom of my family that shaped my life. In the Wilmersdorf district on Fasanenstrasse, at the corner of Pariser Strasse quite a distance from the elegant Kurfürstendamm, we occupied one floor of an ordinary Berlin apartment house. The building next door housed among others a concert pianist and the Social Democratic politician Rudolf Breitscheid.

My father was away a good deal, but whenever he was able to take part in ordinary family life, he was respected as the supreme authority. Guided by highly developed ethical principles and deep affections, as is only fitting for a proper son of Swabia, he seldom expressed his feelings. He was the model for a trait we all shared to some extent: Apparently we must first overcome internal barriers before we are prepared to believe that feelings do not change when they are expressed. While this shyness or reserve may be understandable, it is also a weakness; most people, after all, want to feel and hear warmth and sympathy instead of assuming their existence. Nevertheless, my father preferred expressing himself in rational discourse. If he thought a man's behavior was reprehensible, he merely called him stupid. He had a horror of talking about himself. On the other hand he did reveal his innermost self in the watercolors I mentioned earlier.

He was a good mathematician, and I have him to thank for my interest in history and geography. He preferred the socially conscious Schiller to the more remote Goethe, although he could recite half of *Iphigenia* by heart, and was fond of quoting for example Orestes's praise of his friend Pylades: "With rare skill you manage to combine / The gods' advice and your own wishes." He enjoyed the handsome wording of this verse as well as its successful description of the diplomat's task.

My mother was the heart and soul of the family, bearing the full burden of the work. Her steady hand guided our everyday upbringing, the deep power of her love accompanying the development of each child. Unfailing watchfulness and selfless interest in raising us had become her whole existence. Her personality was marked by strong-willed self-discipline never muddled by nervous excitement. I never heard her raise her voice. It was not her way to be openly strict, nor was strictness ever necessary, given her much more effective use of inexorable logic, which she clearly preferred over compromise.

Of course when she insisted that we do chores we thought were unpleasant, she was aided by highly transparent euphemisms. The harsh "have to" was reinterpreted as kindly permission. When I, the poor baby of the family, was encouraged night after night to be the first to go to bed, I was always told, "Tonight you may start the dance." Everything we had to do, we were "allowed" to do.

Keeping in mind each child's strengths and weaknesses and the eight-year age difference between oldest and youngest, my mother encouraged us individually and yet managed to hold the family to-gether. While we lived in Berlin, my oldest brother, Carl Friedrich, born in 1912, approached secondary-school graduation. There had never been any doubt that he was highly gifted, since he had exhibited high intelligence early on. At age eleven he taught himself astronomy and told his interested mother, "If there's anything you don't under-stand, you can always ask me." It was not only because he was the oldest that he stood out; he was admired but never envied by his sister and brothers. Of course I interrupted him and his friends more than once because, naturally enough, I preferred playing to philosophizing.

My sister, Adelheid, four years older than me, was known as "the font of reason." I never saw her embroiled in a quarrel or spat. Instead she provided consolation to anyone needing comfort, and in her quiet and inconspicuous way she helped everyone. Of course from my perspective in those days she was too soon addicted to reading Hölderlin, Mörike, and similar romantics instead of joining me in more amusing pastimes. But when my protestations against the annoying intellectuality of my older siblings grew too vociferous, she placated me warmly by giving in, explaining to the others that the house was more peaceful if I was happy; how true! Her skill at producing delicate drawings and watercolors, inherited from our father, allowed her to express her nature and feelings through the harsh life that lay ahead. Watercoloring became second nature to her. Never expressing disagreement through the sharp instruments of woodcuts, she preferred the magic of delicate watercolors that rose from deep wells. Blessed with the gift of overlooking others' weaknesses, she stressed only their good points, encouraging and thus transforming them.

The brother closest to me in age was Heinrich, born in 1917. In spite of all our differences, during my childhood he was the person closest to my heart. He had remarkable growth spurts and became a lanky giant, fearless and filled with idealism. Although he quickly came to prefer spending time with his heroes in history to playing with his little brother, he was selfless enough to spend time with me and never made me feel his superior strength. In the youth organizations he found a group of like-minded boys to whom he turned with his gifts for friendship and loyalty and his chivalric nature. Subsequently, when the group was to be absorbed into the Hitler Youth, it disbanded.

This was the challenging environment to which I, the youngest, had to learn to rise. The idea, universally believed, that the youngest "naturally" had the easiest time of it always filled me with appropriate outrage. It was said that those things older children fight and struggle for just fall into the lap of the youngest. No, they were allowed to wear their older brothers' and sisters' castoffs, and if on a Sunday their father asked one after the other who wanted to go for a walk in the Grunewald with him, when he got to the baby he announced that of course the child would come along.

So it was a matter of learning to assert myself as energetically as possible, occasioning my father to see me as the "biggest little rascal of them all." In fact I fear that my siblings suffered more from my unwanted insistence on being given the floor than I did from my worry that no one would pay attention to me. My favorite ploy was to place myself at the spot in the apartment that had the most traffic, from which vantage point I announced my commentaries and judgments concerning any and all praise and reprimands. When I was only seven years old, my visionary brother Carl Friedrich pronounced me a parliamentary speaker in training. One of my parents' friends, a woman with a sharp wit, called me simply "cockadoodledoo"—without of course thinking for a moment of a parliamentary delegate.

I held a monopoly on a single talent within my family: I was the only one who managed to learn to speak the Berlin dialect flawlessly. I was taught early on to use language to express even the most obscure thoughts as exactly as possible. This concept promised a rich field of endeavor to which I too devoted myself happily. Once at supper somebody remarked that the wife of the deep-sea explorer Piccard had given the gift of life to her fifth child. And I in all innocence wondered, "So what you're telling us is that she's had five children, killed the first four, and then gave the gift of life to the next one?"

No one in my family made life difficult for me. I have a lucky talent to spy a safe harbor in plenty of time whenever defeat threatens and to infect the entire household with my joy when I've found a pleasurable activity. Or if I was determined to meet a deadline, I found I could summon up unsuspected strengths. My mother told me later that once, when I was sick in bed, in anticipation of a birthday party I had practically hypnotized myself into getting well. And in retrospect it seemed to my loving sister that pleasure in the baby quite eclipsed any problems in raising him.

The high points of my childhood included trips, games, Christmas celebrations, and music within the family. Vacations were spent at alpine farms in Hindelang in the Allgäu or in Mösern in the Tyrol, at a fisherman's village on Spiekeroog Island in Holland or with a minister in the Mark Brandenburg. When we heard a rumor that leeches lived in Lake Möser, my father used my fear of them to teach me to swim when I was still very young. Taking me out where the water was quite deep and then abruptly letting me go, he shouted at me to make for shore to save myself from the vermin.

At Christmastime we were not allowed to buy presents for our parents—what would be the point? Instead we children wrote the story of that summer's trip. Late on Christmas Eve the family gathered in a circle, the children took turns sitting on the floor at the center and reading the magnum opus, "What I Did on My Summer Vacation." This custom led to a tradition, frequently demanding and yet fulfilling, that we carried on long after childhood.

Some toys appeared only at Christmastime, among them an ancient magical dollhouse for my sister. The oldest child was given a toy theater with an actual curtain, scenery, and figurines, most of it made by adults in the family who had some artistic talent. Each figurine was painted, cut out, and pasted onto cardboard, and a wooden block attached to the bottom enabled it to stand. The pieces could even be moved by wires so they could be maneuvered across the stage. On some Christmas Eves my parents staged a well-known fairy tale such as "Puss in Boots," with lines they had written that were larded with fairly unvarnished characterizations of the children and their mischief, complete with educational pointers tailored to the various individuals. It was an indescribably delightful and uniquely effective entertainment.

Most Sunday afternoons saw a conflict between reading aloud and games. For practice as well as pleasure we read classical plays, assigning each person a part. But when the readings consisted of lyrical sonnets, I looked for escape routes. I responded quite differently to Schiller's ballads. They stirred my boyish feelings deeply, especially "Die Bürgschaft," a preference that I never outgrew.

Another area of endeavor was music. Once again Mother gave the impetus by playing herself and inspiring all of us. A chamber trio composed of the three younger children was formed, but unfortunately I often proved a hindrance to my sister at the piano and my brother Heinrich on the cello because of my slow progress on the violin. My unflagging love of music was greater than my interest in playing, which tended to flag all too quickly. It takes years of practice, after all, to coax a truly good tone from the violin. I thought that my teacher was much too kind and absolutely enchanting; Beatrice Bentz, a native of Switzerland, headed the Bentz Quartet, a women's string ensemble very popular in Berlin at that time. On many evenings our apartment played host to memorable quartet performances. The setting was modest, but the circle of listeners was more than illustrious: Werner Heisenberg, Ricarda Huch, Hans J. Moser, and Ina Seidel attended regularly. Later, in the school orchestra with many other violinists as mediocre as myself, I was retrained to play the trumpet and the trombone. For a while I even had ambitions to become a singer. But in the end neither my talent nor my diligence was enough to reach the goal I had so cheerfully anticipated.

My mother was also a passionate games player, ambitious and skillful. For years her favorite was mah-jongg. She also loved a card game called Racing Devil, a kind of solitaire with multiple players in which speed was of the essence. Only very late in her life did several grandchildren manage to jeopardize her supremacy. Though getting on in years, she still managed to win. The most popular guessing game involved divining the intended person's name from others' statements about flowers, sports, cheeses, paintings, and other categories that could be matched to someone we knew or a historical figure.

When it came to written games, we all liked word dissection— using letters from one word to form others—best. If, for example, we dissected the name Stresemann, we gained a point for a one-syllable word such as "rest," two points for a two-syllable word such as "manner," but six points for a three-syllable word. The game led to weird results whenever several generations played together. Once my grandmother played with us and won with the source word *veranda*. And why? Because she used an extra *h*: in her youth the word was spelled *verandah*.

Chess was also in our repertoire, and of course Carl Friedrich was

the unequaled grand master of the family. He spent hours in his dark-
ened bedroom working out moves for long-distance games with his
teacher and friend Werner Heisenberg, ten years his senior.

Later we added bridge, a game played only within the family.
You had to marry into the family if you wanted to play with us—of
course not because we were such outstanding players but basically
because this game, like all the others, was played not for competition
but for the sake of family togetherness.

In those years we children had the unparalleled good fortune to
find all the stimulation we needed entirely within the family. Was it
family pride that kept us together? Others may have seen it as such
from time to time. But it was more like a tapestry of evocative language
and references to events we had experienced together, which could be
communicated to others only with great difficulty. Familiarity with my
family's habits, our mutual trust, and shared experiences were all responsible for my sense that life was more interesting in my family
circle than elsewhere. Over time I became aware repeatedly that fate
had given me an advantage of incalculable worth when it placed me in
this particular family. My upbringing was and still is the decisive background for—and greatest blessing in—my life. As well as a place
where I could flourish, our Berlin home was also the base for the other
vital element in my life: my circle of friends. In some cases my relationships with them were formed through family co-optation.

And yet all this enrichment took place in comparatively modest
circumstances. Our apartment was spacious enough but unassuming
and fairly dark. A ray of sunlight rarely made its way through our
windows from either the street side or the backyard. By this time the
government was issuing emergency decrees that primarily affected
public services. Our family had butter for breakfast only on Sundays.
When I broke my arm at the age of ten and required relatively complicated and expensive treatment, there was no state aid. Social want was
evident everywhere in Berlin. Every day singers and their accompanists
playing barrel organs turned up in the rear courtyards of apartment
houses and begged for coins, even bread. Occasionally my mother

took me along to the Neukölln section of town, where she served as temporary conservator for children born out of wedlock.

Such glimpses of increasing poverty and the kind of hardship that jeopardized honesty, health, and life itself gave me my first view of conditions beyond my family's horizon. The consequences of unemployment without material state aid were devastating. Even at my young age I saw that productive community living ceases when the chasm between what some people need but must do without and what others take for granted has become too great. As a result I developed an interest in political problems chiefly in the social area. Only much later did I acquire a conscious awareness of the importance of foreign relations, with examples drawn from my father's diplomatic experience. The two realms are not as different as might appear at first glance, since the requirements of living together either in a neighborhood or on a globe are not at all unalike.

After skipping over third grade, I started at the humanistic Bismarck Gymnasium in Wilmersdorf when I was nine. Latin and math were less easy for me than Greek and history, physical education, and music. But our school did not shelter us from the real world. We began to read the newspapers and during recess discussed whatever we had gleaned from the headlines. Of course our youthful curiosity far exceeded our understanding. We registered the fact that unemployment had risen to seven million and that in the fall of 1930, 107 National Socialists and 80 Communists were elected to the Reichstag. I clearly remember our debates—as passionate as they were immature—on current events.

The leading roles in these discussions were taken by Jewish students, almost half the class, who were for the most part the children of doctors, lawyers, businessmen, and academics. During this final phase of the Weimar Republic we ardently analyzed the almost daily Berlin street brawls between the Right and the Left (as a rule we disapproved of both sides), the repeated elections to the Reichstag, and, naively, even the cabinet assignments made by each new administration. Of course we were still very young; but we were not so childish as to miss the growing explosiveness of the times entirely. All the same such glimmerings did not dampen our youthful high spirits and did nothing to affect our total absence of prejudice.

As I went to school in Berlin during the late Weimar period, I saw few signs of traditional and widespread anti-Semitism (sentiment not unique to Germany). And yet I could not help asking myself in later years: What had I known, what had I learned, about Jewish religion, history, and identity? Practically nothing. We sensed that there were differences between us, but we did not shun each other. We were in and out of each other's homes, and at times we might even fantasize about marrying the sister of a friend from that other world when the time came. Of course I also learned the names of outstanding Jewish personalities who had a large part in shaping the culture, science, and economy of Germany and the renown of our country throughout the world. When I first climbed the stairs of the Leo Baeck Institute in New York in the early 1970s and saw the portraits of these great people, I was all the more impressed and moved because I recognized names familiar from childhood.

And yet I knew far too little of their internal tensions and schisms, of the difficulties of Jewish self-awareness, and of the dangers of ignoring a separate identity. Which of my young Jewish friends had felt the pressures of reconciling life in their own families and religion with their daily attendance in school and the culture it represented? Might there have been others whose homes reflected conflicts with assimilation, the concept that for so long was seemingly accepted? What momentous consequences might grow out of the fact that the assimilating Jews were expected to adapt absolutely to the values and objectives, the customs and outward image of their environment? That, in other words, Jews should stop being Jews in order to solve the problem of their position as a minority? And was it even possible for them to adapt to a world made more or less in the Christian image, and would that world ever really accept them? Did not the Jews, even in the liberal Berlin-Wilmersdorf of my childhood, remain friends but always other? In fact, wasn't it true that more often than not assimila-

tion seemed more of a provocation than the choice to remain different? We recall Theodor Herzl's words: "I try to enter into society and
to keep only the faith of my fathers: I am not permitted." What he
experienced then was the futility of wanting to be a true patriot.

All the Jewish students were still in school at our graduation in
1937. Our class closed ranks against the outside world. By this time all
of us understood how dark the clouds over Germany had grown. And
yet none of us had any idea of the horrors to come. The scant knowledge most Germans had of Jewish history and identity remained incomprehensible and came to have unspeakably fatal consequences.

PART TWO

Hitler

and the

War

The Seizure of Power

Once more I must retrace my steps a little. In the years from 1927 to 1933 Berlin was the focus of my mind and heart, my real home, and it has remained so to this day. During these stimulating years my father was transferred to Norway to serve as the German envoy. After the strain of his time at the League of Nations his stay in this country—a land of breathtaking natural beauty and freedom-loving individualists and eccentrics—provided rest and relaxation, restoring him physically and mentally. There he made many friends, among them Bishop Eivind Berggrav, the primate of Norway who subsequently became the heart of the resistance to German occupation and had close ties to German resistance groups.

Only one of the Weizsäcker children made the move to Oslo with my parents: my sister, Adelheid. With her musical talent for languages she quickly picked up Norwegian. When I joined them for three months, I had private lessons from the Swabian Vicar Hermann Häberle. He explained the Lord's Prayer to me and gave me an appreciation of it that has withstood all excesses of faith or depths of doubt.

The wonderful Norwegian literature and painting was avidly appreciated in Germany. Politically, on the other hand, Norway tended to identify more with Great Britain, though the prevailing ideology was Scandinavianism. Nevertheless my parents did not suffer from political tensions, at least for the present.

But events in Germany snowballed dramatically. Because I was a twelve-year-old who had to attend school, I was living with friends of my parents in Berlin. As January 30, 1933, approached, I witnessed its coming in a way that made a lasting impression. One of my uncles had invited me to a horse show in the Berlin Sportpalast. I was happy and excited—I had never been to such a performance. During a jumping event, which I was following with bated breath, newspaper sellers abruptly ran through the rows of seats, converging from all sides and shouting out the headline of their extra edition: "Hitler appointed!" Even though I was unable to understand the full implications of this development, I did grasp that it meant something momentous for us in Berlin and for my parents in Norway. The reaction of other spectators reflected that same realization.

But my parents were far away. My life as a schoolboy simply went on. There was no clarity about coming events. Among the so-called educated middle class there was still little understanding of the shifts and resentments in the lower social classes and just as little awareness of the great lacunae in their own conservative thinking. Many who did have some inkling of these currents were strangely powerless.

The "movement" had been widely underestimated. Even though explicit written declarations of its program and objectives were numerous, they had not been taken seriously or even acknowledged. When my father was asked in 1931 and 1932 to report to the Reichstag's foreign office on the League of Nations and participate in discussions with members of the National Socialist Party, he had muttered about "schoolboys playing at politics." What became clear was the diplomats' widespread, dangerous ignorance of the country's mood.

Soon friction between natives and Germans became evident in other countries. In Oslo as well it suddenly became necessary to place the German embassy under police protection. In his official capacity my father declared that he would carry out orders from Berlin insofar as they could be reconciled with his conscience. Though his experiences in Geneva had taught him that the Hitler administration's first foreign policy catchphrases amounted to a renewed threat of war, he nevertheless believed that in the long run the crisis could be resolved. When Foreign Minister Konstantin von Neurath asked him if he was prepared to become state secretary for foreign affairs, he declined. But like most of his colleagues he held on to his conviction that the established, skilled German diplomatic corps, whose members knew and trusted each other, must not be abandoned in favor of the new dilettantes and that therefore he could not resign his post. Reich Chancellor Heinrich Brüning, who thought highly of my father, encouraged him in this belief.

As a result he saw himself accepting a position dedicated to defending the actions of the new government. But how long could that government continue unassailed? Would it accomplish anything at all, either in foreign relations or domestically? These were and remained the crucial questions of politics and conscience—for my father and many others.

School Days

Early in 1933 my father was appointed German envoy in Bern. After Basel and Geneva it was his third posting to Switzerland, and it served to strengthen the family's ties of friendship in that country, especially as my brother Carl Friedrich met his wife, Gundalena Wille, whose family lived in Mariafeld on Lake Zurich. Gundalena was a doctoral student of Carl Burckhardt's, and her spirited temperament, self-confident style, and warmth became a blessing for our whole family.

Much as I had liked living in Berlin, the prospect of another move soon filled me with eager anticipation. After all, the burden of the actual work fell not on me but on my mother, who in her lifetime dealt with twenty-six moves altogether. Her deliberate and punctilious ways gave the lie to the old adage that five moves were as destructive as a devastating fire.

My problems started when I changed schools. When I left Berlin, I had for the first and only time been the proud recipient of the best report card in the class. When I took the entrance exam for the first year of secondary school in Bern, which corresponded to the grade I would have attended in Berlin, I barely passed in German and not at all in the four other subjects. They didn't fool around at the Bernese secondary school; no outside distractions were permitted and especially not politics. Instead there was a lot of cramming. Intensive tutoring helped me to pass the second time I was generously allowed to take the test, and I spent three busy years with my Swiss companions, with whom I have stayed in touch to this day. Though secretly I

learned the Swiss German dialect, I was embarrassed to speak it in my
classes, which were generally conducted in German anyhow.

Understandably, Swiss feelings toward their neighbor to the
north soon began to sour. Switzerland felt threatened, a sensation that
intensified when the dictators in Germany and Italy formed closer ties.
Shrill verbal attacks from Germany only increased their nervousness.
In an address in Freiburg im Breisgau, Hermann Göring spoke about
southern neighbors whose "brains were coated with muck." Our history teacher, a man whose mind was as sharp as his tongue, took out
his dislike of Germany on me, the son of the German chief of mission.
But my fellow students, no less patriotic Swiss than he, placed themselves protectively in front of me out of loyalty to their classmate.
Though we worked hard, we were also fanatically devoted to sports.
One of us, Marc Hodler, went far: student world champion in Alpine
skiing, later president of the International Skiing Association, he is
today vice president of the International Olympic Committee. My
skiing skills never quite rose to the level of my classmates', but I did
become a pretty fair middle-distance runner, even if I never managed
to break the two-minute record for the 800-meter run.

In spite of more than a few poison-tipped arrows shot across the
frontier, my father was troubled less by binational relations—which
remained reasonably normal—than by events within Germany and
their effects on the international situation. On April 1, 1933, he saw
for himself the shattered window panes of Jewish stores in Altona, and
he grew very emotional when he told us about this experience. In a
church in the Tiergarten district of Berlin he stood by as a swastika flag
was placed next to the altar during a ceremony. The Enabling Act was
issued. When the so-called Reich Bishop Müller was named to head
the Lutheran Church, another group founded the Confessional
Church, establishing its basic aims in the Barm Declaration. Pastor
Martin Niemöller was taken into custody for the first time.

On June 17, 1934, Franz von Papen, who was still vice chancellor, spoke in Marburg; at the time his words were felt to be very bold.

He objected strongly to the "unnatural claim to unlimited authority," to the "plebes," and to the unbridled radicalism of the National Socialist revolution, and added, "No nation can afford a permanent revolution from below if it is to justify itself before history. At one time or another the movement must come to a standstill, at one time or another a firm social structure must emerge, one that is held together by an incorruptible administration of justice and an undisputed ruling power. Nothing can be created by perpetual revolution. Germany must not be allowed to become a one-shot deal." Nazi propaganda minister Joseph Goebbels immediately prohibited any reprinting of the speech.

A power struggle ensued, culminating in the massacre of June 30, 1934—the so-called Röhm Putsch—which eliminated Ernst Röhm, leader of the Brownshirt security organization (SA or *Sturmabteilung*, "storm troopers" in English), and his followers as threats to Hitler's leadership. Hitler and Heinrich Himmler, chief of the rival "Blackshirt" SS *(Schutzstaffel)*—Hitler's bodyguards—then used this occasion to unleash arrests and killings throughout Germany that were both selective and random. Among the victims was Edgar Jung, who had written von Papen's Marburg address. The most basic rules of a constitutional state were blatantly ground underfoot. I remember my parents' agitation that day. They clearly explained to me what was happening and told me to listen to the radio all day and report any news to them immediately.

Shortly thereafter, during a National Socialist attempt at a putsch, Austrian Chancellor Engelbert Dollfuss was murdered in Vienna. August 2, 1934, saw the death of Reich President Hindenburg, who had imposed a last flicker of respectability and political decency on the new regime.

Most nations hesitated to react openly to Hitler's new Germany; many were even eager to cooperate. They accepted Germany's resignation from the League of Nations in October 1933 and the reintroduction of compulsory military service in March 1935. One year later they even accepted the renewed occupation of the Rhineland.

Hitler also crafted a naval agreement with Great Britain, a new concordat with the Vatican, and an understanding with Poland.

The diplomats in the foreign service searched desperately for a way out. For the present the National Socialist leadership was ambivalent about career diplomats. On the one hand the staff of the foreign office was told that "heads would roll"—a threat laconically countered by one of my father's close colleagues with the question "But where are the heads in office?" On the other hand the Nazis were eager to prevent potential international risks by using all the skills their experienced professionals could bring to the table.

German diplomats felt the strain more and more keenly. Many of them, like my father, were horrified by the new rulers' rabble-rousing, their reckless strong-arm tactics in international relations. And yet these diplomats were patriots who loved Germany. At the end of the First World War they had been upset by the harsh conditions imposed by the peace treaty, which they felt to be highly immoral and in the long run politically untenable. Of course the victors are almost always deluded by what they may safely exact from the vanquished, being especially thirsty for reparations. As early as 1914 Germany too had planned to demand considerable sums from its enemies, who had yet to be vanquished. Although by 1930 a good many of the crushing conditions of the Versailles Treaty had been fulfilled, this fact hardly affected the nub of the widespread and understandable feelings in Germany concerning Versailles. You did not have to be a reactionary German nationalist to feel that the Treaty was calamitous, especially if you feared the enormous effect of the Nazis' political propaganda against Versailles.

Some Allies too expressed similar sentiments. As head of delegation of the British treasury the well-known economist John Maynard Keynes had participated in the peace negotiations but not gained enough adherents to his ideas for lightening the burden of reparations on Germany. His characteristically brilliant and sharp pen wrote the shortest and most pointed, though much attacked, evaluation of the Treaty by describing three Western statesmen who played leading roles at Versailles—French premier Georges Clemenceau, British prime minister David Lloyd George, and American president Woodrow Wilson:

> These were the personalities of Paris—I forbear to mention other nations or lesser men: Clemenceau, aesthetically the noblest; the President, morally the most admirable; Lloyd George, intellectually the subtlest. Out of their disparities and weaknesses the Treaty was born, child of the least worthy attributes of each of its parents, without nobility, without morality, without intellect. (John Maynard Keynes, Essays in Biography, vol. 10, 1972 ed., p. 26.)

It came as no surprise to anyone outside Germany but seemed almost a matter of course that German diplomats such as my father would pursue a policy of revisionism concerning Versailles with the unconditional priority of preserving peace in the process. Meanwhile nations permitted Hitler to exploit his first foreign-policy successes. When would the ends be discredited to the point where they could no longer be tolerated because of the means he employed domestically? Would his successive victories go to his head? Might he soon declare any danger of a world war to be a pipe dream and therefore feel even more tempted by a small, limited war?

The crucial moment in my father's professional life came early in 1938, when he was recalled from Bern and asked once more to accept the post of state secretary in the foreign office. In the meantime Ribbentrop had replaced Neurath as foreign minister. My father searched his conscience; the problem troubled his every waking moment. Ambition had never been his driving characteristic. Five years earlier, Neurath had offered him this important position when the international situation had been far less disturbing, and he had turned it down. He consulted his intimates and friends. These included General Ludwig Beck, who told him that a military chief of staff could not wait until war broke out to resign—by then it was too late. The person heading the diplomatic corps, on the other hand, would have to cling to his position and hold out to the bitter end in order to stall or avert disaster.

My father knew far too little about the true nature of the Nazis and had no premonition of the unspeakable crimes to come. When he had formed his concepts of how the world functioned, he lacked the imaginative power to grasp the demonic nature of the evil already at work. He concentrated intensely on the central question of whether the foreign office still had a chance to employ its comparatively intact weight in the cause of peace. To his mind this was the only—and in the long run decisive—argument, and on this basis he accepted the job.

A few months later, in the spring of 1938, the first—and as it would turn out, the last—incident arose that put his thinking to the test: the so-called Sudetenland crisis. War was avoided by a hairsbreadth. Today there is almost universal agreement that if the former Allies had not agreed to a peaceful solution of the Sudetenland conflict with the Munich Pact, the world might have been spared the worst misery. "Munich" has become a symbol of weakness and delusion, a word to tar any thought of submitting to dictators with a brush of moral reprehensibility and political suicide. Today all this seems obvious. But at the time of history's crucial moments, can the people involved ever know as clearly as later generations—instructed by the mirror of history—the right course to follow, the consequences of holding out or giving in, or whether any action or decision will make a difference?

How did matters stand at the time? The dilemma for the French and especially for the British—Germany's rearmament—has been discussed repeatedly by modern historians. What is certain is that Churchill's rise to lead Britain's resistance against Hitler was a consequence of the decline of British prime minister Neville Chamberlain, who had signed the Munich Pact.

In Germany three blocs grappled over policy. One was the war party. Hitler was determined to get the Sudetenland, and more: If military confrontation was unavoidable, he wanted to get it over with quickly. Himmler and especially Ribbentrop also urged brute force. Goebbels—who looking out his window had seen a Wehrmacht unit march down the Wilhelmstrasse to palpable and silent reserve by the crowd—expressed greater caution.

Opposing the war party was the active resistance, still in the process of formation. Generals Ludwig Beck, Franz Halder, and Erwin von Witzleben, Admiral Wilhelm Canaris, and Lt. Col. Hans Oster belonged to this group, as did a number of diplomats including Adam von Trott and Albrecht Haushofer. Should the Sudeten crisis come to a head and end in war, they planned to exploit the people's fears to eliminate Hitler. My father was closely allied with these men and acted as their consultant. Haushofer called him the "nonenrolled member" of the group.

During the entire Sudeten crisis, however, diplomacy kept my father busier than he had ever been or would ever be again. He represented the third position: to keep the peace at whatever cost. Sir Nevile Henderson and Bernardo Attolico, the British and Italian ambassadors, my father's friend Carl Burckhardt, at that time High Commissioner of the League of Nations in Danzig, and of course my father plotted intensively. After some dramatic days Hitler was persuaded to make a minor concession to Chamberlain, though at first this was insufficient. Finally he passed the ball to Mussolini, who at the last minute suggested a compromise that, when the European "Big Four" met, he knew would turn into the successful basis of the Munich Pact. Ribbentrop was boiling mad because the whole affair had played itself out behind his back. Hitler was furious for a long time because, as he believed, he had backed down. Far into the second half of the war he called his yielding at Munich his greatest foreign-policy mistake. Chamberlain and French Premier Edouard Daladier, for their part, departed with relief. The whole world saw photos and newsreels of the two statesmen being enthusiastically greeted at their homecomings: "Peace in our time."

A load had been lifted from my father's heart. His close confidant and colleague Erich Kordt, an active member of the resistance group, had only this to say about the Munich Pact: "The second-best solution."

Who has the right to condemn another? In the aftermath of our all too dreadful experiences, today we hold the conviction that tyrants' international blackmail can be thwarted only if we put no faith in their promises of future good behavior or let ourselves be pressured even in part. Munich is and remains the historical warning. I am as convinced of that truth as I am proud of my father's actions in those days.

At the time he did not foresee the horrors to come. During the Sudeten crisis he was obsessed with the possibility of imminent war, his greatest fear. Every fiber of his being felt the horror and misery of war to be humanity's greatest calamity. The First World War had already wrought terrible sorrow in his generation and his family. It is true that my father worked for changes in specific provisions of the Treaty of Versailles and to that end considered diplomatic pressure a legitimate weapon. But it is also true that he was not prepared for even a moment to court violence to further a policy of revision.

If he did not think that he could play an active role in preventing war, he would not have accepted the position as head of the German diplomatic service. As long as he found ways to stave off war in his office, he employed them. His influence during the Sudeten crisis was comparatively central. Immediately after we had bypassed the abyss of war, he wrote, "A relief without compare; the children, our life—all of it felt like a new gift."

"Remember us with mercy," Bertolt Brecht called to those who came after—at the time he meant, "when the time has come when man is helpful to mankind." Did we become that? Mercy includes understanding that knowledge of history demands of us not to equate events from the past with what we know in the present. Nothing can be compared with past events, but the plea for mercy trickles down from generation to generation. Munich was the last happy day of my father's life. Or so he felt, and that is what he wrote. Every day we, his family, noticed how serious and silent he grew thereafter.

The last happy day came and went, because very soon the

situation grew critical, this time unalterably. At first within the country: On November 9, 1938, the pogroms against the Jews occurred. Anyone who witnessed them, as I did as an eighteen-year-old around the Gedächtniskirche in Berlin, could never forget the expressions of organized brutality. Most passersby, like me, walked past the smashed store displays in silence, uncomprehending. Persecution of the churches also increased. My mother repeatedly intervened in vain with Himmler on behalf of Pastor Niemöller. The sense of Himmler's response was, "We will not rest until Christianity has been destroyed. It is a sickness." One time she and a theologian friend traveled to Karinhall, Göring's home, to plead for the release of ministers. Göring's wife had facilitated the meeting. But Göring gave them a curt "No" and left the room, though he showed himself once more, in a doorway, and with a pacifying remark handed his visitors little packets of coffee—a gesture that made my mother furious. Today we cannot imagine life in those days.

The government's system of informers and surveillance became more and more sophisticated. We began to use simple codes when writing notes and letters to each other. A dash at the end of a sentence meant that the exact opposite of the written statement was true. Pfeifer stood for Hitler, Himmler was called Engelke, Niemöller was Immermeier, Italy represented Aunt Camilla, and so on. When my father had to have minor surgery and the hospital put him under general anesthesia, my mother never left his bedside so she could interrupt at once if he talked loosely in his ether dreams.

The crucial turn in foreign affairs came when Hitler broke the Munich Pact and marched into Prague in the spring of 1939. The die was finally cast in London. Any further Western surrender to Hitler became unthinkable. Poland received a guarantee of help from the Western Powers if Germany attacked. For weeks my father desperately tried to convince Himmler and Ribbentrop that Britain and France would inevitably declare war on Germany if Hitler committed any acts of violence against Poland. But the worst occurred just the same. For the sake of his influence, so successful in the Sudeten crisis, my father vainly spent the following weeks and months mutely accepting the stigma of having remained in the camp of the rulers. Now, as he wrote, the meaning of his work was destroyed.

On the day before the outbreak of war my mother noted, "Can God let it happen that *one* person unleashes this catastrophe over Germany and all of Europe? And our sons? I am not prepared to sacrifice a single one to this war. The circle of the family, the endless riches in the children, all our pride—I know how it is from the last war, when the word was: gone. Then life goes on, and what was ours never, never returns. New people come who never knew those who were our pride." In her passionate love for us she wrote it all down.

The following morning war broke out. The day after that, on September 2, 1939, my brother Heinrich, her second son, fell in the Tucheler Heide in the Polish Corridor.

Graduation

In my own life, during the spring of 1937 final exams were instituted for students in the next-to-last year of school. These boys were exempted from the final year of school, so that they could become new recruits for the Wehrmacht. In January 1937 I left the school in Bern, which I had come to love, and passed the last three months of the school year with my old classmates at the Bismarck School in Berlin. I chose history as my major field for the exam, and my special topic was the French Revolution—a sharp contrast to the reality and mood in Germany under Hitler. Biology was mandatory for the whole class, and we were tested on our knowledge of genetics and race ideology—key doctrines of the National Socialists. Because that obligation suited us as little as it did our biology teacher, we engaged in a mutual conspiracy involving the questions and answers; the teacher was eager to spare us and save himself from having to deliver pseudoscientific avowals of faith. In other ways too a wholesome spirit pervaded the school. The Jewish students were among the best in the class, and our decent teachers managed to make sure that the grading conference assigned them reasonably fair final marks.

My own final exam was made easier for me not only by the excellent schooling I had enjoyed in Bern, but also by the reputation of my brother Carl Friedrich, which had not faded even though it was eight years since he had passed his final exams brilliantly. Thus my weakness in math went largely undetected. Besides, to calm my nerves my mother came up with an effective remedy for the afternoon before the exam: We spent hours at my beloved Berlin zoo. Such a visit certainly is a help in ordering priorities. The teachers I feared most lost their power to frighten me when I saw the striking resemblance they bore to quite different life forms. In the end everything went smoothly.

Although I was now the proud possessor of a diploma, I was far from being mature. Because I was not quite seventeen and therefore too young for conscription into the compulsory Labor and Military Service, I was given permission—quite unusual for young German men at the time—to study abroad for two semesters. I spent the first six months in England. At Oxford I encountered many of the inimitable British traits. I found the students fair and unemotional, helpful and often openly snobbish, slow to start but superior at the "finish." They seemed conciliatory and yet knew precisely the limits beyond which they refused to go. When, as happened at the large university convocations, they spoke their Oxford Latin, all educated humanists of the Continent thought that they were using a British dialect.

They argued hotly for the necessity of a moral politics, without feeling even the slightest scruple in the face of "right or wrong, my country." A country doctor in Wiltshire, with whom I spent two wonderful months of the summer vacation and whose hobby was the study of Napoleon, whom he admired without reservation—something not at all rare in Great Britain—argued with me night after night the whole time I spent with him about the outbreak of war in 1914. If only the Germans had not violated Belgium's neutrality, he believed, the British would never have entered the war against us. There are some things an Englishman just will not doubt—and once he has made up his mind, he will not doubt himself.

The doctor's duties toward his guest were just as indisputable in his mind. During school and semester breaks it was the custom in the county where he lived to hold tea and games parties almost daily. A few of his neighbors indicated that he and his family were, of course, always welcome—but only without the lad from the land of German barbarians. These people were merely reflecting the general mood. My host declared just as invariably that of course his family would bring the guest or would not come at all. Without the slightest hesitation and without ever mentioning it to me, he accepted temporary estrangement from his neighbors for the sake of sacred hospitality.

In 1937 I encountered only one German whose reputation was entirely unassailable in Great Britain: tennis champion Gottfried von Cramm, who won the Wimbledon finals. His combination of a tough competitive spirit and overwhelmingly attractive fairness brought honor to the name of Germany.

I saw firsthand the British monarchy's tradition of splendor at the coronation procession of King George VI and his wife, Queen Elizabeth, today's Queen Mother. The greatest applause during the convoy of coaches was awarded to Stanley Baldwin, the prime minister who pulled the strings that persuaded Edward VIII, George's older brother, to abdicate because of his relationship with Wallis Simpson.

I spent the winter semester of 1937–38 at the French University of Grenoble, which housed a company of international students gathered to learn French. The place offered the ideal opportunity to observe the differences in behavior between the two cultures. When at the end of the semester we had written a common final exam in a large lecture hall, it became clear that the majority of Anglo-Saxons and Scandinavians had failed while students from southern and southeastern countries had passed with flying colors. The reason was simple: one group, keeping rigidly to the rules, had not used any additional study aids nor copied from each other. The southerners and Balkan students, on the other hand, had taken advantage of reference books, crib sheets, and oral resources of every kind. Of course they were not morally inferior—they were merely conforming to the culture in which they were raised.

For me these were exciting, liberating months—the first I had spent far from home. Only little touched by events in the world, I set out on exploratory trips into achieving adulthood, not always an easy undertaking. Young people, changeable in their moods and not at peace with themselves, try to appear more grown-up than they are. In my case this state of mind was complicated by the consequences of traditional pedagogic maxims learned at home and in school. I was left to my imagination, the perusal of encyclopedias, and cautious reconnaissance patrols to solve the great mystery of what it is that divides humanity into male and female. No wonder, then, that today we have fallen prey to the opposite, an all too early explanation that holds nothing back—though that, too, is not always particularly helpful. Youth is a wonderful time but not always to be envied.

When matters come to a head, criteria for selecting recruits may be relaxed. On orders of the German consul I saw a French doctor in Lyon who examined me for the German army. What he then dutifully did was attest that I indeed possessed the physical requirements to go to war against France. In those days that was how matters were arranged between two states preparing to make war against each other.

I returned to Germany, where I was not allowed to continue my studies before doing my Labor and Military Service. So I put on a uniform. Seven years passed before I was rid of it.

National Labor Service

My memories of my superiors in the Labor Service are not favorable. Many ended up there because they could not get into the armed services. Most of what we did was a primitive imitation of army life. In the absence of a weapon, the spade became the sacred object of the drill book. Each of us had a second spade beside the work spade, which we had to keep shining clean and handle like a rifle. We even practiced presenting it so that it sparkled in the sunlight. We could just as easily have presented a broom, but our platoon leader provided an ideological explanation: "Everything we know about history we owe to excavations. Spades are used to excavate. So history is only the history of the spade."

We were deployed to the Schorfheide at Lake Werbellin north of Berlin to uproot tree stumps and plant new seedlings, but I do not believe that many of our baby firs grew to full height. Though I was the only one in my platoon of fifty to have graduated from an academic secondary school, the camaraderie we developed taught me a lot in more than one way. My support came primarily from a small group of Berlin stove fitters who initiated me into the solemn mysteries of life. They were highly amused at the lacunae in my knowledge regarding the relationship between men and women, but they were quite willing to rectify my ignorance.

The Outbreak of War

In the fall of 1938 I was conscripted into a machine-gun company of the Ninth Potsdam Infantry Regiment. My brother Heinrich had joined the same company two years earlier as an officer cadet senior grade and risen to the rank of second lieutenant. Though his heart and professional aspirations were dedicated to the Middle Ages, especially the period of the Holy Roman Emperor Frederick II, he was unwilling to submit to the political indoctrination of the increasingly brown ideology taught in history departments; he therefore decided to become a professional military officer.

His intellectual interests and Swabian origins made him an outsider in this traditionally Prussian regiment. The prevailing worldview in the Potsdam officers club was nationalist-conservative, and these men were well pleased with the advancement and new standing of their soldiers. After all, on March 21, 1933, so-called Potsdam Day, Hindenburg had made Hitler an honorary Prussian and had so sworn him in—while our regiment presented arms.

The more time passed, the clearer it became that Potsdam had not entirely forgotten what was permitted to be considered genuinely Prussian. Sitting around the fireplace in the officers club, the young men, following an old Prussian tradition, spoke openly among themselves—more openly than they did outside these walls. Prussia was the source of the constitutional state. The regimental officers considered the arbitrary arrests and killings by the SS on June 30, 1934, to be serious offenses and passed contemptuous judgment on the vulgar forms of expression used by party leaders. They felt that they were a "republic of free grenadiers."

But there was no help for it—the soldiers inevitably embodied a contradiction. On the one hand the regiment became for many a refuge from the propaganda and infiltration of the despised party. Even if the well-known statement by Gottfried Benn—that the army was the aristocrats' form of emigration—need not be considered a generalization, it did apply to many of the bright young men in the Ninth. On the other hand they were dedicated to restoring the Wehrmacht and to the military as the model of society, marked by a sense of duty to the state and united under the oath that Hitler—with his sure instinct—had directed to himself personally immediately after Hindenburg's death.

Outside the barracks the bells of the Garrison Church rang out a familiar tune every hour on the hour, its words exalting loyalty. Sincere loyalty—to what? To tradition? Or to the new regime? Loyalty or distance? In my superiors I saw a mixture of both. One, the leader of my own company, Lieutenant Ekkehard von Ardenne, was incidentally the grandson of the woman many of us came to love as "Effi Briest" thanks to her story as told by Theodor Fontane in his novel. Ardenne was ordered to muster his troops to commemorate Hitler's and Ludendorff's march of November 9, 1923, at the Munich Feldherrenhalle, also known as the Beer Hall Putsch. Because this ceremony suited him not at all, he discoursed at length on the topic of November 9, 1918, the end of the First World War, merely closing with the remark, "The newspapers will tell you what occurred on November 9, 1929."

Another leader who set the tone for us younger officers was Captain Graf Baudissin, who held the key position of regimental adjutant. After the war he became a general in the federal armed forces and the father of the concept of "citizens in uniform."

At the end of August 1939 general mobilization was announced. I had completed a scant year in uniform. As ordinary soldiers we could not know about the political developments that transpired just before war broke out. We knew nothing of the secret agreements between Stalin and Hitler that created the decisive prerequisite for the German attack on Poland. The German newspapers were full of reports describing Polish acts of provocation and attacks on German minorities living there. Who could know whether the reports were true? We believed the greater part of them.

One night we marched from our barracks to the railway station. A few family members and passersby lined the streets, as silent and worried as it is possible for a crowd to be. What a contrast with the enthusiasm the populace showered on our troops at the start of the First World War!

At the time we soldiers were no better or worse than our fathers, who had gone to war twenty-five years earlier, or our children, who today pass judgment on us. Like soldiers all over the world we had ties to home. We had been trained and compelled to obey. And so we marched, without enthusiasm but aware that we were doing our duty.

Early on the morning of September 1 we crossed the Polish frontier. The following day we had our first engagement with Polish troops, on the railroad embankment of Klonowo on Tuchel Heath. The first officer of the regiment to fall was Heinrich, a few hundred yards away from me. I spent the night watching over him, my dearly beloved brother, until morning when we buried him, together with the other casualties, at the edge of the forest. Then we marched on. How to describe my feelings on that day? Hardly begun, the war changed my life forever. Nothing was ever the same again.

War and Resistance

The war ran its course, bringing misery to all sides, incapable of being understood in what was then the present and quite incomprehensible in retrospect, especially for younger generations. Why think about it again at this late date, when more than half a century has passed? What can we expect to gain from such a backward look? Though I generally place contemporary history at the center of the reflections I share with younger people, I hesitate to tell them about my own wartime experiences. The story of one young soldier can surely contribute little to the universal significance of the war, which is of interest to everyone and affects the life of all concerned. And yet the fact remains that the young soldier is forever changed by the experience. How can we reconcile such a discrepancy?

Should we even try? One individual's story seems insufficient to strip history of its abstract nature. Who could possibly believe that one personal experience can serve as an example for the whole complex course of events?

But of course I cannot narrate the larger history; I can only add my own small set of explanations to the many others. Thus, while at best I can make a contribution to "history written from below," there is little I can do to help historians in their meticulous work. What matters to me is being true to what I remember. My memories are my constant companions in any case, recalling both the bad and the good events I witnessed and lived through during a period fraught with problems of every sort.

There is no doubt that, like everyone else's, my memory is subjective. For the most part unconsciously, it is selective. But even though it skips over or perhaps alters events, it cannot change the nature of the person whose memory it is. Even if it were to try, the reader would hardly be fooled.

Today questions put to those of us who served in the war are asked primarily to learn how it could have happened. What we young men did and thought—did it reflect what we knew and were able to understand? Many older people say that they did not know they knew nothing because they did not know there was anything to know. I'm not about to pass judgment on that claim. The only important question—the question each of us can put only to himself but one that must be asked—is not what we knew but what, given the actual situation, each one could have known and was willing to know. To find those who are guilty is a separate task, and performing it does not give any of us the right to a clear conscience.

Our regiment fought in Poland, and when those battles were completed, we were sent to the border with Luxembourg. I will never forget the mood of the crowds in the villages we passed through in Germany's western Eifel region. We had just come from the area of the so-called Polish Corridor, thus restoring Germany's direct link with East Prussia that the Versailles Treaty had severed, and of course the East Prussians cheered us. At Germany's western frontier, on the other hand, we were considerably less welcome. Talking to us quietly in the night, local farmers explained that it didn't matter to them one whit whether they lived under German, French, or even European rule if only they could be spared a war.

But the victorious campaign against France soon followed, unleashing an enormous response in Germany. Our regiment was involved and then sent back east, first to the Weichsel River near Thorn and later to the new Polish-Russian border. From the beginning of the war against the Soviet Union to its end we remained on the eastern front.

In the summer of 1941 I suffered my first war wound, but after four weeks in the field hospital I was fit to rejoin my unit. In the winter of 1941–42 my regiment was almost entirely wiped out only a day's march from Moscow, almost within sight of the capital. After a short period in Jutland while the regiment was reconstituted, we were sent back to the front, first to a position near Leningrad south of Lake Ladoga. Later, during the retreat, we were moved to Nevel, the Baltic islands, and Lithuania until finally we arrived back in East Prussia, where in March and April 1945 what remained of the regiment fought its toughest battles of the whole war. I was lucky to escape Russian captivity; a new wound spared me. During the first half of April I was transported to Potsdam by way of Königsberg (now Kaliningrad) and the Baltic.

So what had we experienced, those of us who had been no more than twenty or so and had lived through the entire war? One of my friends answered simply, "We survived." This friend, Axel von dem Bussche, felt this survival as a heavy burden all his life—and this was a man who in war proved his willingness to sacrifice his life in a plot against Hitler.

Nevertheless these years influenced and tested the lives of all the young soldiers, Axel included. They were full of contradictions, a mixture of cold and warmth, youthful lightheartedness and deadly seriousness, decency and hopeless ethical dilemmas. Isolated within our units, we lived more intimately with each other than we ever would again, and we experienced day-to-day events together and dealt with them within ourselves. Before the war, in basic training, we had often enough bellowed out the song with Friedrich Schiller's words on liberty, with its ideal of fearlessness as the element that makes us free. But none of us felt any such sense of freedom; after all, Schiller had not been writing a poem to fit the current situation. But our war sorely tried our hearts, and we too were tested on our readiness to risk our safety for another. A few were so brave that they never seemed to know fear, but that kind of man was merely strange and of little help to others, especially if he served under an ambitious superior officer or suffered from what we called a "sore throat"—the glaring effort to win a medal to hang around his neck. A man with that kind of temperament stood alone, apart from those who struggled bravely with their fear, concealing it from others so as not to infect them. Unlimited trust could grow among these men. We formed friendships seldom possible under other circumstances, and these friendships never faded. Many of us were assigned greater responsibility at an early age than we ever had in later years, no matter in what positions we found ourselves.

And yet we never had a sense of Max Scheler's "moment of truth" and "the secret of a culture's self-assertion," which separates the genuine from the fake and reveals the true substance. At the time none of us was interested in what Scheler, writing in 1915, thought to be "the nature of war." Even without taking into account today's devastating weapons systems and recalling only my own experiences of war during the Hitler period, I, like most of us, cannot see war as anything but the cruel destruction of life.

Cruelties of another sort than the kind I saw at the front have been shown in a traveling exhibit, "War of Destruction," which the Hamburger Institut für Sozialforschung (Hamburg Institute for Social Research) assembled in 1995. Designed to demolish once and for all the belief that the German army had remained "clean," the exhibit set out to show that the Wehrmacht had been an increasingly active participant in war crimes. Most of the examples were taken from White Russia, the march on Stalingrad, and Serbia. It is difficult to remain unaffected by the sight of the texts and pictures in the exhibition. In an order to the troops concerning their behavior "in the Eastern region," Field Marshal Walter von Reichenau had decreed that the major focus of the campaign was to be directed against the "Jewish-Bolshevik system"; the objective was the extermination of Asian influence on European culture. Some commands and units in the Wehrmacht did take part in barbaric outrages against defenseless Jews, civilians, and prisoners of war. We did not need the exhibit to tell us that we cannot keep claiming that we were an army of unassailable integrity, an uncompromising haven of decency in the midst of evil.

All that I have seen and lived through led me to two separate observations. The first is that it is really no less necessary to make distinctions. Though there can be no question that the Wehrmacht committed crimes, it would be quite another matter, and quite wrong, to speak of *the* criminal Wehrmacht. It would make no sense to ignore the differences in conditions prevailing during the French campaign, in the Afrika Korps, at the Eastern front, and in the rear echelons of the East. Lumping them together would produce collective judgments of guilt or innocence. Any such approach would quickly lead to an ethical no-man's-land, effectively aborting the process of perception, and yet that process is what is most important, not only for succeeding generations but also for the war veterans themselves, especially in the area of ethics. But that process—and this is the second observation—cannot be satisfied merely by people's refusing to generalize. It can be realized only in the individual's willingness to look straight at the abysmal situation the war brought for him in his military unit and his personal situation.

Therefore I must once again start with how I experienced the war within my unit. Basically the only concrete knowledge we had concerned losses in our own ranks. We practically never had an overview of the military course of the campaigns and hardly ever received reliable news about outrages against defenseless victims in the rear echelons. We heard vague rumors—which, admittedly, we failed to check out adequately for far too long. But in the front lines we rarely saw war crimes committed by soldiers in fighting trim. The very few instances we witnessed involved wounded German soldiers who, as the front lines moved back and forth, had fallen into enemy hands and, when they rejoined us, were found to be mutilated. The very thought of capture by the Soviets inspired fear and terror.

One time we received an order from above not to take prisoners. I vividly recall our outrage at this thinly veiled command to commit murder. Those of us at regimental headquarters—I was regimental adjutant at the time—simply did not pass the order on; as far as I could tell, no one in our regiment ever carried it out. Further, on the German side we had the notorious "commissars' order," which specified that all political commissars assigned to Soviet units were to be shot upon capture. To us this decree was itself an atrocity and a violation of the rules of war. I know of no single instance when anyone in my regiment followed this regulation.

Since all the men facing each other across the battle lines worried chiefly about their own survival, we can assume that our foes were not so different from ourselves. We saw examples of this fact everywhere. I remember a silent night march in long lines in which we suddenly sensed, coming in the other direction, an equally silent line. We could barely make each other out, and yet we realized abruptly that the others were Russians. Now the crucial point for both sides was to keep calm, so we felt our way past each other in silence and unscathed. We were supposed to kill each other, yet we would have preferred to embrace each other.

Our inner tension grew as the war went on. The greater our losses, the more we were bombarded with shrill propaganda from home. In 1941 we had been marched forward to the middle sector of the Eastern front toward Moscow until we were near the capital in the depth of winter, in bone-chilling cold without winter clothing or equipment, where we grew numb and bogged down in the snow. A short while later Reich Press Secretary Otto Dietrich opened a radio address with the unforgettable statement, "When winter took us by surprise in Russia in December. . . ." For the first time a wave of bitterness shook even those soldiers who had faith in the regime. What kind of leadership could be so totally mistaken about relative troop strengths and the time required for the campaign, and then, apparently, confuse the climate of central Russia with that of the Riviera?

During the long retreat headquarters more and more frequently issued orders to hold a defensive line, which, as any normally intelligent person could not help but realize, was indefensible. How in the light of our own understanding could we officers pass such orders on to others, for whose lives we were responsible? Was it enough that as superior officers we demanded more of ourselves than we did of our subordinates? Could any answer stand up to our own conscience?

Whether or not we were in a position to pass valid judgment on such orders, whether we knew a great deal or only a little about crimes—one thing grew increasingly clear: By fulfilling the duties assigned to us, our attitude toward evil and all our feelings were numbed. We were caught in this trap—that was crucial—and sooner or later we knew it. Where were the ethical standards broad enough to encompass these extreme situations? Who among the younger generation can today be certain that if he had lived through that time he would have all the answers? As soldiers we tried to make decisions based on our personal standards of values and decency we had been raised to uphold so as to deal with the incredible situations we faced daily. At the same time we were made aware of the inscrutability of all human existence, and in the face of this mystery ethical judgment must fail completely.

But that was not the end of it. As soldiers we had a duty to follow orders. Even as conscripts we had sworn to this duty, not in the abstract but very specifically and personally, swearing an oath not to the state but to the Führer. This oath protected Hitler—though not other Nazi leaders—from revolt within the Wehrmacht in a very special way. Nevertheless within our small circle of friends we discussed the matter more and more openly. What could this oath mean to us, given the long tradition of an oath as a contract between free men bound by mutual loyalty, when there was no loyalty from above?

We did not, of course, talk among ourselves with the dispassion of a formal seminar in ethics. Once, while we were briefly holding a reserve position, six of us—friends for some time—met in a farmhouse. Emotions ran high, until one of us, excited beyond reason, drew his gun and shot at a picture of Hitler hanging on the wall. It was a dangerous shot, straight from the sharpshooter's heart, requiring protection with a demonstration of solidarity. I therefore immediately aimed a second bullet at the picture, and the others followed suit. None could and none wanted to be excluded from the event and what might follow. The picture disappeared into the stove, the spot on the wall was covered with a map, and the entire occurrence was disguised as a tussle among friends, in anticipation of the subsequent arrival of the regimental commander.

But such naive outbursts of impotent rage were not the only ways in which we expressed ourselves. Though our regiment was far removed from the centers of power, we eventually cared about only one thing: resistance. Two officers were my models and mentors.

One, my friend Axel Bussche whom I have already mentioned and who was my age, showed us how to demand the most of oneself when it came to obeying questionable orders. Time and again he was wounded because he had taken unsparing risks. After one incident he was transferred temporarily to the rear echelon near Dubno in the Ukraine. In the fall of 1942 he was an eyewitness there as deep trenches were dug before defenseless people were shot en masse and thrown into them. They were Jews, victims of the infamous Einsatzgruppen (Special Action Groups; actually mobile extermination squads). When Bussche returned to the regiment he told us about this unimaginable horror. We were deeply upset and discussed the incident among ourselves. Bussche's determination to sacrifice his own life in a possible attempt on Hitler's life solidified.

We talked with my other friend, the much older Fritz-Dietlof Graf von Schulenburg, called Fritzi, a reserve officer in our regiment, about what such an attempt would entail. Fritzi had already lived a dramatic life. Seeking a form of national socialism, he had joined the Nazi party in 1932, eventually becoming vice police commissioner of Berlin and later deputy president of Silesia. But his original enthusiasm quickly turned to harsh disappointment. Outrage at violations of the law and crimes led him step by step into the resistance, where he became a central, driving force. An exceptional case, he was as uncompromising and stimulating in his thinking as he was unhesitating in his actions.

According to plan, he gathered a group of friends who shared his feelings. The time came when Graf Claus von Stauffenberg in Berlin saw the opportunity for an attempt on Hitler's life during the Führer's personal review of new uniforms. Schulenberg suggested that the young officer, Axel Bussche, be the man to model the new overcoats Hitler had ordered, then throw himself on Hitler and blow them both to kingdom come. At regimental headquarters I organized the technically complicated code communication with Stauffenberg that Bussche needed and the travel permit allowing him to go to Berlin. He was ready to act when at the last minute an Allied air raid destroyed the uniforms, canceling the ceremony. Bussche returned to the front, and before another uniform inspection could be arranged, he was wounded once again, this time so severely that any further participation on his part was out of the question.

The regiment transferred Schulenburg back to Berlin, and I saw him for the last time in June 1944 during a leave in Potsdam. Without going into detail, he briefed me on an imminent new attempt headed by Stauffenberg and discussed the steps that would follow, making sure of my willingness to do my part when I received the signal. Four weeks later the assassination attempt of July 20, 1944, failed. Fritzi was arrested that same night. In the courtroom he confronted the shouting judge, Roland Freisler, with fearless calm and replied to demands that he repent by expressing the hope that someone else would have better luck. On August 10, 1944, this bold and unique man was put to death.

After July 20 inquiries and investigations were carried out even in our regiment and in the division. Telegrams signed by Stauffenberg came to light in which Bussche had been ordered to Berlin months earlier. Through indescribable miracles, removal of other papers, and the determined silence of his comrades under interrogation, Bussche and others came through undiscovered. But not everyone; in the end no other Wehrmacht unit lost so many members who had participated in the resistance as our regiment.

The nine months from July 20 to the end of the war were unmitigated agony. Many bitter disputes erupted between people with opposing views as to whether there was a correct moment to make an attempt on Hitler's life. Some argued that it must not come too soon, to prevent another stab-in-the-back legend like the one that arose at the end of the First World War. Only when the Allies had made their way deeply enough into Germany did the populace understand what was at stake. I remember one such heated discussion, lasting all night, a few weeks before July 20, 1944, in my brother's home with him and our close friend Hellmut Becker. It is as painful to think back on these debates as it is to recall the many obstacles and omissions in the resistance. How could clever and brave men not realize that the war had long ago stopped being a matter of legends or what future generations would think of historical actors or actions and that what really mattered was the loss of human life day after day? The number of victims in the death camps and among the fighting forces, in air raids and in flight grew at a greater rate during the months after the failed assassination attempt than at any other time of the war. We never did bring it off.

PART THREE

Germany

in a

Polarized

World

Germany Surrenders

On May 8, 1945, Germany surrendered unconditionally and the country was occupied by the four victorious powers. Everyone was liberated from the National Socialist dictatorship, and those persecuted by the regime could finally stop fearing for their lives. But many others went on living in misery and deadly peril. The suffering of innumerable people started only when the war ended. Their homes were destroyed. The fate of family members was uncertain. All who had survived searched for a new beginning.

The last house our family occupied in Berlin had burned in an air raid. Above Lindau on Lake Constance sat a small chicken farm worked by my father's mother, who was over eighty years old. She transformed the old farmhouse into a new refuge for her children and grandchildren. I too found room and board there when I came home.

On this "hillside," as we called it, I joined a household made up entirely of women—a result of the war. My sister and her two little girls, forced to leave the East Prussian home of her in-laws, now found a haven here. She waited in vain for news about her husband, who had been declared missing in action at the front in 1944. My aunt Olympia, who had married my father's brother Viktor, had come from Breslau, the capital of Silesia, with her two daughters; both her sons had died in the war and her husband was interned in a camp. The same fate befell my brother Carl Friedrich; with Otto Hahn, Werner Heisenberg, Max von Laue, and several other German physicists he was taken into custody on orders from the United States and sent to England.

The Americans mistakenly suspected these German scientists of having worked on an atomic bomb for Germany. At that time the American bombs were being readied to be dropped on Hiroshima and Nagasaki.

In the summer of 1945 another fleeing couple joined us on the hillside—my sister's in-laws. During the First World War her father-in-law, Siegfried Eulenburg, had commanded the first infantry guard regiment, whose traditions were later transferred to my Potsdam regiment. Early in 1945 he harnessed three horses to a landau, placed his wife in the carriage, and seated himself on the coachman's block. And so these two, both eighty years old, left their home in East Prussia to cross all of Germany until they reached Lake Constance.

Today it is almost impossible to imagine all the stories or understand the immeasurable burdens borne mainly by the women. They had labored and feared, given birth and then protected these new lives. They mourned their fallen sons, husbands, brothers, friends. No one who lived through these times and felt their pain can forget the women's sorrow, their self-denial, and their quiet, supportive strength.

Study in Göttingen

During the first months after the war we reverted to pre-technological living. Currency transactions gave way to barter, rumors replaced newspapers. Relay runners from local parishes and private messengers on bicycles took over regular mail service. Concentrating all our energies on the bare necessities of survival, we managed pretty well.

One day in October 1945 one of these private messengers, the former head of press relations in our regiment, surprised me in Lindau. Axel Bussche—released from the field hospital soon after the war and living in Göttingen—had sent him to draft me, in a manner of speaking, into the ranks of university students in Göttingen. Axel had already obtained a place for me through the university's thronged admissions office.

The roundabout journey from Lake Constance to Lower Saxony—a journey of several days—was aided by wildly overcrowded trains that crossed all the zonal frontiers established by the victorious powers, making it significantly easier for me to conceal the fact that I lacked valid papers and passports. Since in Lindau I had ignored the orders of the French occupiers that all former Wehrmacht members must register, I was not properly discharged by the authorities—a situation that has not changed to this day.

I had studied for two semesters at the university before the war, but since then I had spent seven years in uniform. I was at an age when, in other days, people had long since taken their degrees. Now a new and different generation had arrived at the universities and colleges. Struggling with clashing feelings of innocence and guilt, confused by the Nazi era and the war, we were nevertheless more mature. Even though basically ignorant, we had acquired a sense of good and evil and learned to distinguish the important from the unimportant. Now we set out on a life of unaccustomed freedom we hoped would take us in a new direction but in which it was easy to become lost. On the one hand we were impatient at the thought of spending so many years in endless study before real life could begin. Conversely, we were curious and full of basic questions about even the most fundamental matters.

We put the university to a hard test. What could it offer us? How could it prove its worth? Take, for example, the centuries-old intellectual structure of civil law—what possible connection could it have to the problems of everyday life? What good would the great intellectual ideas and ideologies do us as we struggled to acquire bread-rationing cards, cigarettes, and iron stoves? The city and the university, nine miles from the Soviet occupation zone, were crammed with refugees. Even if you could find student housing, it was probably unheated. Lecture halls were filled to bursting, and it was almost impossible to get into the smaller seminars. Of necessity we accepted whatever came our way, without indifference or even cynicism but still with a great deal of skepticism, especially about the older generation, our professors. During the time of the terror they must have done and thought something. What values had they found and practiced in their scholarship? Had they accepted any responsibility in the community?

At first we were more concerned with their character than with their fields of expertise. But the two soon coalesced. Our thirst for knowledge grew stronger. Like dried-out sponges, we longed to be infused with more than the bare tools for a practical profession. We wanted valid guideposts for every aspect of our lives. Not all the professors sensed our needs, but the leading figures on the faculty knew exactly what we wanted. They did not present themselves as privileged tenured full professors exercising their superior learning and keeping their distance. Instead they knew that our questions were the same as theirs, and they asked them quite openly of themselves and their disciplines. And so it became an exciting and emotional time, in which the university, thanks to several outstanding figures, ironically passed all our tests.

After the war the University of Göttingen became the first in Germany to resume research and teaching, and it quickly acquired a leading academic position, not least because of the influx from the nearby Soviet zone.

Traditionally Göttingen owed its prestige to its faculties in mathematics and the natural sciences. The leading German mathematicians of the last 150 years, Karl Friedrich Gaus and David Hilbert, had taught here. Now the great tradition of the Göttingen physicists, among them James Franck and Max Born, was joined by the Max Planck Society as this research institute, by far the largest and most important in Germany, moved to Göttingen. In 1946 I was present at one of the last lectures given by the aged Max Planck. The Nobel laureates Otto Hahn, Werner Heisenberg, Max von Laue, and Adolf Windaus, as well as other outstanding research scientists and teachers—among them my brother Carl Friedrich—quickly formed a strong magnet attracting scholars from Germany and abroad.

These years saw an increasing symbiosis between the humanities and the sciences. Physicists grew philosophical, theologians took an interest in quantum theory, the medical faculty debated the realities of psychosomatic symptoms. All those who prided themselves on their eminence within their specialty tried to contribute to the store of general knowledge. And for the many interested students in all the schools it was the heyday of general studies, subjects borne aloft by a few extraordinary academic professors.

One of them, Herbert Schöffler, a scholar in the field of English studies, taught us not only to appreciate his own special interest, William Shakespeare. He also helped his students to avoid the pitfall they encountered as they acted out their deep aversion to the perniciously abused idea of a national community that had been prevalent during the Nazi period; the logical end of that aversion could easily lead them to the absolute opposite of community, utter isolation. Of course it took no great effort to persuade us, the war generation, to avoid an excessive sense of honor and the dueling ethos of the old student fraternities. Few of us were interested in these organizations. But Schöffler wanted to show us how to arrive at a sense of community without its traditional questionable elements. It was an achievement I was frequently reminded of in later years, the more it became watered down in the course of time.

Schöffler, who died at an all too early age, also left us an unassuming, delightful little book, *Kleine Geographie des deutschen Witzes* (A Little Geography of German Wit). By organizing his material in the form of a comparative typology of wit, he created a persuasive and helpful tool for the study of our national psychology. In this way he expounded his belief that culture is the art of learning how to coexist harmoniously.

One of the great and brilliant Göttingen figures was the historian Hermann Heimpel. His constant search for a "delicate, or at least a nervous conscience" led him to grapple with the history of the late Middle Ages just as sensibly as he did with the conflicts of his own generation in the first half of the twentieth century. Familiarizing me with the material to which my brother Heinrich had dedicated himself, Heimpel's courses were deeply serious even as they celebrated the art of communication. He could teach the matter closest to his heart: to love history without denying the difficulty of accepting responsibility.

The professors in the evangelical-theological faculty devoted themselves to reconciling their field and current history. Hans-Joachim Iwand lectured on the struggle between church and state during the Nazi period, when the church fought the "German Christians" and their so-called brown agenda—a battle in which he had participated actively. Friedrich Gogarten took the church as his topic; besides Karl Barth and deviating from that theologian, he was crucially important to the establishment of dialectical theology. But his thinking was not always easy to follow. When I listened to his lectures, I was reminded of Werner Heisenberg's recipe for a stimulating and profound lecture: one-third easily understood, almost trivial ideas; a second third demanding and difficult concepts that were lasting, constructive, and comprehensible; and the final third theories incomprehensible to the entire audience to the end of their days. Heisenberg, a friend of my brother Carl Friedrich, never tried to explain physics to me. Instead, I learned to play table tennis from him and greatly enjoyed listening as he brilliantly played the piano. These arts, then, belonged in his second third.

Gerhard von Rad, who taught the Old Testament, made a deep impression on me. To him I owe my understanding of the power of memory in human existence, perhaps most deeply embodied in a religious sense in the Jewish faith, in which belief in God is the belief in God's works in history. The Old Testament, the Bible of the Jews, is also their history book. Their memory is therefore their experience of God's works in their own history and at the same time their hope for salvation—that is, for transcending every conflict, the reconciliation of the separate parts. To forget is to lose one's faith.

Public lectures on every subject, held in the largest lecture halls, always drew huge audiences. The university's rector, Ludwig Raiser, taught the fundamentals of the law of company codetermination; before long I had to deal with that subject in my professional life. The renowned philosopher Nicolai Hartmann lectured with great clarity on ethics and aesthetics, but I'm sure that Heidegger would have fascinated us more. Maximilian Braun, the Slavic specialist, established in me the conviction—which I never abandoned—that of all the contributions to world literature in the nineteenth century, Russian works were the ones I would be most reluctant to lose. My brother Carl Friedrich gave a lecture on the history of nature, a bold and powerful interdisciplinary view of the whole, which led to heated discussions.

All this may seem to imply that in those days a law student could ignore the dry and factual training of his own field. We completed our assignments, collected our certificates of attendance, and sought out the best tutors. But we also interacted with the wider world of ideas and experience, even if it had no direct relation to the professions to which we aspired.

I say so little about my own department, the law faculty, because difficulties often crop up at the beginning of the study of law. In the most prestigious section, civil law, we learned a wealth of complicated details that had no easily discernible context or relationship. It was a very long time before we understood how these details coalesce into a systematic, impressive structure designed to provide a humane way for people to live together. We also had a hard time with the other object of our desire—the grounded assurance that criminal law represented the highest attainable level of justice—since the subject was taught item by item, listing the criteria of each statutory offense.

Many professors deployed all the brilliance at their command to counter their colleagues' ideas with the "correct view"—their own, of course, and generally just as subjective. Often they engaged in hair-splitting, in a fairly repellent dogmatism. Especially in law, surely, self-criticism in view of the very recent past and the search for a directed new beginning should have gained a clear and unambiguous hearing. That was what we, who had been shaped by war, were looking for; too many faculty members abandoned us and left us dangling.

There were important exceptions, including Rudolf Smend, the expert in public and church law, and Franz Wieacker, who taught civil law. The latter made us see the reciprocal relationship of exacting details and the ethical-legal whole and made us understand not only how much the law is shaped by the culture of its day but also the degree to which culture finds and expresses its character in the law. He called his subject the history of civil law in the present day, but in reality it was a most persuasive course in cultural history, taught by a gentle and charming man.

One other professor addressed my questions about injustice, justice, and civilizing evolution, though he was not a legal authority nor did he live in Göttingen. This was Viktor von Weizsäcker, my father's brother, a clinician in Heidelberg and founder of psychosomatic medicine in Germany, who thought in terms of the whole being. I cannot describe accurately his new beginnings for general medicine, about which he had been thinking for a long time, but he had also looked deeply into religion and philosophy and into society as it was constituted socially and by law. In close intellectual exchange with Gustav Radbruch, who taught law in Heidelberg and who had been the attorney general in the Weimar government, Uncle Viktor had developed an ethical line of thought I understood more clearly than most of my professors' lectures in law. I owe this uncle, who had lost three of his four children and who treated me, with all my questions, like his own son, for the help and support we all needed so much at that time along with his help in training me for a profession.

A university cannot do everything. But the opportunities to broaden the horizons of a generation given to us by Göttingen University were so valuable that they left us beholden for the rest of our lives. We were faithfully instructed to follow the slogan penned by Georg Christoph Lichtenberg, the great man from the university's early days: "We must teach people *how* to think, and not always *what* they should think." This was our greatest lesson, and we learned to cherish it.

It is difficult to compare the mind-set of different generations and other times. Experience shows that parents and grandparents are generally not very successful when describing the sacrifices and successes of their own educations in order to be helpful to young people of the present. All we can do is report on what we believe occurred and tell our story without an ulterior motive.

Living conditions in these first postwar years were harsh, but the life was not hard to bear because everyone was in the same boat. Shabby and discolored uniform coats or trousers were common, and no one had to worry about being overweight. Government support for students was still unknown. We had and needed little. Clever people lived, as they always did in such times, off the black market. Some took unskilled night jobs, others tutored. My first source of income was Radio Bavaria. The night program, under its outstanding head

Gerhard Szczesny, aired fascinating cultural reports and hired free-lance reporters from far and wide. I became one of them, broadcasting on the life of the wartime generation at the universities.

Politically the times were pregnant with unrest. The victorious powers were moving toward Cold War and the air was full of rumors. Many of us kept our backpacks packed and ready, prepared to set off on new travels should Soviet troops advance westward.

The zones of occupation had not yet officially partitioned the country. But as time went on, the frontiers between East and West became firmer, cutting us off from one another more and more—as I had occasion to find out for myself. Textbooks were still in short supply, and when a rumor circulated that secondhand bookstores in Halle and Leipzig had some books at a good price, I made my way by night along a secret path across the green frontier into the East Zone. But my adventure ended when armed border guards on the eastern side put me in a quasi prison—a house in the woods—where the women were kept in the upper story while the men were held on the ground floor. All were people who had tried to cross the border in the dark. How was I to get out?

Halfway up the stairs I met an attractive and strong-willed young woman. We devised a plan: She would start screaming loudly in the middle of the night, then explain to the Russian guard that she was pregnant and was having labor pains, that the bags she had brought were heavy, and that her boyfriend was downstairs and would have to take her and her things to the nearest doctor. We pulled it off as planned; the guards were eager to keep peace in the house. I, as the supposed boyfriend, was alerted, and both of us were sent out into the night. My first engagement to a charming and clever woman—made memorable by the heavy luggage I carried for her—ended twelve hours after it began at the nearest railway station. In Halle I found the books I needed so that I could study to my heart's content.

These student years immediately after the war marked a fulfilling and impressive epoch in our lives and offered another opportunity to forge lifelong friendships. Many years later someone said of me that the best thing about me was my friends. He could not have said anything that would please me more.

Axel Bussche was the moral authority and outstanding representative of our generation. In the very first postwar semester he was elected chairman of the student organization and delivered a major lecture on the topic "Oath and Guilt." The university administration as well as the British occupation forces heeded his suggestions. Unfortunately he remained in Göttingen only briefly. Soon after, he was invited to England, where he helped to put up the first bridge between the wartime generations that had so recently stood on opposite sides. His invitation was all the more remarkable as it was very difficult at the time to travel abroad. A respected law professor, later a judge at the European Court, invited me to Lausanne in Switzerland for two semesters, but, as was customary at the time, I was denied an exit permit.

One friend I made in Göttingen was Klaus Ritter, whom I had first met in the war. A law student like myself but with a more decided philosophical bent, he wrote his doctoral dissertation on "Natural Law and Positivism," a basic topic in the philosophy of law. His adviser noted that he had not understood the work and therefore gave it a grade of excellent—an expression of the professor's honesty and his high regard for the exceptional quality of his doctoral student. Later Ritter became a true pioneer in the scholarly study of politics. Happily, this circumstance gave me an opportunity to combine a close professional relationship and constant personal friendship with him. With none of my other friends have I kept up such a continuous—and, for me, always illuminating—exchange of ideas about the basic structure of international policies. His intellect, softened by his heart, is a wonderful gift.

During my years at the university I also forged a friendship with Hartmut von Hentig. Our fathers had worked together in the old foreign office, though they were not particularly close. We completely changed that state of affairs in our generation. Hartmut demanded a lot of himself and as a result did not have an easy life. One day as he was hitchhiking, he was picked up by an American car in which

Thornton Wilder was a passenger. This writer and humanitarian had already earned our gratitude. Now he did his part in enabling the young German, whom he had never met before, to obtain a two-year stay at an American university. This act and the following years did Hentig a great deal of good, and in the course of time he made a name for himself as an educator working in pedagogic theory and practice. I always believed that his policies were determined by his original field of study: ancient Greece. No profession today is more difficult than pedagogy. His willpower and imagination always succeeded in finding new ways to create models for education, inspire people to be independent and form their own opinions, and work with them to find a better life.

I already knew the brothers Peter and Konrad Kraske from the army. Peter studied theology in Göttingen, and the sermons he delivered when christening three of our four children became a spiritual basis of our family. For our youngest son, Fritz, he took on the additional office of godfather. His younger brother, Konrad, became a historian. His talent for writing was extraordinary. To this day I suspect that he wrote his excellent dissertation on Martin Luther in one night. The first of our Göttingen group to make politics the object of his daily activities, he became a member of the Bundestag. There he brought great competence and integrity to one of the most delicate jobs in our party democracy: the office of general secretary in a large national party.

The youngest of our group was Wolfgang von Buch, from the Uckermark in Brandenburg. During the final phase of the war he had been drafted at the age of fifteen. After almost dying of starvation in Russian captivity, he came to the university still too young for everything and yet unnaturally mature. It was contradictory and yet so characteristic of him that for a long time he totally absorbed himself in the systematic study of legal theory while becoming the compassionate and humane supporter of the most significant and intellectually brilliant legal theoretician, Professor Franz Wieacker, whom I mentioned earlier. From Wolfgang Buch, long an active lawyer, I learned anew that legal theory is only the tool but not the substance when it comes to what is right and just.

We all led busy and at times turbulent lives in Göttingen. The occupying forces continued to govern with a certain amount of harshness, and our nighttime activities were restricted by the so-called curfew: After ten o'clock no German was to be on the streets without a special permit. Since our nightly bull sessions were usually far from over by that hour, quite often we simply stayed up until curfew was over—at six in the morning. Guessing games were a favorite pastime. For example, one required players to illustrate a concept without explaining it in words. Once I tried to nonverbally represent "opium of the people" by setting a lit cigarette on a Bible, but no one solved this simple puzzle. Another time Ritter was supposed to guess "nothingness" by asking questions answered with yes or no. Thus, he could ask whether the answer was present in the room, whether it was large, alive, a member of the animal kingdom, and so forth. His first questions were, "Abstract? Concrete?" Hentig and I fought about the correct answer for hours—literally until the curfew was lifted. We continue the debate to this day.

Unforgettable evenings were spent at the Göttingen municipal theater. At the time Fritz Lehmann, the great oratorio director, headed the theater. He and the other artists gave us ignorant and hungry students of the arts a unique view of the speaking and musical stage. We saw *Murder in the Cathedral* by T. S. Eliot, *Les Mouches* (The Flies) by Jean-Paul Sartre, *The Skin of Our Teeth* by Thornton Wilder, and plays by O'Neill, Tennessee Williams, Brecht, and others. During the first two years after the war Lehmann mounted all five of Mozart's major operas, Beethoven's *Fidelio*, both *La Forza del Destino* and *Un Ballo in Maschera* by Verdi, *Carmen*, and *Der Rosenkavalier*. A seat in the back rows cost just one mark. We went to operas whenever we could and so truly made them part of ourselves—a lifelong treasure with only one drawback: the temptation to sing along softly each time they are heard. My wife does not appreciate this predisposition for one moment—and of course she's right.

I encountered a number of my fellow students again in later years: Wilhelm Hennis, the Max Weber scholar who taught me many important things about the programs of political parties; Walter Russell, the wonderful physician and humanistic philanthropist in Bonn; Horst Ehmke and Peter von Oertzen, who went into politics; Uwe Jessen, later the presiding judge in Berlin; and Schroeder-Hohenwart, the industrialist. We all were lucky enough to spend the years right after the war putting down an intellectual foundation on which we could build for the rest of our lives.

In political and economic life the first great break was currency reform in the summer of 1948. The time of stable money began; of course none of us had any. We also had to start learning how to manage our affairs in our private lives. On the day of currency reform each of us was given forty deutsche marks. By that night mine was all spent on a decent secondhand suit and a used bicycle.

But for me an interruption in another form arose, concerning my parents.

My Father's Nuremberg Trial

In 1943 my father was named ambassador to the Vatican, where he continued to enjoy the hospitality of the papal government until well after the war. We did not see each other again until we met in Nuremberg in the winter of 1945–46. Escorted as a guarantee by the Allies, my father had been asked to be a witness at the war crimes trial in that city.

In Göttingen, Marion Dönhoff, Axel Bussche, and I decided to travel to Nuremberg to see for ourselves what legal processes the Allies had devised to deal with crimes of the Nazi period. On the way we called on Pastor Martin Niemöller, a close friend of my mother's and one of the earliest clerics to be sent to a concentration camp. With his unique ardor he argued that judgment must not be left to the Allied High Command but that Germans themselves must assume responsibility for a new moral order.

When we reached Nuremberg, we saw that the splendid medieval city, made up almost entirely of half-timbered buildings, had suffered extensive destruction. But the Wilhelminian Palace of Justice survived in all its splendor, fully prepared to pass judgment on the living. Still in the car when we saw the main entrance guarded by two American tanks with full crews, Marion Dönhoff remembers that Axel and I became quite agitated: "Get rid of those guys, make room for *us*." Marion, somewhat shocked at this demonstration of our apparently still unassuaged military blood lust, stared at us. But of course it wasn't that we wanted the war to continue. What bothered us was that the process of denazification seemingly continued to be carried out by the victorious powers alone. We believed that Germans should sit in judgment of the crimes that had victimized the people of so many nations, not the least our own compatriots. When it came right down to it, something more substantial than merely the word "reeducation" would be needed to express the American occupation policy toward the Germans. The American chief prosecutor, Robert Jackson, wrote in January 1950, after the Nuremberg trials had ended, that if the Germans had overseen the proceedings, all the accused would have gone free. Is that really what would have happened? Despite the diffi- culty of finding competent judges, isn't it more likely that a trial of the true criminals under the German penal code would have raised aware- ness in Germany much more and strained the sense of justice less than the trials that were carried out—a kind of victors' justice? As it turned out, the reality was different.

My feelings during our visit to Nuremberg were concentrated entirely on the reunion with my father. The terrible years had taken a heavy toll on him. All of his efforts had been in vain: preventing the outbreak of violence, stemming the wildfire raging throughout Europe, shortening the war if he could not prevent it, putting a spoke in the wheels of crime, and finally halting the destruction of his own country and removing the taint on his name.

My father's nature had always been to keep his feelings to him- self. But now, at our reunion, his emotions got the better of him as his thoughts dwelled on the inferno, the son and the son-in-law who had not come back, his bereft daughter, and the rubble left behind in every heart.

But because he wanted to help in any way he could, he had come to Nuremberg a free man, to testify to whatever he knew. At that time he was working on drafts for a constitution for his country and on plans for shaping the future Europe. He described the disastrous dis- crepancy between public and private morality and said that he had a strong desire to live in Germany again.

However, once he had testified at the International Tribunal, he returned to the Vatican in Rome. After the French authorities, follow- ing on the actions of the Americans, had assured him of an unrestricted stay in their zone of occupation in Germany my parents left the Holy See early in 1947 and established themselves in simple quarters on the Halde near Lindau.

Then, in July 1947, my father was recalled to Nuremberg. He accepted this invitation to testify once more without the slightest hesitation; but as soon as he arrived in the city, he was arrested. Hearings followed, bargains were offered, and finally indictments were handed down, culminating in a trial that dragged on until 1949. My father did not regain his freedom until the following year.

At the time the trial attracted a great deal of attention both in Germany and abroad. I took a leave from the university and moved to Nuremberg. Although I was only in the fifth semester at the Göttingen school of law, the American judges at the tribunal granted me formal standing as an assistant to the defense, and I worked with my father's attorneys for a year and a half. At first my father was deeply disturbed at this turn of events; he was firmly opposed to my devoting so much time to him and delaying my own career to help him in his legal predicament. But I look on my decision as anything but a sacrifice. It represented a unique, even central chapter of my life. No matter how difficult the period was, the work was deeply fulfilling. The intense, often daily sessions with my father allowed us to develop a strong bond. Besides, I received an education in contemporary history more thorough than any I could have found in a regular course of study.

The defense team worked together as friends. Hellmut Becker, along with the American lawyer Warren E. Magee, headed the team. Becker's friendship with my brother Carl Friedrich, dating from their college days, had grown into a close relationship with my whole family. His brilliant analytical mind and tireless energy steered us through the proceedings. Sigismund von Braun was also prepared to work with us. A friend of the family and most recently a member of the embassy to the Vatican, he later served in the Federal Republic as ambassador to Paris, London, and the United Nations before serving as undersecretary of state in the foreign office. Albrecht von Kessel, one of my father's former colleagues, became my close friend. He helped us in Nuremberg from the outside, just as he had stood by my father during his most difficult times in office. A member of the inner circle of diplomats who had taken part in the resistance to Hitler, his courage, good sense, and refinement made him a central social and political figure in the postwar reconstruction of the diplomatic service.

My father's trial threw light on a question that is crucial to understanding the incomprehensible time we had lived through: Was it possible, was it even conceivable, to abhor and struggle against the nature and crimes of the regime and still work in its ministries? Did some particular circumstance even make such a situation necessary? Or was there no occasion that could justify such a life? What price must a man pay for deciding not to abandon his post—and thus collaborate—in order to exert some influence from his position so as to change policy into something more acceptable and bring about change, or at least to prevent worse? But what could the phrase "to prevent worse" mean, since the unthinkable worst had happened? Thus the prosecutors argued that a man who claimed to have searched for the lesser evil had in fact been interested in the lesser evil only for himself.

Since a criminal trial deals with the guilt or innocence of the accused, the debate is not about the politics of a period but about the actions of one human being. From the beginning, however, I was convinced that in this case it would be impossible to arrive at any reasonable understanding if the proceedings attempted to separate these two aspects. The tribunal for its part needed to gain a true picture of the person. But the defense would also have to analyze unreservedly the political conditions of the time.

This dual approach was both necessary and at the same time hugely difficult. The three American judges were not even familiar with the details of European and German history. And, of course, citizens of a nation that was and had always been a democracy of free men could have no idea of conditions prevailing under a dictatorship controlled by a secret service.

In addition, public discussion in Europe brought to the surface opposing camps that advocated divergent opinions and exhibited a mixture of old and new preconceptions. Did the sequence of Luther-Bismarck-Hitler constitute a direct line? There were those who had always suspected that the Germans were typically more dangerous than other nationalities; this group stressed the German tendencies to nationalism and militarism and an aversion to democracy. Others, who believed that the same tendencies existed during the 1920s as well and were typical even of such republicans as Stresemann and Wilhelm Groener, saw Nazism as the obvious end stage of that fatal German weakness. Lord Robert Vansittart, the well-known diplomat who at the time headed the British foreign office, was in this group. His belief in the Germans' moral bankruptcy culminated in the statement "No sane man can trust the Germans." This camp truly believed that if a German such as my father claimed that he had always thought of Hitler as something of a foreign excrescence in the nation, he must be resorting to some kind of subterfuge.

It could not be denied that everything that had happened was horrible beyond belief. Of course we could not limit our efforts to struggling against such age-old anti-German prejudices. Even those who kept an open mind had a hard time understanding the immediate past. At that time none of us had the advantage of temporal distance, of having digested Alan Bullock's and Joachim Fest's major biographies of Hitler. Nor could we have read Sebastian Haffner's *The Meaning of Hitler,* which described not only the consequences of the mistakes made at Versailles but also, astutely, the process of domestic disintegration that began during the Weimar period: "a whole army of enemies of the constitution in its own [i.e. the republic's] public service"; the few sensible republicans in the " 'republic without republicans' "; Hindenburg's election to the Reich presidency as a "piece of luck" in that, at least for a time, it forced the right to help support the republic; the death of the Weimar Republic for all practical purposes as a result of the international economic crisis, unemployment, and the government of Brüning with quasi-dictatorial powers; the road to the Fascist corporate state as dreamed of by Kurt von Schleicher; the appointment of Hitler by Hindenburg at the instigation of von Papen; the heroic, hopeless resistance of the left, which Hitler eventually saw as a job for the secret police and which ended in internal or actual emigration.

Wasn't it true, as Haffner believed, that there were officials, officers, and conservatives in important positions who presented a serious problem for Hitler because at the time he was dependent on them? Could those who—given their particular traditional attitudes—remained in office have made it harder for him? Or were they basically a help to Hitler because their experience was useful to him and gave credence to the regime's appearance of legitimacy at home and abroad? In the last resort, wasn't it equally true that until July 20, 1944, some sectors of the resistance were also marked by romantic-conservative ideas of the state that were just as unrealistic?

This argument was the background behind the questioning to be answered in the so-called Wilhelmstrasse Trial, in which my father was one of twenty-one defendants. Granted, the activities and views of these twenty-one varied so much that the media quickly dubbed the proceedings the omnibus trial.

A huge battle of documents unfolded. The evidentiary material came to 39,000 pages while the English-language trial transcripts, complete with witnesses' testimony and arguments, filled 28,000 pages.

The tribunal brought to light the abysmal extent of crimes committed during the National Socialist period. Almost all the surviving players of the time testified. The sheer number of statements from abroad could not be ignored.

The accusations focused on the conduct of wars of aggression and on crimes against humanity, especially the deportation of Jews from other countries into the concentration camps and death camps. The prosecution depended largely on principles established in the main Nuremberg Trial, which were not codified but were based largely on natural right. The case brought against my father, however, did not involve a dispute on the basic question of criminal law—that is, the central principle of *nulla poena sine lege* (no crime without a law). None of us had any doubt whatever about the criminal nature of the atrocities that had been committed, whether or not any existing explicit laws could be applied.

The whole world was shaken by what came to light about what was done to the Jews in the death camps. These facts must be placed at the center of the Nuremberg trials and lead to charges of the widest magnitude. Who had planned what, executed it, known about it, let it happen? Did no one protest? Where were the guilty? Or, as one of the prosecutors asked, had each one saved the few while none had killed the many?

In one of the Nuremberg proceedings against industrialists who had run manufacturing plants near concentration camps, the defense presented a large volume of exhibits under the title "The Great Belief of the German People" (Der Grosse Glaube des deutschen Volkes). There can be little doubt that only a very small number of Germans knew with certainty and in detail about the many millions of killings in Auschwitz and other camps. Most Germans not only lacked the necessary information, it was simply beyond anyone's power to imagine that something so monstrous could occur. But the road from such ignorance to "good faith" in what might be happening to the Jews is long—far too long. Such questions torment us to this day.

Anyone reading the moving diaries of the Jewish scholar Victor Klemperer encounters vivid episodes of open mistreatment of Jews. Klemperer describes them with great self-control and specificity; at the same time he makes us understand how the fatal illness of Nazism developed under the conditions of the German citizenry's immune system, which had been weakened over a long period. No one could innocently and in good faith witness the burning of synagogues or the yellow stars Jews were forced to wear, not only in the streets but even in their private rooms. These actions were not described in the old, threatening tract Mein Kampf, written by the young and still powerless agitator. But well before the war Hitler, speaking in the Reichstag, told the German people loudly and publicly: "Should the international finance Jewry within and outside Europe succeed in plunging the

nations into another world war, the result will not be the bolsheviza-
tion of the world and thus the victory of the Jews, but the destruction
of the Jewish race in Europe." According to the official minutes, the
legislature responded with "sustained tempestuous applause." After
such instances, was it still possible to pull the rug out from under the
alleged good faith of the German people?

When, forty years later, I said publicly that it could not have
escaped the notice of those willing to open their eyes and ears that
deportation trains were rolling out of the railroad stations, serious and
reliable contemporaries rebuked me: They had not known, they said,
nor could they have known. I have to believe them. Each case must be
judged individually. But seen as a whole the discussion now concerned
a tempting reaction: To stay as ignorant as possible when rumors and
then evidence about something fishy start circulating; to let a pliable
conscience be distracted, to look away, to keep silent. Hardly any who
lived through those years as adults were entirely free of this evasion,
including myself.

The proceedings against my father focused on his actual position.
He had not wielded power directly, but he had been close to the
centers of power. Even if the facts at his disposal, his suspicious nature,
and his imagination had not been enough for him to form a correct
picture of the Holocaust, he did know from documents and oral reports more than enough to make a reasoned decision. He was completely aware that he accepted the stigma of remaining in the service
of an infamous system. He never tried to justify staying at his post by
citing the great number of individuals whom he protected and whose
lives he had saved in Berlin and later in Rome, of which there is public
evidence. Conversely, he never had an opportunity to prevent serious
crimes, especially against Jews—a central question raised at the Tribunal—crimes he knew about or might have suspected.

His only reason for accepting and keeping the post was the possibility of truly taking a hand in the course of foreign affairs to prevent
the outbreak, expansion, and prolongation of war, especially the attack
on the Soviet Union. No one saw more clearly and felt more deeply

the fact that he had failed in all his intentions. But to keep trying—
that he saw as his duty. It became the substance of his activities.

The first point of the charges against him concerned the conduct
of wars of aggression and took up most of the proceedings. The prosecutors tried to show that my father had enthusiastically supported
Hitler's military policies and even made them possible. But evidence
for the defense could not be easily obtained because it required the
testimony of my father's negotiating partners abroad, many of whom
were inaccessible to us. The most important were members of the
British foreign office and diplomats who had personal knowledge of
my father's efforts, especially in trying to prevent the outbreak of war
in 1938 and 1939. But now the British foreign office ordered these men
to keep silent. Most of them obeyed, to our detriment. One exception
was Lord Edward Halifax, the foreign secretary at that time, who gave
honest and helpful testimony in my father's favor.

Since then, the extensive literature on the contemporary history
of both Germany and the rest of the world has left little serious doubt
about the inappropriateness of the charges against my father. In the
words of Klemens von Klemperer, he put himself in the service of
preventing war "with the appropriate insistence and cunning," risking
high treason for the sake of peace. He remained unsuccessful. But even
if his activities warranted a trial, Freisler's People's Court would have
been the appropriate venue rather than the Allied Military Tribunal in
Nuremberg. Thus witnesses also confirmed Ribbentrop's earlier statement, that the Gestapo had not arrested my father after July 20, 1944,
only because they could not reach him; by that time considerable
Allied territory stretched between his residence, the Vatican, and
Germany.

I do want to report on an aspect of the trial that has less to do
with politics than human temperament and concerns American criminal law procedure, which is structured quite differently from ours. In
Germany the presiding judge conducts the proceedings himself. It is
his job to arrive at the truth through examination and instructions. In
Germany, unlike the United States, there is no "prosecutor"; instead

there is the state's attorney. In contrast to the defense attorney, he is equated with the judge—even outwardly, by his robes. He is required by his office to serve only the truth, though he might at times be tempted to hunt down the accused rather than follow the scent of truth even if it might exonerate the accused.

In the American trial system, on the other hand, prosecutor and defense attorney face each other as two equals in a dispute. Fighting not only with documents and arguments, prosecutor and defender also use every means at their disposal to prove that witnesses for the other side are unreliable, to discredit them as human beings. The result is a verbal wrestling match without mercy. The judge sits above the battle and rules on motions at the outset of the trial and for the rest simply listens. In the end the judge or jury decides which side came closest to the truth.

In addition the Nuremberg tribunals practiced a method, admissible in principle according to American trial law, of obtaining state's evidence. This practice—which by now we have introduced to a lesser extent—may be practical but can also lead to problems. We had dramatic evidence of such an outcome in Nuremberg.

The American prosecutor was Robert Kempner, himself a one-time fighter in the German army during the First World War, subsequently a Prussian official and legal adviser to the police department in the ministry of the interior. Having lost his job in 1933 because he was Jewish, he emigrated first to Italy and then to the United States. He had traveled a thorny path.

Now that the end of the century is near, few in Germany can still remember what the need to emigrate meant for the people who were persecuted and driven from their German homes. Some of them came to Israel later and established a new home through herculean efforts. Among them was Yohanan Meroz from Berlin, the same age as myself almost to the day, a splendid diplomat and philologist with whom I struck up a close friendship during his time as Israeli ambassador in Berlin. Others looked for a way back to Germany after the war. It was difficult for all of them. The great scholar of German literature Hans

Mayer went to Leipzig to be part of a clear alternative to fascism on German soil before moving to Tübingen for reasons of intellectual honesty. The art historian Otto von Simson—great-great-grandson of Eduard von Simson, the president of the national assembly in the Church of Saint Paul in Frankfurt in 1848 and the first president of the Reich Supreme Court in Leipzig—emigrated to the United States, where he was very successful; but he returned to Germany in 1949 and there served indispensably to restore culture and science in his country of origin. The chemist Eric Warburg also returned to Germany as an American officer and chose to remain, setting an example to all Germans of humanity and selfless communitarianism. Everyone who returned to Germany had a different history. All had at one time been brutally torn from the life they had known, an experience that resulted in lasting wounds.

And that is how Robert Kempner felt. He, the onetime German official, suffered more than most from memories of what had once been his. It was understandable that now, as the American prosecutor, he would concentrate on the type, effect, and guilt of the Germans in government service, although he practiced some strange methods. To prepare for the trial, he made use of a number of Nazi officials, including the astute specialist in public law Carl Schmitt. Schmitt had supported the change of the parliamentary system into an authoritarian one and a "dictatorship of commissars." Kempner and many others thought of him as the "chief justice of the Third Reich"—this is not the place to debate whether the epithet was fair or not. In any case, because Kempner thought that Schmitt could be useful for the prosecutions Kempner had in mind, Schmitt was given immunity at Kempner's instigation and set free in May 1947.

Kempner's attempt to enlist a leading official from the foreign office, Under Secretary Friedrich Wilhelm Gaus, became particularly well known. By accident I succeeded in finding the transcript of Kempner's interrogation of Gaus, who was then in custody. We submitted the relevant passages in evidence, and they were widely reprinted in the German press. "We need your help to clear up this matter," Kempner had said to Gaus before adding, "If I could save my own neck, I wouldn't stop at a little perjury." I do not believe that Gaus later perjured himself, but Kempner did persuade him to exchange the role of defendant, which loomed large in his immediate future, for that of collaborator with the prosecution. Two days after that interrogation he was released from isolation. A few days later the front page of the *Neue Zeitung* trumpeted a long, handwritten declaration from Gaus in which, as the newspaper itself commented, he confessed the collective guilt of the German government service. Further, it was made absolutely clear, Kempner himself had given the text to the newspaper.

During the first interrogations of my father by the court similar unreasonable requests for cooperation came from the prosecution. Taken aback, he refused. Kempner immediately shifted to the stance of hostile investigator. A deep abyss of distrustful dislike opened between the two men. My father was unable—and continued to be unable—to fathom morally and humanely just how the causes of truth and justice were served by turning a defendant into a more or less manipulated collaborator of the prosecution by rewarding him with immunity. He was keenly interested in holding a deep and very open discussion with the prosecutors to clarify the political and moral possibilities of resisting a dictatorship by remaining in office. He did not fear penetrating questions about the appearance of ambiguity in his choice, nor did these offend him. But what he found unbearable were Kempner's tactics of treating him from the outset as untrustworthy, an enemy of the truth. The more he sensed that each of his words was being twisted, the more he felt surrounded by mistrust and traps, the more he found himself unable to speak.

Apparently Kempner was not given to such scruples as he applied his trial methods—and why should he be? He acted according to his nature and the rules of American trial law. He was the prototype of the accusing prosecutor. Without a doubt his subsequent contributions to clearing up crimes, to knowledge of contemporary history, and in general to vigilance as the price of freedom as well as the liberal constitutional state are considerable, and I have always had the utmost respect for them. Though in the following decades we occasionally exchanged letters, no closer friendship ensued, certainly not in Nuremberg nor ever. During the proceedings Kempner once said to me that though our defense was very good, it suffered from one error: We should have turned him, Kempner, into my father's defense attorney. Was it really impossible for him to understand that I felt his words were nothing more than pure cynicism? In any case my store of humor was not full enough to enjoy his wit.

Family and friends made every effort to melt my father's icy, offended silence. He knew what we were doing. Once he sent me a note in the courtroom, "Some even think that my job today is more important than my job of the past"—that is, to collaborate by laying bare what he had learned in a key position in the past. But it was not easy for him.

All his life he had talked little about himself. It had always seemed presumptuous to him to tell others about his personal motives and actions. This attitude also made it difficult for him to conclude and publish his memoirs, which we had urgently begged him to write. Finally he was persuaded to do so only because the book would allow him to contribute to his wife and daughter's support.

In his life up to that time people had generally responded to him with reason and confidence. His only weapon against the mistrust he now encountered—which he found so inexplicable and hurtful—was the worthless weapon of silence. His form of self-protection, it was seen as a kind of pride and arrogance when combined with the tacit expectation that he would be understood correctly. He found it difficult to defend himself against the prosecution's mentality and methods. His heart counseled silence.

This characteristic caused him the most difficulty, with which he struggled again and again, and for me it was the most moving human experience of my father. He never tried to win favor for himself and his nature, with his adversaries no more than with his friends. And yet this difficult period of the Tribunal allowed me to see that nothing about him was more evident than his essence, perhaps more understandable than many of his actions. The instructive element in his example was not so much the political role he had played; what was much more attractive was his human dimension, as inaccessible as it seemed to his prosecutors and some historians. Nuremberg taught me to wish for nothing more—for myself and especially for other young people—than never to find ourselves in my father's situation. But if such a situation must occur, then I would wish that I and they could live and act with the same depths of conscience as I saw him do through the years.

He exemplified a human being thinking and acting in an extreme situation. How could he explain his role in a historical drama that overwhelmed us even as we were its cast? To act and to suffer are one and the same, T. S. Eliot says. No one is free of guilt. The survivor of the extreme situation lacks the concepts to describe it, while anyone who has not experienced it must develop some understanding for it; no road avoids it. But how can we do justice to the drama of history even with all the thirst for justice at our disposal?

After the proceedings had dragged on for a year and a half, two of the three judges sentenced my father to seven years' confinement, then commuted this sentence to five years. The third judge voted for complete acquittal in both verdicts, submitting a dissenting opinion that was carefully annotated. It took three days to read out the sentence. As it was pronounced, my father's earphones clattered to the floor. But this fall did not indicate an emotional outburst—merely a coincidental accident. But it is certain that at that moment I did not wish to be anywhere else in the world than in that courtroom, separated from my father by only a few yards. It was April 13, 1949, the middle of Holy Week. "The day serves to turn our thoughts in the right direction," my father said. "The actual self becomes the fitting nothing."

A little while later the High Commissioner of the American occupation forces, John D. McCloy, took action. Though not a formal professional authority—no such position existed—he took a stance and ordered my father's immediate release, his first response to any Nuremberg sentence. This occurred in the fall of 1950.

In its editorial of October 16, 1950, the *Frankfurter Allgemeine Zeitung* commented, "The many persons who were saved from death and concentration camps by Weizsäcker were not able to persuade the court at the time. The demands that he be given justice did not fall silent. . . . [McCloy] considered the many voices, especially those from abroad, that considered the Nuremberg sentence to be unjust and came to believe that in 1949 the Nuremberg verdict had been arrived at too lightly. He reversed it de facto."

Churchill himself, speaking at a public debate in the House of Commons at an earlier date, had characterized the proceedings against my father as a "deadly error" on the part of the American prosecutors.

Great Britain and German Resistance

Allow me one more generalization in the form of a footnote to modern history. I want to focus on Great Britain, the key power in the struggle focused on the outbreak of war, in the resistance against Hitler's aggressions, and in preparing the postwar order. In the spring of 1939, after the occupation of Prague, London sent a crucial warning that any further aggressive action on Hitler's part would lead to war. It was the British who declared war on Hitler immediately after the invasion of Poland. Great Britain was the leading political and moral power in Europe against the National Socialist demon. After the fall of France, Great Britain supplied the bulk of the resistance during the hard times before Hitler dissipated his strength in the war with Russia and before the United States entered the war, which turned the tide.

Covert back channels were used before and during the war for intensive contacts between German emissaries and their leading British counterparts. These Germans, my father foremost among them, hoped to persuade the British to take a public and unambiguous stance against Nazi plans for aggression and so prevent Hitler from taking steps that would inevitably lead to war. Once war had broken out, these same Germans felt it important to demonstrate to London the existence and extent of resistance within Germany, hoping by this proof to win agreement to end the war without Hitler's involvement. This resistance group needed help from outside the country if it was to explain its actions to the German people subsequently.

Today an extensive literature, with generally accepted findings, relates the German contacts with Great Britain. Adam von Trott, executed after July 20, 1944, established these contacts, as did Theo and Erich Kordt, brothers and diplomats, and others. They thought of themselves as a group of friends who, according to their own statements, worked under the protection and at the direction of my father. At his urging, the Swiss historian and High Commissioner of the League of Nations in Danzig, Carl J. Burckhardt, and the Primate of the Norwegian church, Bishop Berggrav, head of the resistance to Hitler in Norway, also brought their influence to bear on the British.

But in vain. The British democrats and the German resistance could not find a point of agreement.

Of course it was difficult for the British to make a reliable picture of the extent and impact of these voices within Germany. Furthermore, many of them must have lacked the will. In London outrage at Hitler was not an undiluted emotion; it was merely part of a greater anti-German sentiment. Anthony Eden, the foreign minister, made no secret of his disinclination to distinguish between a Germany under Hitler and one salvaged by the resistance. Some in the foreign office were even relieved at the failure of the assassination attempt of July 20, 1944. Notes from the files of this department written by John Wheeler-Bennett are revealing. A close friend of Eden's, an official in the Foreign Office Intelligence Department, and author of *The Nemesis of Power*, one of the first books written about the Nazi period after the war, his notes include the following passage:

> It may now be said with some definiteness that we are better off with things as they are today, than if the plot of July 20th had succeeded and Hitler had been assassinated. . . . The Gestapo and the SS have done us an appreciable service in removing a selection of those who would undoubtedly have posed as "good" Germans after the war. . . . It is to our advantage therefore that the purge should continue, since the killing of Germans by Germans will save us from future embarrassments of many kinds.

Anyone holding such a view could hardly care about the specifics of internal opposition to the regime in Germany. The unfortunate phrase *unconditional surrender* is part of this context, since it could make it harder to organize a coup d'etat in Germany. Wheeler-Bennett once more: "We should not put ourselves in the position of having any dealings with whatever Germans, good or bad. . . . This goes along with the principle of unconditional surrender." (Quoted in Richard Lamb, "Das Foreign Office und der deutsche Widerstand 1938–1944," in Müller and Dilkes, *Grossbritanien und der deutsche Widerstand,* 1994.)

Churchill agreed with this Allied principle. After the war he conceded that he had been misled about the resistance in Germany. The appropriate signals had been allowed to die in the foreign office. When Roosevelt speculated about the name history would give to the war, Churchill suggested, "The unnecessary war." In his opinion Great Britain had allowed Hitler to exert his blackmail for far too long before the war and during the war had ignored the resistance in Germany.

No thinking person given such information will be tempted to minimize Hitler's crimes against humanity and the crimes of war by comparing them with other outrages in history. And yet today we can view the events of the first half of our century in a wider context. To start with, Great Britain and Germany were both imperialist powers that, thanks to their colonial and naval policies, increasingly engaged in rivalry. Hitler's crimes and his attacks on all of Europe finally exposed Germany to the condemnation of the whole world. Great Britain, a leader in this assessment, therefore justifiably witnessed not only the punishment of evil but also the final settlement of its old conflict with Germany.

The two world wars, however, brought about a new world order, detrimental not only to Germany but also to the United Kingdom as new, shared problems gradually arose from the consequences of the conflict. Most of the British, however, were still far from such premonitions until the end of the Second World War. Once again Churchill was one of the first to take notice of the signs of coming events. His great appeal to Europeans in his speech in Zurich in 1946 is proof.

Choosing a Profession

I was done with school, and the Nuremberg Tribunal was behind us. Now I had to decide what to do with my life. I was past thirty, high time to get on with it. An older friend advised me not to place too much emphasis on the particular job I took; sooner or later I would be able to work my own special interests into whatever career I chose. In the long run, he said, another consideration would be even more important to my happiness: to work without a boss and with as few colleagues as possible. Independence, he believed, was an unbeatable asset.

Easy for him to say, I thought to myself. At the time his advice seemed pretty cavalier. I did not have the advantage of being born into a family business, but I was not entirely free to choose, either. There was no one to smooth my path—I had to make my own way. And so I learned to work under a great variety of bosses, good ones and bad ones, horrible examples and genuine models. Nevertheless, as I gathered more experience, I learned to value that friend's advice more and more. His opinion and his faith in me were good incentives.

I was most interested in politics and contemporary history, and I hoped to use these interests to maintain and make use of the contacts with my friends from the war and the university.

The first offer I had to consider concerned the Institute for Contemporary History (Institut für Zeitgeschichte), established in Munich under the superb direction of Hermann Mau. During my work in Nuremberg I had been one of the first Germans given access to documents from the National Socialist period, and I had taken more than a thousand pages of notes on them. The decision to continue this work in Munich seemed obvious. And the institute was not averse to taking me on.

But after a great deal of thought I arrived at a different conclusion. I had not inherited the family's scholarly bent. Even more important, I had no wish to spend my life devoting myself to the study of National Socialism. I was much more interested in doing all I could, together with my friends, to draw concrete inferences from the lessons of the immediate past, most of which we had experienced at first hand.

If I thought in terms of politics, I could imagine several ways to begin. Should we, for example, set our sights on elective office right away? But how, and where? The established parties and their leadership did not immediately welcome us into their arena. They were still defining their mission, and the process of forming a viable party was a slow one, since it involved internal power struggles and debates concerning the best direction to take.

Heading the CDU (Christian Democratic Union), Konrad Adenauer tenaciously pursued relations with the West, while Jakob Kaiser and his friends in the same party were more interested in an all-German option. The situation in the SPD (Social Democratic Party) was similar. In that party Ernst Reuter, the mayor of Berlin, supported the American demand that West Germany establish a state as soon as possible. However, other Social Democrats, Kurt Schumacher among them, were hesitant to take such a step because they feared that it would contribute to the permanent division of the country—an outcome they were determined to avoid. The FDP (Free Democratic Party) in the southwestern part of Germany, with Theodor Heuss, Reinhold Maier, and Wolfgang Haussmann, carried on in the traditional liberal way. But the party's branch in Lower Saxony was at that time clearly far to the right and insufficiently liberal.

In spite of internal sectarian struggles, however, the leaders of all the parties were alike in one respect: The generation of the fathers and grandfathers was back in place. The old veterans from the Weimar Republic and those who had returned home from internal and foreign emigration were back at the helm, and we—the younger generation, who had fought in the war—were supposed patiently to wait our turn. At that time there was no demand for youth in politics. The practice, which lately has flourished like weeds, of choosing the profession of politics practically from the tenth grade and to do so by the Jacob's ladder of party politics, had not yet become customary. Of course I am not opposed to this newer practice in principle. It is still better for an interest in politics to arise very early than not to occur at all. Without parties, democratic politics are unthinkable in a society such as ours. Further, there will always be strong and impressive people who know what direction their lives will take at an early age and who, like young Napoleons, will use every means their epoch offers to rise to the top.

But in most cases these youthful careerists do not exhibit any laudable strengths in Germany. They make themselves prominent at an early age in the political youth organizations by demonstrating a fairly provocative energy. Then, when they have won their first interesting open-ended mandates, they gradually let themselves be domesticated. With little or no independent experience in ordinary jobs, they seldom have opportunities to move into the private sector. All too quickly they may become psychologically and materially dependent on political benefactors, whose bread they are allowed to eat if they will only dance to their tunes in return.

My generation was saved from such temptations, if only because the older men thought that they could carry on very well without us. Not seriously troubled by this state of affairs, we were driven much more by a fundamental need for political independence. We wanted to acquire our own professional experience and amass enough material wealth to remain free to act according to our own lights.

Interpreting *politics* broadly, a career in the public sector was another possibility I could seriously consider. I made several approaches in this direction, but I was really serious about only one of them. At the instigation of an undersecretary in the foreign office, I sent my papers to the office's personnel department. I had done quite well in both the legal examinations and my doctoral orals, and I had a pretty good command of the required two foreign languages, English and French. I could also give a satisfactory reply to the question—asked frequently at that time—concerning any political taint acquired in my activities during the Third Reich. The denazification tribunal had certified my lack of involvement, adding that I was "not affected" by denazification. Bonn took a favorable view of all my qualifications, and the foreign office notified me that I would soon be asked to appear for an entrance examination.

But this never materialized. Later I heard hints that the rejection had come from the highest echelons in the foreign office. Who could have blackballed me? At the time Germany did not yet have a foreign minister; Adenauer combined the offices of both chancellor and foreign minister. But my rejection could hardly have come from *that* high an echelon. Surely Der Alte, as Adenauer was known the world over, did not take a personal interest in the next generation of diplomats and would not find much to object to in my name. There must be someone else who found my name a stumbling block, and there was: the state secretary of the foreign office, Professor Walter Hallstein. He was the high authority who was troubled by my application.

This type of roadblock was fairly common in those days in the liberated part of Germany. Unanimous in condemning guilt by association as practiced in the recent past, we now found isolated signs of a timidity that I considered shameful and lacking in self-assurance. But my opinions carried little weight, and as it turned out, the incident did me no lasting harm.

My personal relations with Hallstein were more harmonious later, when we met as members of the same parliamentary group, and at the beginning of the 1970s, when we crossed swords on the question of the Eastern treaties. In the intervening years I had come to appreciate the pioneering European policies he promoted as head of the Brussels Commission. However, I thought less of the doctrine named for him—the Hallstein Doctrine—that dealt with domestic policies.

It was my own fault that I lost the first real opportunity—at least first in terms of time—I had to enter public service. Private reasons were behind this omission. After my legal internship I routinely applied for permanent employment in the justice department, a common practice, since this career option was always considered a fallback position. The justices were, of course, completely free to decide on candidates based on their review of examination results.

Though I was not in the group both admired and infamous of those who had received perfect marks, my grades in the second exam were good enough to actually earn me a summons—which arrived later—to serve as a judge. But three days after the exam I left on my honeymoon. The postal service did not forward my summons and reminder notices from the president of the higher regional court to Ravello on the Gulf of Salerno. On my return I therefore found the punishment I deserved: I was dismissed from the civil service! I'm afraid this fact remains in my personnel files to this day.

This too was not a catastrophe, professionally speaking. I had not pursued a career in the judiciary very seriously, in spite of my respect for this field. And in the meantime a private company had offered me a real job; I was asked to become a "scientific intern" in the mining division of the Mannesmann Corporation, a major firm in the mining industry.

Quite contrary to the tradition of my family I now took—even before the second state law exam and my wedding—my first professional steps into the world of business. I acted out of a desire for independence and to broaden my personal horizons in an industry that, at the time of our country's reconstruction, was crucial. The salary certainly did not exert an irresistible attraction. Rather, I began with the modest monthly remuneration of 120 DM along with a per diem of 6 DM for each day spent working in Gelsenkirchen, the site of the company's bituminous-coal pit.

Almost thirty years later, as vice president of the German Bundestag, I paid another visit to Gelsenkirchen. On this occasion and after a successful descent into the pit, the colliery staff council presented me with a voucher for 6 DM because, according to my old work contract, I was entitled to the compensation. The gesture came from the heart, was typical of the miners, and meant a great deal to me.

I found the people of Gelsenkirchen enormously likable. I lived across from a large colliery on Bismarckstrasse, where I rented a room from a mining deputy's widow who initiated me into the benevolent and calm atmosphere of the Ruhr area. Here some life-changing private events occurred.

In honor of Saint Barbara, patron saint of mining, the town held an annual festival to which my boss, Hans J. Braune, head of the Mannesmann mines, always brought various family members. His sharp eye and warm heart made him particularly fond of a young niece, whom he wanted to invite to the festival. A kindly fate made him choose me to escort the altogether charming young woman, who was just finishing school. Though her name was Marianne, she was often called Barbara at that time, and so the patron saint shed her grace on me as well. In short, it was not long before Marianne accepted my proposal, and ever since she has been the joy of my life and of our family.

Marianne von Kretschmann's family came from Schleswig-Holstein on her mother's side. Her father's family came from Franconia, and the family chronicle records more than a few unusual histories. One ancestor, it is believed, was a Hussite who died at the stake. Another, a master shoemaker in Nuremberg, had been a contemporary and fellow guild member of Hans Sachs, though, sadly, Richard Wagner never discovered him. Still another headed a Nuremberg regiment.

Early in the nineteenth century an earlier Kretschmann, chancellor of the exchequer to the then Duchy of Saxony-Coburg-Saalfeld, freed that state from an enormous burden of debt. At the same time he raised the level of culture at the Coburg court by persuading Jean Paul and other leading figures to choose this city over Weimar. Jean Paul referred to him as "a splendidly philosophical and deeply respected mind." Subsequently Kretschmann tutored Coburg's Prince Leopold in thrift, which turned out to benefit the kingdom of Belgium, since the same Prince Leopold was crowned in 1831 as the first Belgian king. Ever since then, Belgian history books have mentioned the name of Kretschmann with great esteem.

Later my wife's family resettled in the Mark Brandenburg. There a grandson of the Coburg Kretschmanns became a minister, while his brother served as a Prussian general who distinguished himself by bravery in the Franco-Prussian War of 1870–71. He was in the habit of writing almost daily to his wife; his letters described with a meticulous devotion to truth and compassion the sufferings of the civilian population and the soldiery during the war. This habit was to win him unsought fame in France and Germany. Years later one of his daughters, Lily, found these letters at home and was deeply moved. Because she directed all her energies to the cause of peace, she decided to publish her father's letters. A French publisher got hold of this book at a time when a wave of revanchism was sweeping France, and Prussia was the great enemy. The confessions of a high Prussian officer reporting on the misery of war perfectly suited the times. Under the title *Lettres de Kretschmann*, the work became a bestseller in French bookstores. The letters did not serve the purpose Lily had intended—to turn people against war; instead, they turned the French against Prussia.

Kretschmann's daughter had an even harder time of it at home, in the military-conservative Germany of Wilhelm II. Her idealistic temperament made her a pacifist and follower of the reform socialists, which resulted in vehement confrontations with Clara Zetkin. Lily— now writing under her married name Lily Braun—began to write very popular books that went into large printings. The best known is her *Memoiren einer Sozialistin* (Memoirs of a Socialist), a significant work recently reissued. Without agreeing with all the author's views, my mother read this courageous woman's books with great admiration before the First World War.

Marianne's family made its home in Potsdam until the Second World War, then the partition of Germany divided the Kretschmann family. Direct ancestors and other family members lie buried in the Bornstedt Cemetery in Potsdam, which in its own way continues to testify to the good sides of the history of Prussia.

Mannesmann's Economic Section

As far as work was concerned, I spent the next few years in the world of coal and steel, which provided me with an opportunity to learn a branch of the German economy that was vitally important during reconstruction of a country destroyed by war. For one thing, everybody needed what the mining industry produced. For another, that same industry established the bases for new economic and social structures in the country.

Certain clear characteristics of our system were gradually developed during the immediate postwar period. Among them were comprehensive reform of labor laws, the Labor Management Act, codetermination by the executives in the larger corporations, and activity in the international European Coal and Steel Community; these were the first and crucial steps on the way to today's European Union.

As head of the economic-policy division in Mannesmann, I had to deal with these structural questions of sociopolitics. Not infrequently they were hotly disputed topics among corporations, the parties to wage agreements, and the political parties. I brought a deep conviction and had some success in bridging these conflicts between management and labor, business and politics.

For example, one vehement confrontation concerned "coal and steel codetermination"—that is, the innovation, introduced only in the coal and steel industries at first, of parity between representatives of management and labor on boards of directors and the inclusion of directors chosen by the labor unions in the corporations' executive committees. One side saw these innovations as a strong turn for the better in the social climate, while the other side saw dangers for the freely responsible business community, which had a chilling effect on foreign investors.

Using our corporation as headquarters, I conducted empirical social research on this disagreement. We retained the Frankfurt Institute for Social Research, which had won an international reputation under the leadership of Max Horkheimer and Theodor Adorno. While they worked on the project, I had a lot of fun watching these great sociological intellectuals express great curiosity and not a little awe when they met with my bosses—that is, the captains of industry along the Rhine and in the Ruhr, with whom they were also a little ill at ease. In this context they openly tested their highly critical theories of late-capitalist ruling structures against the postwar practices in the mining industry. I felt that their expert opinion was helpful in clearing the air. Codetermination in coal and steel did not work any miracles, but it did contribute to social harmony in the nation and became a crucially positive accomplishment.

Social Teachings of the Churches

On a more general level I was particularly interested at that time in the social ethics of our newly won democracy, which was jelling into its final form. It was a field noted for lively theoretical discussions, active social programs, and practical social initiatives.

The ideas of the Frankfurt School and other emerging secular academic trends competed with more traditional Christian-theological social ethics. At this time both Protestant doctrines and Catholic social teachings attained a new flowering. What was at hand was a third way, between capitalism and communism, marked by changes in the world of work, and the first steps toward a developing policy on north-south differences. Today similar pioneering contributions of Christian social teachings to help solve our great contemporary problems—the population explosion and worldwide migrations, unemployment and German xenophobia, the conflict between work and family experienced by many women, permissive affluence here and growing poverty there, globalized amoral capitalism, exploitation of natural resources—are, sadly, relatively rare.

In the early 1950s the situation was quite different. At that time Catholic social doctrine in particular exerted a strong influence, not as theological dogma or prophetic social criticism but as a helpful guideline, a way to test the ethical values of a sensibly responsible freedom. It derived the principles of solidarity, subsidiarity, and the public welfare from its conception of human values.

The basic differences from the views of the Protestant church were minimal. Of course I was always pleased when, in specific cases the Protestant side chose responsible action over public opinion—not unlike the well-known difference between the ethics of responsibility and of opinion elaborated by Max Weber. Thus the way to proceed meant not simply doing what was right in principle and leaving the consequences to God but considering responsibly and in advance the repercussions of one's actions in each individual case.

I belonged to an association of professional colleagues from a number of corporations, and we compared the promises of the various social programs against our everyday experiences. Our group was formed at the instigation of Horst Rheinfels, a lawyer in Cologne and a member of the Rhenish CDU, where his role was as individualistic as it was selfless. For obvious reasons we were interested less in social theory than in practical applications. We discussed the action that would be required to bring about co-ownership, stock held by employees, and salaries reinvested in our branches of the mining industry. That was easier said than done, then and now. We looked for political support.

Support from where? With what amount of active contribution on our own part? The question of membership in one party or another became more pressing for me.

Until that time my relationship with political parties had been fairly impartial. While I had no doubt that parties were indispensable, I also realized that none could ever come close to the ideal. I always respected the fact that some members saw their party as a kind of home, especially when they had endured and shared hard times within the party structure. For me personally the vitality of our democratic constitution is enough to make me feel politically at home.

Of course I was not a freelance artist or scholar. My activities and interests tied me to Germany's sociopolitical evolution. The direction it took mattered to me. Gradually it became a problem to keep my distance from the political centers that were charting this course, the political parties.

James Reston, the legendary editor of the *New York Times*, once coined the phrase, "In politics as in love there comes the moment when you have to kiss the girl." That notion, of course, would confer too much honor and love on the prosaic application for membership in a political party. But I could not wait cautiously forever; you have to take a stand.

But how? In the first political election of my life, soon after the war while I was in Göttingen, I voted for Adolf Grimme, a religious socialist, because I knew and trusted him. I respected the history and current position of the SPD (Sozialistische Partei Deutschlands—Social Democratic Party), but I would have felt strange within its ranks.

The liberals had fought for universal democracy in the nineteenth century and turned us all into liberals in the sense that we were democrats. The Liberal Party proclaimed no secular message of salvation—a plus. Did that mean that the FDP (Freie Demokratische Partei—Free Democratic Party) was for me? In principle its economic moderation made sense to me, but I was looking for a broader sociopolitical philosophy, not a narrow interest group.

I was most drawn to the basic principles of the Union parties— the CDU and its Bavarian subsidiary, the CSU—especially the aspects designated by the U: to learn from the shared experiences of the Nazi years, to deny a political arena to the old sectarian differences, to be inspired by the social teachings, to strive for parity between management and labor, to steer toward a truly national party—such a concept of union was very attractive to me.

What caused me problems was the C in the names of the Christian Democratic Union (CDU) and the Christian Social Union (CSU). Surely it served only to deepen the abyss between pronouncement and realization, between word and action in our policies. Was it permissible to derive a political party program from the Christian faith? Was there anyone even capable of doing so? Christ himself did not proclaim a political program. He did not say, "This is the truth." Instead he declared, "I am the truth." He committed Himself to no abstract law but to a specific course of action—to active love.

If human beings were capable of acting according to the precepts of the Sermon on the Mount, the problems of this world could be solved by political means as well. Perhaps that would be the only way to solve them. To keep the peace, safeguard all against want and hunger, practice justice, strive for the freedom of others—how often we fail in these attempts! The C must never be allowed to fall silent as a demand we make on ourselves; but to use it as a political slogan? To advance it as a distinguishing mark in rivalry with other democratic parties, when there are believers and unbelievers in every grouping? And where some believers are not automatically paragons of humaneness and democratic thinking?

Of course I was far from the first who felt such misgivings and found it always easier to ask questions than provide answers. For me the decision whether to join a party became acute in 1954. It would have been much too naive for me to renew the debate over the name of the CDU. By now the C was a permanent part of the name, abused by some, an inspiration to many, an annoyance to others. However, I felt that there was one response the name would never provoke: indifference, among the party's friends or its enemies. So I made up my mind to join. It always seemed useful to me when political opponents asked where the CDU's full name could be seen in action. It is good to have an explicit standard for others to measure us by. Equally valuable were the internal debates, not only in commissions—in which I became deeply involved in subsequent years and where such self-examinations were the order of the day—but also in everyday power politics. The C in the name is and continues to be a thorn in everyone's side; that is its most important asset. At the same time it is a reminder of what Luther described as *sola gratia*, our justification not through our good deeds but solely through grace—in light of our shortcomings.

The composition and motivation of the party membership at that time can be compared with today's only with some modifications. In those days the CDU successfully exploited every opportunity as a newly created national party. Its reach extended from slightly left of center to fairly far to the right.

The preamble to the program, composed in Ahlen in 1947, to which Adenauer himself contributed, contained the terse statement, "The capitalist economic system has not done justice to the governmental and social interests of the German people." In the decades that followed, such high-minded declarations did not arrest the triumphant march of capitalism, which by now has advanced beyond the necessary moral boundaries. The Ahlen Program contained a call to nationalize the mining industry, which at the time was in its heyday. Today only losses are socialized.

At the same time, from the moment the CDU assumed the mantle of government with Ludwig Erhard at the helm, it advocated an economic policy that, while socially directed, was unequivocally liberal. From the start the party membership included a significant number of conservatives; for them no serious party alternative existed.

From such beginnings the new type of colorful and broad-based national party came into being. It grew into more than an ideal arena for leading party strategists; most important it was helpful, even essential, in assisting the new democracy to become firmly established. By regularly combining the relatively strong right-wing electorate with other sections of the party into a cohesive group with shared interests at election time, the party made a crucial contribution to avoiding the sad experiences of Weimar.

Important preliminary political decisions binding on the whole were made in its pluralistic ranks. Both the CDU's achievements and its failures were frequently deciding factors that determined the country's course. Time and again the same age-old concern was felt within the ranks of the CDU: It was impossible to keep alive something that was doomed to ossification. The only good conservative is one who is capable of accepting renewal. And the only good restorer is one who can successfully advocate the overdue changes of the conservatives. These are precepts learned from Benjamin Disraeli. Anyone, then, eager to bring about reform, who looked to smooth the path for difficult but unavoidable decisions of the Federal Republic, had to pick just the right moment to influence the direction of the CDU's long convoy. In the following years I too became concerned with this task, especially in the areas central to my active interests, domestic and Eastern policies of the 1960s and 1970s.

But to start with, I was merely a silent member who did not even try for a seat.

Fifteen Years in Private Industry

Pursuing my career, I worked in the industrial sector for another fifteen years. After Mannesmann I became acting manager of a small private banking firm, Waldthausen & Co., in Essen and Düsseldorf. Owned by a distant relative of my wife's, the bank was mine to run for five years, until a family heir was old enough to take on the responsibility. During this period I learned how to be an independent entrepreneur. Success and failure depended largely on me. It was hard work but highly instructive.

My third and last position in industry led me to Ingelsheim on the Rhine, into the pharmaceutical firm of C. H. Boehringer Sohn. The managing director of the branch, Ernst Boehringer, who had recruited me, was energetic, forthright, and large-minded. As head of the family business for forty years he took it to the top of the German pharmaceutical industry. He made a specific point of ensuring that the constantly growing family fortune was treated not as privately disposable capital but as an economic resource dedicated to the good of the company and the community, as Robert Bosch and Ernst Abbe had already done in their firms. Boehringer was passionate about research and development of new medicines to effectively treat and cure persistent diseases. The older he grew, the more he felt morally responsible whenever third parties abused a company product to make it dangerous for humans or nature, even though he could not have foreseen the particular misuse of the medication in question.

Such modest restraint was not a noted trait of German businessmen, but at the time there was little reason for such a stance. During the first twenty years after the war the success of the Federal Republic rested squarely on its economy. With Ludwig Erhard's active support and triggered by the Marshall Plan, German industry became known all over the world for creating an economic miracle. Accordingly many industrial leaders were not shy about stepping forward and demanding political influence. I will cite only two examples, drawn from my experience.

Mannesmann once sent me to Baden-Baden for a so-called industrial institute, to last three weeks. About twenty of us participated in the course, which was intended to train us at every level to become the next generation of managers. Funded by the federal industrial association, the leading lights of the business world lectured and discussed with us not only research and production, marketing and sales, accounting and human resources but also society and politics.

The final lecturer was Fritz Berg, president of the association. Speaking frankly, he told us his vision of what it meant to be a business leader in society. A revolt broke out during his discussion, instigated by me because his statements touched me personally. Berg had attacked the so-called Göttingen Declaration, made by eighteen German physicists who voiced their absolute refusal to participate in any way in the research and development, deployment, or disposition of atomic weapons. These included the nation's leading nuclear scientists, headed by Otto Hahn, Max von Laue, and Werner Heisenberg. The Declaration caused quite a stir, with sharp criticism in the Bonn government camp and a press campaign that seesawed back and forth. My brother Carl Friedrich, who had drafted the Declaration and was one of the signers, even managed to become a cover idol to illustrate the lead story in *Der Spiegel.*

Fritz Berg took the strongest exception to the Declaration. Industry, he announced, would categorically refuse to tolerate such illegitimate interventions by arrogant intellectuals, who irresponsibly damaged the economy and thus the whole country. Here too, he noted, business must fulfill its leadership role. I contradicted him: We were talking about basic political decisions, I said, and in these matters the voices of researchers—with their scientific-ethical responsibility—carried no less weight than economic interests.

At the break the moderator—a cousin of Erhard's, as it happened—asked me with deep concern to please practice greater restraint. He pointed out that we did not want to offend the industrial association, which was sponsoring the institute. Surely it would be better to learn from President Berg than to contradict him. But I was not the only member of the course who rejected industry's outspoken claim to leadership. Our quarrel ended without reconciliation, but apparently Fritz Berg had enjoyed the open exchange; a few weeks later I received an inquiry from him about joining his firm.

The Bonn government's principal fighting cock opposed to the Göttingen physicists was Franz Josef Strauss. As a one-time cabinet member for atomic matters and now minister of defense, he was close to the issues. Regarding almost all military or peacetime uses of atomic energy, he had little sympathy for my brother's position. The Göttingen group was, for all practical purposes, summoned to Bonn. There Adenauer, Strauss, Hallstein, and Generals Adolf Heusinger and Hans Speidel argued with the mutinying physicists. At dinner the highly regarded originator of all the evil, Otto Hahn, sat next to dry Walter Hallstein and across from Strauss, who with all his combativeness was always ready for a pointed joke. Accompanied by his neighbors' laughter, Strauss complained that the only reason for the disagreement was a failure of vocational guidance: If Hahn were state secretary in the foreign office instead of a scientist, there would be no messages coded in legal mumbo jumbo but only diplomatic memoranda, the kind anybody could understand. And if Hallstein had become a scientist, the atomic bomb would never have been developed. Thus Strauss dealt with his anger at the physicists by seizing the chance to make fun of Hallstein.

I had one further opportunity to observe the thoughtless self-assurance of the industrial association when it asserted political claims.

Shortly before the 1957 elections to the Bundestag I received an invitation from the industrial association's general manager, Gustav Stein. He asked me to run and guaranteed me a seat in the Bundestag as an FDP representative. When I pointed out that I was enrolled in the CDU, he assured me that it didn't matter; I'd simply have to resign "in a dignified manner." There it was again, industry's astounding claim to the power to arrange the political landscape according to its will. There is nothing wrong with being close to an association and having its support. But what about the representative's independence? Our conversation ended quite quickly, "in a dignified manner."

From the Patriarch of Rhöndorf to
the Revolution of '68

During this time, when the German economy was recovering so successfully, Adenauer had a firm hold on the political helm. With all his support of the industrial sector, he took a strong interest in maintaining social and political peace in the country by cultivating a cooperative relationship with Hans Böckler, the grand old man of the unified trade union, now firmly coalesced in the DGB (Deutscher Gewerkschaftsbund—Association of German Labor Unions).

This ploy left Adenauer free to expend his energies in the two areas where he concentrated his powers: foreign policy, in order to secure the legitimacy of the new federal republic, and elections, to safeguard his course against enemies from within. Early on, bitter disputes centered on domestic and Eastern policies—for example, the so-called Stalin Notes in the spring of 1952 and rearmament. Adenauer steadfastly followed the course he had set himself. This tough and plainspoken man, as skilled as he was power-conscious, succeeded magnificently in putting his stamp on the times. He helped our nation win worldwide respect by firmly establishing a democratic constitutional state in the domestic sphere and steering a clear, reliable Western course in foreign affairs.

I met Adenauer for the first time in 1957. He invited Fritz Berg and several young men working in industry and interested in politics for tea in his official residence. When Berg and I, seated at a small table, promptly found ourselves embroiled in another minor altercation, Adenauer joined us and took my side. He clearly enjoyed keeping his powder dry while others squandered their energy arguing. He was a shrewd and ironic debater but always exercised a relaxed, paternal kind of humor. No one could miss his self-assured superiority.

But of course he was not infallible. One important task he neglected, even when talking with us: He did little to encourage the younger generation to actively participate in democracy. Young people saw in him the leading statesman, who could wage polemical political battles without growing unnecessarily emotional. They lived under a fairly authoritarian chancellor whose opinion of his colleagues—both friends and opponents—was clearly none too high; in fact, he seemed hardly to need them at all. What the younger generation saw was a cool skeptic, at times a misanthrope. Whether or not this impression corresponded to reality, the effect was what mattered. And thus a whole "without-me" generation, as they were known, gradually grew up.

Without a doubt other causes contributed to this phenomenon, which had nothing to do with Adenauer. Deeply disillusioned by the devastating failure of the National Socialist state, with its claim to totalitarian politics, we were reluctant to become committed once more. Most of us were also busy enough building our own private and professional lives. These concerns were strengthened by our fearfulness of all politics. For these reasons some recruiting on the part of the political leaders could have made a big difference. And no one else would have had as much authority as Adenauer to mobilize the next generation for the newly established democracy. He steered the republic excellently; but during all the time he was at the helm, he persuaded only a few exceptional young figures to become active in the democratic state.

A long time passed before a new generation asked for the floor. During the 1960s remote passivity gradually turned into the protests of an aggressive minority. This evolution moved the center of the country away from the Rhöndorf Patriarch and toward the youth revolt of 1968.

In spite of its illusions and brutality, the movement of 1968, with its sweeping rejection of everything, was a sharp turning point in the postwar period. It was, in the words of Hans Magnus Enzensberger, a "civilizing necessity." We paid a high price for it, though.

On the one hand the uprising brought about a new, more honest response to the Nazi past and changed people's attitudes to the government in irreversible ways, giving our democratic society a new character. On the other hand the many absurd, antiauthoritarian tribunals, the determination to violate every social and ethical taboo, and the obsession with theory alienated many people who were otherwise quite ready to accept reforms. The majority of workers found little they could use in the ideological campaigns. Though the facades of the traditionally privileged classes quickly collapsed, the next step saw the beginning of an ongoing search for a fundamental ethical consensus, without which no humane society can function for long.

But the new age of civil initiatives and the movement of 1968 did not drop from heaven without warning. The 1960s as a whole, anything but a colorless, sleepy decade, were characterized by a turbulent, finally wild vitality. An explosion of technical-electronic innovations was matched by ferment in culture and the arts. Young people began to explore alternative lifestyles.

Joseph Beuys taught his theory of artistic creativity: All those who affect the world and the future, he claimed, are creative artists in their own way. Imagination is not a musty nook where a few talented artists can hide but a creative impetus to anyone living in the world of technology.

Hans Werner Henze composed his stirring polyphonic oratorio *The Raft of the Medusa*, which deals with the dramatic death struggle and fight for survival of people in the Third World and ends on a drumbeat that scans to the name of Ho Chi Minh.

Along with contemporary literature, the new cinema made indelible inroads. Unlike "your father's movies," the art form developed a vitality that shaped the sensibilities of the young. The generation that wrought the change was represented by Alexander Kluge, Werner Herzog, Rainer Werner Fassbinder, Volker Schlöndorff, and others with ties to Max Frisch, Heinrich Böll, and Federico Fellini.

The Beatles performed in Germany, the pill made its debut in the United States, and Yuri Gagarin successfully orbited the earth for the first time.

At the center of such turbulence bubbled profoundly impressive political and scholarly initiatives. The opening measure was sounded in 1961 by the newly elected United States president, John F. Kennedy. His thrust toward new shores also echoed the thoughts of many Germans who felt that Kennedy was speaking to them when he said, "Ask not what your country can do for you—ask what you can do for your country." Surrounded and advised by the intellectual elite of his nation, he used his unique combination of dynamism and rational calculation to find ways to lessen the tension with the Soviet Union and reduce the danger of world war. His was a fascinating personality. The world fell silent at the news of his assassination; Germany mourned almost as deeply as the United States.

Another internationally significant figure who helped to shape the times was Pope John XXIII. This pontiff, elected to the papacy at the age of seventy-seven, understood the signs of the times and the sensibilities of the next generation. His important reforms stemmed from a new way of thinking. He cared passionately about reconciling the Church with the world and abolishing divisive economic frontiers. His genuine contemporaneity defined his faith. Believers and unbelievers alike revered him and felt motivated to act in accordance with his vision.

The Pope's influence was particularly strong and lasting in Germany, a country that since the Reformation had harbored a number of denominations, with all the problems attendant on such variety, even in the private sphere.

I found new directions in my own life that would determine my future. For me, lay activity in the German Protestant Conference, long-term membership in the council of the Protestant Church of Germany, and an assignment to the World Council of Churches in Geneva were at the core. Though it was not these activities but my subsequent political work that placed me in the larger world, I owe thanks to these organizations for giving me the strongest influence for the period just ahead. These organizations attracted me and gave me my formal education, and their atmosphere and the friendships I formed there created a place where I could put down roots. Since they were so influential in forming my views and later actions, permit me to describe these years before I discuss politics in the narrower sense.

German Protestant Conference

T he German Protestant Conference dates back to 1848. At the founding assembly in Wittenberg, Johann Hinrich Wichern gave his famous speech promoting ecumenism and the Christian-social movement. By laying the cornerstone for the Inner Mission, which continues its diaconal work to this day, he helped establish the Conference, which had a long, eventful history before it perished in the disturbances of National Socialist rule.

Reinhold von Thadden-Trieglaff, the Pomeranian Pietist who was a courageous and contentious participant in the struggle between church and state during the Third Reich, decided while in Russian captivity near the Arctic Ocean that he would revive the Conference. He had a flair for touching a contemporary nerve, and his energetic leadership resulted in a Protestant lay movement much more extensive than any seen previously. The first large-scale convocation took place in Essen in 1950.

What does the word *layman* connote? It does not mean a lay person as the word is understood in the Latin nations, which use the word *lay* to distinguish secularism from religious initiatives. Nor does it indicate a distinction between ordained clergy and unordained members of the congregation, a difference of little significance in Protestantism; Martin Luther used the concept of the general ministry of all believers to oppose precisely such a division. According to his admiring critic Karl Marx, Luther "shattered the faith in authority by restoring the authority of faith. He transformed the priests into laymen by turning laymen into priests."

Of course we attended the resurrected conference not as Marxists but as Germans defined by a steadily increasing secularization. The society in which we live tolerates the churches and supports their functions but no longer acknowledges any ecclesiastical mandates. Society today determines its own guiding ideas and sets its own ethical norms.

Laymen as understood by the Protestant Conference are professionals active in secular society who take their bearings for life in this world from the Christian faith as best they can. Not intent on increasing the power of the church, they simply want to share the responsibility for living in committed harmony with the church. If they have any motive, it is to comprehend the standards learned from historical experience. They have no interest in or possibility of declaring a policy in God's name, unlike both revolutionaries and ultraconservatives. Thadden, the devout and sensible founder, would never have permitted such a claim.

The response to his appeal exceeded all expectations. At the convocations—at first held yearly, then every other year—huge meeting halls were thronged with thousands upon thousands of participants whenever the burning questions of the day were discussed in ways both controversial and open to reconciliation. Many who felt isolated in their everyday lives looked for togetherness at the German Protestant Conference. For them the Conference was an assembly, a meeting of the faithful who were scattered at other times, where they hoped to transcend the limitations of congregations, dioceses, and sects.

Lively discussion on inter-Christian and current social topics dealt with reform of the popular church and the role of military chaplains. Theological workshops saw verbal altercations between those who favored literal readings of biblical texts versus others who advocated interpretations that tended to demythologize the text. Discussions concerning peaceful relations with our wartime enemies were just as heated as those on aid to the Third World. Hermann Ehlers, the president of the Bundestag, and the theologian Helmut Gollwitzer, in spite of their diverging positions, joined in calling for political commitment. Labor leaders and managers debated the social benefits of the market economy. The Christian Democratic minister of culture, Edo Osterloh, spoke openly with the Social Democratic party leader, Fritz Erler, about the parties' campaign slogans and was willing to admit, contradicting statements that came from the Chancellor's office, that he did not believe Germany would collapse if the SPD won the election.

The study group "Jews and Christians" made a deep impression on me at the Conference. It sponsored the first serious dialogue since the Holocaust in which Israelis and Germans participated, foremost among them Jewish and Christian theologians. I will never forget how Ernst Simon, who had emigrated from Germany to Israel, recited Jewish biblical interpretations that could prove instructive to every Protestant professor of systematic theology. Rabbi Robert Raphael Geiss from Düsseldorf appealed to our conscience with his implacable but not unforgiving commitment to truth by comparing actions of Christians throughout history with the principles of their faith. But the participants from Israel were not spared searching questions regarding their treatment of Palestinians in the Middle East.

Today it is hard to imagine the atmosphere that prevailed at these encounters. No one displayed excessive religious zeal; we were much more likely to practice the sobriety the Bible enjoins on Christians so that each one could rationally realize his share of responsibility for his time and his world. "Love thy neighbour as thyself" we are taught in Sunday school, but the Conference recognized the more precise interpretation of the saying given by the great Jewish theologian Martin Buber: "Love your neighbor because he is the same as you"—that is, relate to him as to yourself. This does not mean transferring the love you feel for yourself to him but seeing in him your own weaknesses and selfishness and overcoming them in the encounter with him. When you help your neighbor, you help yourself. Consequently building new bridges between people, groups, and societies traditionally at odds was one of our primary goals.

One scene from the Cologne Conference of 1965 remains indelibly etched in my mind. It was shortly after the promising conclusion of the Second Vatican Council under Pope John XXIII. Though we were Protestants, this overwhelmingly Catholic city on the Rhine welcomed us warmly. The Catholic prelate, Cardinal Josef Frings, hosted a reception for us in the Cathedral museum, but he did not give the usual welcoming speech; instead, the frail, almost blind old man recited from memory the verse in Galatians that became the basis of the Conference: "Stand fast in liberty." It was a truly gripping, moving ecumenical high point among Christians in Germany. No one could resist the moment. Konrad Adenauer and Martin Niemöller, standing near me, embraced—these two men who had always met only on opposing sides of what it meant in the real world of politics to stand fast in liberty.

I was fortunate enough to meet with Niemöller frequently. At one occasion, his retirement from the presidency of the Protestant Church of Hesse and Nassau, about fifteen speakers took turns praising him—governors, bishops, and secular figures. After listening with growing emotion, he finally rushed to the podium, first expressing regret that his wife—who had been killed in an accident—could not have been present to hear what a fabulous husband she had married, then loudly calling to those of us who had spoken: "But everything you said was untrue." This valiant Christian then confessed his failings. His autobiography, entitled *From the U-Boat to the Pulpit,* told the story of his days in the navy. My father used to say that a better title would have been "On a U-Boat to the Pulpit."

The Conference was uniquely effective in a divided Germany, and soon it became the strongest, most visible organization embracing both Germanys. At the close of the Conference in Leipzig in 1954 over six hundred thousand people from both parts of Germany gathered on the Rosenthal Meadow. Catholics and Protestants, Christians and non-Christians, all were driven by the desire to gain strength through solidarity. The Protestant Conference was among the first to choose a road that led more and more clearly to the final phase of the

East German party government; people assembled under a protective church roof, not primarily to share in a Christian communal life in the everyday world but to experience liberty and to defend it.

Responsibility for the Protestant Conference lay with its president, and elections to this post were held in both parts of Germany. With the erection of the Berlin Wall in August 1961, which occurred only a few days after the last Conference in Berlin attended by participants from all over Germany, contact became difficult to maintain but was never entirely severed.

Soon I found myself taking on a much larger role. Thadden, citing his age as the reason for resigning the presidency, asked me to succeed him. His request took me completely by surprise. I lacked many of the strengths that had defined his presidency, such as his dynamic Pietistic temperament and his history and experience in the church. To borrow an expression from Paul Tillich, I felt more a part of the latent church than of the manifest one, and my attitude toward the church was not always free of doubt, though always hopeful. Not last, I feared that my profession would not leave me even the little time that the office, though an honorary one, would require.

But as with everything else he set his mind to, Thadden pursued this idea with the determination characteristic of him. And so I was sworn in. There is no doubt that I was fascinated by my work in the Conference. I got more out of immersing myself in this organization than I did from diving even more deeply into the waters of private industry. Now forty-four years old, if I were ever to make a decision about my future, this was the time. Of course I could not foresee where this road would eventually lead, but it was obvious to me that I stood at a crossroads. Fully aware of these implications, I agreed to take on the office.

Although Germany was hermetically divided by this time, the election involved both parts of Germany. The West German members who made up the electoral committee, known as the presidential assembly, traveled to East Berlin and did their job together with the members from the German Democratic Republic (GDR or East

Germany). Given the sharp political division and highly uncertain future for both church and state, we found it an exciting and emotional meeting. Great expectations were expressed, but we had no idea how we might fulfill them. And as I thought about the leadership role that had now fallen to me, I could only recall Luther's saying about fear and trembling.

But of course I could not let myself be afraid. I could not let feelings dictate my work, what was needed were substantive arrangements for upcoming Conference themes. Fortunately I had little time for anxiety; immediately after the election I had to meet the press in West Berlin. Even though I had no previous experience with press conferences, no special treatment was accorded the neophyte. When I finished speaking at the television camera for the first time, the reporter instructed, "That was fine, you spoke for ninety seconds. Please repeat what you said, but this time say it in half the time." This was my baptism by media.

In the following years I paid countless visits to our friends in East Berlin and the GDR. I saw firsthand the harshness of their existence and the strength of their faith within a system that kept them under observation at all times. The GDR authorities were equally aware of my visits; my entry into the country was not always smooth. At times I was turned back after a long wait at the Friedrichstrasse crossing with the words, "You are not welcome in the GDR." The countless contacts and meetings in East Germany, always stirring, and the information I gleaned from them about life in the GDR quite naturally led me to subsequently focus my political energies on domestic and Eastern policies.

The Ecumenical World Council
of Churches

The ecumenical nature of the Protestant Conference led to close collaboration with the World Council of Churches headquartered in Geneva, whose membership includes all the world's Christian denominations except the Roman Catholic Church. *Ecumenism* is derived from the Greek word for the whole inhabited world. The objective is unity. But what kind of unity, and how is it to be achieved? Is inter-ecclesiastical, interdenominational contact the crucial element, or is the intercultural dimension—that is, justice and peace in one united humanity—the goal?

The Roman Catholic Church is not only the largest Christian church by far; it is a worldwide church, linked in one way or another with the lives of all peoples. The member churches of the Geneva ecumenical council, on the other hand, generally have local, national, or regional roots and frequently suffer more from interdenominational antagonisms; resolving these is especially important. But as far as I could see, in the World Council of Churches—especially concerning the secularization and de-Christianization of the world—no serious argument took place over the view that responsibility for the church and for the world are inseparable. We were only too aware that the world felt pressured by the question not of *what* but of *whether* the church believes. The church can respond only by finding itself in the world, speaking and acting in the world, so as to make a contribution toward progress and change in the world. Though the search for church unity is important, it is not an end in itself. Contributions aimed at the revivifying and peaceful unity of humankind and to preserving the Creation for all were our central concerns.

For seven years I was on the executive committee of the World Council of Churches, a group of about twenty representatives from member churches from all over the world. We met two or three times a year in various places around the globe, each meeting lasting a week. Our chairman, M. M. Thomas, was a Methodist from southern India. Our South African fellow was Archbishop Desmond Tutu, who, next to Nelson Mandela, is the person who deserves most of the thanks from his nation for exerting the energy and courage to overcome the plague of apartheid. He must still carry the principal burden of the work of reconciliation with South Africa's recent history.

The Russian Orthodox Church was represented by Metropolitan Nikodim, head of the Moscow ecclesiastical foreign office. Stout and bald, he was a cunning prince of the church with a great sense of humor. Once we were swimming in the ocean, and all I could see in the distance was a majestic beard bobbing on the water as he pushed it in front of him like a camouflaging wall. Unfortunately Nikodim was too much under his political rulers' thumb. A central topic of all our agendas was how to protect and preserve human rights in many parts of the world. When cases of rights violations in the Soviet Union were brought up, Nikodim refused to discuss them. There was nothing to investigate, he insisted, since the Soviet constitution guaranteed human rights. Of course other Orthodox priests who did not hide behind the altar's decorative icons when injustices were evident displayed greater courage as advocates for the oppressed.

The member who lived the greatest distance from Geneva was the archbishop of New Zealand. He persuaded us to hold one of our sessions in his homeland. Meeting us at the airport, he pointed out that the purpose of the meeting had already been accomplished: during our long trip, he hoped we had finally come to see what a chore it was for him and his compatriots to always have to travel to these "damned" conferences in distant Europe or the Americas. He was absolutely right.

We even held meetings in Addis Ababa. The local Coptic Christians were extraordinarily hospitable. Emperor Haile Selassie invited us to a prayer breakfast, while his granddaughter thoroughly familiarized us with the misery and poverty in her country. From Nairobi, where the Ecumenical Council held a three-week-long plenary conference in 1975, I traveled to the South African Christian Council, whose white general secretary, Christiaan Frederick Beyers-Naudé, was a strong rock against the racist tide. When I called on then Prime Minister Balthazar Vorster, not only did he offer endless explanations on foreign policy, he almost literally assailed me with biblical quotations that, he believed, constituted a strict Christian commandment to separate the races. I cannot think of a more disagreeable and fruitless political argument.

Representing the Council, I visited South Korea three times, once with another member of the executive committee, the then Indonesian chief of staff, Tahi Bonar Simatupang, a courageous Christian from an overwhelmingly Muslim society. In Korea we were charged with aiding oppressed and incarcerated priests in Seoul, whose felonies consisted of helping as best they could the many needy people living in the overpopulated slums of the South Korean capital. The authorities believed that such work constituted open political opposition and as a consequence accused the priests, unjustly, of contact with North Korea, which was illegal. South Korean presidents had long known that suspecting troublesome citizens of being crypto-Communists was a foolproof method of holding on to their power. To guard against North Korean propaganda was certainly necessary, but misusing this protective measure to wield power at home prevented the emergence of democracy in South Korea for far too long.

The East-West conflict that dominated great areas of the world at the time also put its stamp on the work of the Christian churches. Pope John XXIII, seeking ways for the church to contribute to détente, had already initiated what became known as the Vatican's Eastern policy. The Cold War repeatedly affected relations among members of the World Council of Churches and even caused some of them to ask Geneva for help in their politically risky situation. In response we frequently held executive committee meetings in nations of the Eastern bloc. When we visited the Orthodox Patriarchate in Sagorsk, we found the atmosphere cordial but the discussions less substantive than the meals and drinks. In Moscow we met with the Soviet minister in charge of religious questions. In Sofia and along the Black Sea we also tried to assist Balkan Christianity.

The Protestant churches in the GDR tried to hold a session of the executive committee in East Germany but were balked at every step. Thanks to the detailed records kept by the Stasi (the East German secret police), I have since learned that I was the one who both caused and resolved the problems. The East German authorities were unwilling to give me an entry permit as the West German member of the committee. But I learned from the Stasi records that World Council General Secretary Philip Potter, a delegate from the Caribbean, made it clear to the East Germans that the World Council would cancel the conference and issue a press release explaining that the meeting was rescinded because they had denied me entry into the country. At that, the East German authorities made sure I was granted the permit.

This meeting took place east of Berlin at Bad Saarow on Lake Scharmützel. At a reception hosted by the government I met the head of the Catholic Conference of Bishops in the GDR, Cardinal Alfred Bengsch, who had grown up in the Schöneberg district of Berlin. A man of strong character and firm in his faith, he was a real Berliner, with a ready tongue. He avoided public appearances; when I asked him why he had surprised us all by attending the reception, he admitted that he was making an exception, but he had no intention of keeping me in the dark about his main purpose: to do his part in helping the Catholic Church survive the next two hundred years in the double diaspora imposed by Communism on the one hand and Protestantism on the other. Though his words fortunately turned out to be less than prophetic, they were pessimistic enough and meant seriously. All the same, he added that he had no wish to withdraw from the community of believing Christians in an atheistic society, and besides, he was curious to see for himself what we were up to.

Transition to Détente

In the meantime my activities had shifted more and more from economic and social concerns to domestic and foreign policy. Even though I held no political office, the 1960s offered me many opportunities to participate in social protest as part of the international debate on the East-West conflict.

It is generally agreed that the Cold War had its roots in the Second World War. Russian historians are pretty well united today in identifying the Allies—who opposed Hitler as well as Germany, the aggressor nation—as a Western interest group hostile to the Soviet Union. Very soon after the war the treatment of Germany became one of the decisive questions in the conflict between East and West. In 1948 American political leaders asked the governors of the West German provinces to found a democratic state, with the idea that this entity would be the West's front-line bastion in its ideological conflict with the East. As early as 1950, only five years after the war ended, the United States secretary of state, Dean Acheson, declared that West German military contributions to strengthening the West were essential. Only France objected, and Stalin was alarmed. Since Lenin's days it had been one of Moscow's prime objectives to prevent a German military presence in the Western Alliance against the Soviet Union.

Of course Stalin himself had contributed greatly to this course of events, which he feared so much. It was he who had forced the ideological conflict, closed all elements of the emerging East bloc to the Marshall Plan, and started the Berlin blockade. This attempt to prevent the establishment of the Federal Republic of Germany and isolate Berlin from the rest of West Germany failed in the face of the Western

airlift and the attitude of the Berliners themselves. Instead of succeeding in neutralizing the free sector of the city and finally co-opting
it, Stalin had achieved the exact opposite: West Berlin became increasingly valuable to the Western Alliance and the Western idea of freedom. It remained the most important test area in all inter-Germany
political conflicts.

After these setbacks Stalin soon switched songbooks and began
to whistle the Moscow version of the peace tune. In the two Stalin
Notes, which have since become well known, he suggested free elections for a united and neutral Germany as early as the spring of 1952.
But the West would not be seduced into agreeing to a deadline for a
test of Stalin's new advances. Adenauer was especially firm in his opposition. Today all sides can calmly discuss the matter, but at the time
the sharp controversy between government and opposition over a
possibly missed national option left a long-lasting sting. Adenauer did
not reach the summit of his foreign-policy career until the Federal
Republic was recognized as a sovereign state with membership in
NATO. The policy of strength prevailed.

Gradually, however, new elements emerged. The Kremlin initiated a second attempt at détente. The victorious powers withdrew
their forces from Austria, which became an unaligned nation. Adenauer
received an invitation to visit Moscow and persuaded the Russians to
release the surviving prisoners of war. The German people may have
appreciated this achievement more than any other of his great successes.

But by this time the Soviet Union had performed its first atom-
bomb tests. Given the balance of fear, the Cold War had arrived at its
triple theme: ideological conflict, dispute over Germany, and the
atomic arms race.

The coming years were difficult for West Germany's foreign policy. Hardly any of the Western Powers still believed that the Soviet
Union would agree to German reunification. Just the opposite, Moscow attempted to strengthen the status quo—that is, legitimize its conquests in Eastern Europe and establish the GDR's absolute dependence

on the Soviet Union. Given these conditions, how could steps toward détente be reconciled with domestic policies satisfactory to us? A conflict within the West began to take shape. Would détente make a solution of the German question easier in the long run? Or, conversely, was détente possible only by reuniting the separate German states?

Bonn pursued a composite policy, as it was called at the time, but we never encouraged an East-West agreement that did not address the reunification question. The Hallstein Doctrine began to predominate, with the intent of preventing the primary goal of Soviet policy—to establish the diplomatic and international legitimacy of East Germany. It is in truth hard to say how strong the desire for German unity might have been if something like the Hallstein Doctrine, which reflected our reluctance to enter into a treaty with the Soviets, had never existed.

In time the Hallstein Doctrine grew into a dogmatic foreign-policy armor that was not conducive to a separate Bonn Eastern policy. The Federal Republic's Eastern policy essentially consisted of Western policies—that is, of inducting the Western Allies into the principles of Bonn.

But by now none of the Western powers were interested in shaking up the status quo. The first suggestions for an arms limitation agreement with the Soviet Union appeared in the United States. Soviet premier Nikita Khrushchev had seized the reins in Moscow. Eager to loosen United States ties to Bonn and its composite policy, he made an initial attempt in 1958 by creating a new and serious Berlin crisis. West Berlin, he threatened, must become an independent political entity, free of the presence of troops from the Western Alliance. On August 13, 1961, Walter Ulbricht's urging and orders from Moscow resulted in the erection of the Berlin Wall. The following year Khrushchev built missile installations in Cuba only 90 miles from the United States.

The most critical moment of the Cold War was now at hand, but as sometimes happens in history, it became the turning point instead.

Washington forced the withdrawal of the Soviet rockets from Cuba. Military confrontation was avoided. Both superpowers respected the nuclear balance, with each acknowledging the other's sphere of influence. The Berlin crisis waned. The Wall remained, but Moscow stopped wholesale questioning of the Western presence in Berlin.

With this situation, a new and important period of postwar history began. Détente became the dominant theme, with Kennedy preeminently representing the West in this effort. Even before Kennedy assumed the presidency, Albert Einstein, along with Bertrand Russell, had seized the initiative in favor of arms control. Kennedy then engaged American scientists to work with their Soviet colleagues as well as specialists worldwide to explore steps to control nuclear weapons and keep their proliferation in check, though this initiative had no results.

With Kennedy's support the so-called Pugwash Conference was established. Consisting of leading consultants from the worlds of science and technology, it was intended to smooth the way to collective security in the atomic age. Soon pacifist idealists began to infiltrate this group of rational scientists, and their presence did not always make agreement between Western and Eastern policies easier. Nevertheless, the larger topics of arms control—from the first Test Ban Treaty of 1963 through the Nuclear Non-Proliferation Treaty and Strategic Arms Limitation Talks (SALT)—are among the heirs of Pugwash. Only in December 1995—that is, after a thirty-year delay—did it occur to the members of the awards committee to confer the Nobel Peace Prize on the surviving veterans of the Pugwash Conference.

Nikita Khrushchev also participated constructively. Many people think of him only in connection with the Berlin and Cuban crises, and they recall most vividly the shoe he banged against his desk at the United Nations General Assembly. The British delegate to the United Nations, William Ormsby-Gore, even suggested at the time that one standard measure should apply at all future disarmament talks: No weapon should be allowed that was larger or louder than Khrushchev's shoe.

And yet this rough and energetic figure had restored life to Moscow, which had become petrified under Stalin. As a flesh-and-blood man all could understand, he became popular even in the West. Today's scholars are trying to verify the speculation—granted, a very controversial one—that perestroika could have come about under his regime in the 1960s if the "old men of the Presidium" (Oleg Grinevsky) had not hounded him from office.

Everywhere, including Western Europe, the desire for a new, relaxed relationship between East and West now became widespread. If you can't beat 'em, as the saying goes, join 'em.

In Western Europe, General Charles de Gaulle was the first to pursue this policy seriously. Particularly concerned that the attainment of détente not be left entirely to the United States, he wanted a European form of collaboration with Moscow "from the Atlantic to the Urals." He also shifted the question of German unity from a political to a historical perspective—that is, to a far-distant future, the same policy Gorbachev preached to me twenty years later in Moscow, two years before the Wall fell.

Naturally the full course of these events also strongly influenced the political debate in Germany. West German officials continued to take their bearings from the Hallstein Doctrine, while our two most important allies, the United States and France, prepared to enter into a kind of détente competition. De Gaulle's tabling the question of German unification to a distant historical future upset Bonn as much as did Kennedy's new tune. These initiatives threatened to shove Bonn aside.

Adenauer has been accused often enough of dragging his feet in the serious pursuit of German unification because he saw hidden and uncontrollable dangers to the Federal Republic's security in the policy of détente. These reasons, it was said, were behind his putting on the brakes whenever any kind of reconciliation between East and West began to stir.

I always thought such judgments superficial and unfair. It is true that Adenauer's visions for Germany and Europe were defined more by Cologne than by Berlin. He never denied the Rhenish sentimentality that was deeply wounded when at the 1815 Congress of Vienna, Prussia was given not Saxony, as Karl Hardenberg had hoped, but the Rhineland. In Adenauer's view, Great Britain had "destroyed" Europe because it thought only of a strong counterweight to France and therefore dispatched the rulers of Berlin to Cologne. But Adenauer was much too skilled a statesman to overlook reality. Earlier than others he discussed with the Soviet ambassador the possibility of a solution for the GDR that was modeled on the position of Austria. Four months after the Berlin Wall went up, he proposed a ten-year truce to Moscow, of course without listing the specifics he had in mind. Considerations of human rights weighed more heavily with him than did nationalist objectives. He himself admitted at the time that he thought the primary task for the rest of his life was to achieve a more tolerable relationship with the Soviet Union.

And yet in the early 1960s a public debate began, concerning the correct attitude of the Federal Republic toward the Eastern bloc. As time passed the arguments became more heated and controversial, culminating in the early 1970s in an emotional confrontation in the Bundestag over the Eastern treaties.

The first step, which resonated far and wide, was not taken by the political parties but emerged as a private initiative. Eight men, representing the world of science, issued the Tübingen Memorandum—as the document came to be called—to express their critical view of the Federal Republic's political situation. All the signatories were Protestants and close friends. Each was already well known in his own field and had taken a public position on the subject. Werner Heisenberg; Georg Picht, the philosopher and educator; Ludwig Raiser, the president of the German council of science; Hellmut Becker, subsequently director of the Max Planck Institute; Klaus von Bismarck, manager of West German Radio; and my brother Carl Friedrich were among them. Their most outstanding adviser within the church was Bishop Hermann Kunst, the representative of the Protestant Church to the Bonn government.

These men were not malcontents who passed the time writing

long screeds. Their motive was alarm over a growing rigidity in the political landscape. Putting forward detailed arguments, they accused government policies of not telling the full truth to the people and of avoiding difficult but necessary decisions. They cited as an example the unplanned concessions made to the electorate in order to sway the election, and they demanded a thorough revision of the educational system. A core section of the memorandum was devoted to foreign policy. Here the writers primarily addressed German-Polish relations and demonstrated the inevitability of recognizing Poland's new western frontier at the Oder and the Neisse.

Reading the text of the memorandum today, we find arguments that are now generally accepted. At the time, however, all the points still seemed controversial, and the document aroused heated public reaction.

Since I had personal ties to all the writers and had participated in drafting the foreign-policy section, I joined the public debate. I wrote my first full-length newspaper article on the topic of domestic and foreign policy, with particular emphasis on relations with Poland. I argued against the stereotypical and outdated formulas that in my opinion could only serve to isolate us. I suggested instead that we take control of relations with our neighbors, no matter how difficult this might be, rather than barricade ourselves behind the idea that only a freely elected government representing all of Germany could address territorial questions and could do so only in a peace treaty. Who, I asked, could possibly have an interest in offering us such a treaty if we ourselves did not become active?

Nevertheless the response of the parties was at that time largely negative on precisely this point. My only success was my first author's honorarium, which I used to give myself the consolation prize of a secondhand old twenty-volume edition of *The Oxford English Dictionary*.

Viewed as a whole, the Tübingen Memorandum represented a symptomatic and important step, a sign that the motto "To risk a greater amount of democracy" was already a thread running through all of the 1960s. In a not entirely legitimate way this slogan became famous only later, in Willy Brandt's inaugural speech when he became chancellor.

In spite of official political reserve, the memorandum's sections on foreign policy and especially relations with Poland got the ball rolling. The "Protestant Mafia," as the writers, their friends, and commentators were soon called, went on with its work.

The Protestant Church also officially took up the topic of policy concerning Poland. Its Board for Public Responsibility, which drafted and issued statements on political questions, was headed by Ludwig Raiser, one of the authors of the Tübingen Memorandum and, as head of the synod of the EKD (Evangelische Kirche Deutschlands, the Protestant Church of Germany), president of the national Protestant governing body. I was a member of the board and second vice president.

During the decades after the war the Protestant Church frequently took positions on social and political questions—in the opinion of some, too frequently and not always happily. Be that as it may, I feel that frequency was less of a problem than was occasional ambiguity and the absence of clarity. The reasons for this state of affairs lie in the nature of Protestantism.

The English poet W. H. Auden, who married Thomas Mann's daughter Erika in 1935, is credited with the saying "The truth is Catholic, what's Protestant is the search for truth." If that were true, it would be enough for Protestants to concentrate on seeking out one Catholic. In reality, we are all searchers. The difference is merely that each church has different traditions and rules to guide our journey and unique ways to arrive at agreements and decisions.

Like the local congregations, religious leadership committees reflect a free, pluralistic community whose members hold varied views and struggle with different difficult situations in their lives. To be united in faith certainly means having the dedication and will to take the Ten Commandments and the Sermon on the Mount seriously. But nowhere is it written that we must agree on all worldly questions.

Dietrich Bonhoffer distinguished between the Last Things and the Next-to-Last things, between belief in God's truth and responsibility for fulfilling our purpose in this world. If a synod or organization takes a stand on a contemporary problem, it is dealing with Next-to-Last things. And when opinions differ, what matters most is that we discuss them with each other as calmly and honestly as possible instead of attacking each other in the belief that we alone are in possession of the truth of the Last Things. To communicate is often a complicated process. More than one public statement from the churches has handled the truth so respectfully that it sacrificed clarity and effectiveness.

In the mid-1960s, however, the Board for Public Responsibility issued one declaration on a central topic with clarity and lucidity, achieving a highly unusual effect. This was the memorandum entitled "The Situation of Displaced Persons and the Relationship of the German People with Its Eastern Neighbors," a document drafted and signed by board members from both the East and the West.

The statement caused heated controversy but finally touched the political parties so deeply that it moved them to advocate a policy of détente, especially in German-Polish relations. Thus the Federal Republic for the first time shifted the topic of Poland to the position appropriate to it. The source of this new awareness was not any political organization but rather society itself—and the churches in particular—both in Germany and in Poland.

For Germany, France and Poland represented the two most pressing areas for reconciliation. But these were radically different tasks, both in their historical roots and in the ways they could be solved. What succeeded between the French and the Germans is one of the great successes of the postwar period. Both nations' political leadership brought it about, while the idea of a united Europe paved the way. Neither the French nor the German people seriously question this understanding.

When it came to German-Polish relations, on the other hand, statesmen's hands were tied for far too long in both countries. For Germany the reason was the greatest and by far the most painful consequence of the war—the loss of its eastern provinces; politically, this motive was strengthened by the connection between the open German question—that is, the future of East Germany—and recognition of the Oder-Neisse Line. For the Poles it was a matter of security from future German claims, and even more crucially to become the nation of Poland, free from encirclement by Russia and Germany, a condition from which the nation had suffered since the partitions of the late eighteenth century. Hitler could start the Second World War because he and Stalin had forged an agreement at Poland's expense. However, because of the continuing Soviet presence a free Polish nation remained unattainable far into the postwar period.

Providing outside aid to Poles in their effort at freedom and finding willing collaborators within Poland for this endeavor required a willingness to agree on a single social and historical view. The churches in West Germany and some of their committed lay members took the lead in this effort. Polish counterparts besides the powerful Catholic Church hierarchy included Catholic intellectuals, writers, and—as members of the Znak Group—such independent Sejm members as Stanislav Stomma and Tadeusz Mazowiecki. Toward the end of Vatican II the Polish bishops wrote a letter to their German counterparts that contained the widely publicized sentence "We forgive you and beg your forgiveness." In Germany the most important role, next to that of the Catholic bishops who replied to the letter, fell to the Protestants. This moment demonstrated the great importance of the memorandum. For me too it was the actual point of departure for taking part in a new German-Polish relationship, which was particularly dear to my heart.

The main reason the Tübingen Memorandum was so effective was because consideration of the subject was long overdue. It was high time the Federal Republic took the initiative to improve relations with its eastern neighbor and, to the greatest possible extent, normalize them. It was neither humanly reasonable nor politically smart to keep alive the hopes of those Germans who had been driven from their homes in the territories ceded to Poland that there might soon be a peace treaty allowing them to return home because the old German eastern provinces, or at least a part of them, would be returned to Germany. The loss of their centuries-old homeland aroused the most profound emotions, and it was the churches and congregations that had to deal with these concerns. Consequently understanding also grew as to how irresponsible it would be to continue to deny this reality, as previous policies had done.

The topic of the memorandum was a good example of the special care the church must take in distinguishing between Last Things and Next-to-Last Things. History teaches that ecclesiastical authorities were many times prepared to impose their personal beliefs with the claim that they were carrying out God's will. It was allegedly on orders from an angry God that Jeanne d'Arc was burned at the stake; and yet not long after that act an all-merciful God commanded her canonization. Granted that such examples are taken from the Middle Ages, even in our own day in composing the Eastern memorandum we had to avoid a danger already penetrating the synods—that is, citing the authority of the Bible and the name of God either to demand that Poland renounce territory beyond the Oder-Neisse Line or, conversely, to insist with the same authority on our right to a homeland.

This time our board members agreed that honesty and truth were paramount in an approach to peace in the East: We were thinking of Next-to-Last Things. After all, the effectiveness of the memorandum would depend on the clarity of this statement.

A small delegation of the EKD, which included the current chairman, Bishop Scharf, as well as Professor Raiser and myself, held discussions with the heads of the Polish parties. Ernst Lemmer and Johann Baptist Gradl, delegates from the CDU, were troubled by the possible effect of the memorandum but still joined the discussions seriously and honestly—especially Gradl, who had a fairly clear idea of the consequences to foreign policy and who did all in his power to help displaced and persecuted persons deal with their taxing lot.

Fritz Erler, Herbert Wehner, and Helmut Schmidt represented the SPD in our group, with Erler acting as spokesman. He argued responsibly, intelligently, and circumspectly. Wehner opened his mouth only rarely, but when he did, he erupted like a volcano to remind us that we in the church would not be the ones suffering the consequences of our proposals. But he as well as Schmidt frequently attended the Protestant Conference.

On the whole the party leaders did not seriously question the legitimacy of the Memorandum. Rather, they more or less obviously welcomed its influence on the ever more inevitable discussion of the issue, just as the response among the larger public was overwhelmingly positive.

Two years later the same board issued another paper, entitled "Germany's Peace Missions." The drafts had been discussed and altered in numerous sessions, held almost exclusively in East Berlin, and the topic dealt with Germany's shared responsibility. Erhard Eppler, at that time federal minister for economic collaboration, and I were the principal writers. He was an active politician, I was not.

Later the two of us had a number of disputes over the basic principles of our parties, each of us contributing a great deal of work on their concepts and wording. At the same time, however, we shared many beliefs—for example, that on the whole parties seem to care more about getting elected than promoting basic principles, though perhaps my problems in this area were somewhat greater than his. Furthermore, we both held strong personal opinions, which we preferred to air in our respective parties rather than keep to ourselves—a trait we were teased about by some in the top leadership echelons, who called us at times "brothers in principle." And why not? I often encountered Eppler at the board and the Conference and learned to value him highly. Possibly each of us might have benefited from some minor adjustments in his idealism and my level-headedness. Nevertheless, his thinking is clear and interesting, his positions sincerely held, his promises reliable. As a political writer he was extraordinary because his papers were always worth reading. In the course of the years many of us agreed to speak on the anniversaries of June 17, 1953—not always an easy job. Our compatriots in East Germany always listened alertly to the ways we West Germans spoke about the uprising of 1953, as if we had performed the heroic deed we were commemorating. I cannot remember a speech on such an occasion that was more impressive in content and tone than the address given by Eppler in the Bundestag on June 17, 1989—only a few months before the fall of the SED government.

Another duty that helped unite us was working together on church committees. These collaborations were often encouraging to us and sometimes provided relaxation from our professional political daily work.

First Encounters with Helmut Kohl

By now East-West policies were progressing from the Adenauer era to the Willy Brandt government, and in this transition period society—and the churches, with their memorandums and open letters—played a more significant role than before or after. This effort involved me as well. Of course the government controlled decisions on any shift in direction. Before I discuss further events in policy making, let me briefly describe how this situation affected me.

Because of my work on papers and conferences dealing with Eastern policies I had one foot in politics, though I still did not hold and had never sought elected office. But only a short time before, I had been seriously tested on this matter when Helmut Kohl put the question to me. He visited me in the spring of 1965 in Ingelheim and suggested that in the coming Bundestag elections I become a candidate from his home district, Ludwigshafen.

Kohl, thirty-five at the time, was working energetically to make the Rhineland-Palatinate section of the CDU more liberal and raise it to national status. When it came to strengthening his own ranks, he did not hesitate to demand that various local parties or the delegates responsible for making up the voting lists include candidates from other provinces. Over the years his methods persuaded Heiner Geissler, Bernhard Vogel, Hanna-Renate Laurien, Norbert Blüm, and eventually Walter Hallstein and Roman Herzog, to name only a few, to work with him in his province. Such successes made an impression throughout the nation.

Of course everyone realized that with all his efforts on behalf of the party, Kohl was also keeping an unswerving eye on his own political future. And why shouldn't he? Responsible for enhancing his regional party, he struggled to win even greater influence in national political circles for both his party and himself. That is the nature of democratic competition. Because he never tried to moderate the views of those he recruited—being much more interested in displaying them exactly as they were—the party he created was quite extraordinary in its inclusiveness and vitality.

Some years later a leading journalist wrote a detailed character study of Helmut Kohl entitled "His Appearance Is His Message." That phrase always reminded me of our first meeting. His straightforward plan of action and his cordial openness in our long conversation made a deep impression on me. Of course he was acutely aware that my statements up to this time and my involvement in church affairs were not compatible with the positions held by the CDU, especially on the subjects of Eastern policy and on détente. But he seemed to feel that this disparity was a plus. I certainly could not deny that the CDU had a pointed interest in nominating the president of the Protestant Conference to a seat in the Bundestag. The idea of the Union as a religiously ecumenical organization had been largely accepted in political circles, to the extent that it was not always clear at first glance whether some of the best-known CDU leaders were Catholic, Protestant, or something else altogether. However, the Catholic element remained predominant in the party, especially in the Rhineland-Palatinate area, so that any additional Protestant affirmation of the concept of *union* was welcome.

Now for the first time I received a letter from Adenauer, who appropriated Kohl's suggestion and repeatedly urged me to accept. A second letter sent from beautiful Cadenabbia arrived only a short time later.

But I could not accept. The year before, I had assumed the Protestant presidency, which forbade any advocacy of political positions. I could not and would not combine it with an electoral office. But I always remained indebted to Kohl for the idea and for the very personal way he proposed it. I had no doubt that sooner or later I would campaign for political office; but 1965 was not the time. We agreed to talk again at a later date.

Eastern Policy Initiatives from Berlin

The rigidity of West German relations with the other Germany and the Eastern bloc nations began to soften. Gerhard Schröder, who became foreign minister in 1961, set out to loosen the strict application of the Hallstein Doctrine to the European nations under Communist rule and to establish various relations short of full diplomatic exchange. His so-called Peace Note of the spring of 1966 was an enormous step in including the Federal Republic in the West's policy of détente and charting a new relationship with Eastern Europe. This note proposed the first nonaggression agreements, which later became the heart of the Eastern treaties. Schröder, an intelligent, experienced, steadfast politician, was immovable in matters of principle yet responsive to new historical events. Many within and outside the Union saw him as the man of the future.

The most important initiatives, however, came from Berlin, where erection of the Wall had sent out shock waves. When no one in the Western Alliance made a move to oppose the physical division of the city, the last illusions dissipated. Willy Brandt, then mayor of West Berlin, often described the situation by saying, "The curtain went up, and guess what, the stage was empty." He was referring to the stage where the play chronicling the Four Power governance of Berlin was to run—a play that in reality had simply ceased to exist.

At first, Berliners harshly blamed President Kennedy for standing idly by while their city was newly divided. But the relationship changed quickly when the Berlin senate initiated an Eastern and German policy of its own. A few months after the Wall went up, contacts with a representative of the East German government were undertaken—something quite unheard of in Berlin—initiating the policy of small steps. In December 1963 the first agreement on frontier-crossing permits was signed, allowing the people of West Berlin to visit their relatives in the eastern part of the city for one day during the Christmas holidays. Almost 800,000 people, more than a third of the population, made the pilgrimage. Subsequent similar agreements were even more far-reaching. It became a common saying that small steps are better than big words. As would become clear, in spite of all domestic discord, there was no turning back from the path so recently cleared.

At that time too the famous and infamous phrase "change through reconciliation" gained popularity. Coined by Egon Bahr, it became the key concept for both followers and opponents of Willy Brandt's Eastern and German policies. Bahr was not looking for a confrontation with East Germany; he wanted that state's transformation. He admitted his belief in the paradox that overcoming the status quo was possible if we did not immediately ask for it to be abolished. His plan was to make partition easier on the people by making the Wall more permeable. And to accomplish this end, Bahr believed that cooperation from the authorities on the other side of the Wall was necessary. If, he thought, the lives of the people over there were gradually bettered, the improved situation might also ease the tension and in the end bring about change in the GDR.

Arguments have raged about just who would change because of such a rapprochement, and what kind of change it would be. That question has now become moot; in any case, at the time both Brandt and Bahr pursued a course that stopped far short of recognizing East Germany. Keeping a peace treaty in reserve protected German unification interests and made certain that our Western friends would not let the subject drop. West Berlin had always maintained close ties with the United States, which on the whole was quite pleased with these initiatives coming from Germans in Berlin.

The reliable protection of the West was needed for a policy concerning the two sectors of Berlin and the two parts of Germany to make its way to the East.

The next step was taken when the so-called Grand Coalition—of CDU and SPD—took over the reins in Bonn in 1966, with Kurt Kiesinger as chancellor and Brandt as foreign minister. The Federal Republic's old position now changed fairly radically. The claim that East-West détente depended on Germany's reunification was dropped, replaced by its converse—that German unity could be achieved only through détente, provided that détente would lead to a loosening of the system that ruled the East.

Within NATO too a common course was agreed upon. The so-called Harmel Report, named for the Belgian foreign minister, became the blueprint for the further work within the Alliance. Accordingly, NATO adopted a double strategy: on the one hand to guarantee the military security of all its members firmly and unequivocally, and on the other to wage an active policy of détente under the protection of an assured balance in military confrontations.

Soviet feelings seesawed back and forth. Their leaders were concerned that a Western policy of détente might cause disintegration within their own camp. In the Soviet view, some member nations of the Warsaw Pact went too far in their contacts with the West, Romania in particular. Poland and especially Czechoslovakia under Alexander Dubček in the Prague Spring of 1968 started internal reform movements that the Soviet Union suppressed by force because they threatened the Eastern status quo.

But on another front Russian President Leonid Brezhnev sought relief for the Soviet economy through arms-control agreements with the United States. Hope for technological and economic cooperation with the West began to grow, and the Soviets looked chiefly to West Germany to help implement this plan. Though Moscow did not abandon its two basic demands on Bonn—recognition of the GDR and the Oder-Neisse Line—it no longer insisted on compliance with them as a precondition for negotiations. Instead the demands themselves were to become subject to discussion. This concession almost immediately placed Bonn in direct contact with Moscow near the end of the 1960s.

Who Will Succeed
Federal President Lübke?

Who would conduct the negotiations in Moscow? And what authority would this representative be given? Anticipating the elections to the Bundestag scheduled for the fall of 1969, differences of opinion over Eastern policy had grown more acute within the Grand Coalition in Bonn. These elections would determine future governing coalitions.

But another democratic decision had to be made much sooner, one with consequences lasting over a longer period of time—the election of a new federal president to succeed Heinrich Lübke. I must begin by describing the election to this office, especially as I became personally involved, to my great surprise.

The election of a federal president is a peculiar process. Generally such elections are preceded by long campaigns, when the media frequently engage in imaginative speculations about the popularity and suitability of the aspiring candidates (as happens whenever a poll reveals the head of the house of Hohenzollern as the popular favorite). But the decision rests ultimately with the Federal Assembly, which in effect means the parties. These try, legitimately, to use the election to promote their political positions and increase future opportunities at wielding power.

Election to the presidency also brings additional tension because the powers of the office have never been clearly defined. On the one hand the position is less important than the office of parliamentary leader or prime minister, since the center of power as defined in the constitution is a considerable distance from the office of federal president. On the other hand the president is in a position to affect important future developments, for example, by confirming the existing division of power among the parties, by signaling an emerging change, or by expressing the deeper tendencies of an age.

Our federal constitution does a very good job of defining democratic institutions and rules by dictating the separation and control of power. Of course the constitution hardly mentions the content and objectives of this exercise of power. Nor can it show how democratic activities will support the power structure created by the constitutional regulations, on which the vitality of the constitution depends to such a large extent. In other words, the Basic Law derives its dynamism from preconditions it is unable to bring about itself that are based on contemporary attitudes and society's consent.

The office of the federal president is not about institutional power but about these assumptions. To identify them, to articulate them, to mobilize them in order to advance the democratic organism—that is within the range of this office, that is its "power." For these reasons the election of a federal president is uniquely and deeply linked to the spirit of its day.

All these considerations came into play in the election of a successor to Heinrich Lübke. These were the late 1960s, a time of steadily growing disturbances, especially among the younger generation. The Grand Coalition then governing in Bonn was one of the very rare government coalitions whose achievements tended to be underestimated rather than, as was more common, being overblown. At the same time all the parties were preparing for the next elections to the Bundestag. The date of the presidential election, set for six months earlier, could introduce crucial changes.

As I already mentioned, the atmosphere among the parties to the Grand Coalition was characterized by great fluctuations. While the heads of the two parties in the Bundestag, Rainer Barzel and Helmut Schmidt, worked together more competently, more reliably, and in increasing amity as time passed, the relationship between Chancellor Kiesinger and Vice Chancellor Brandt was generally tense. Kiesinger preferred dealing with Wehner; Lübke's second term, largely shaped by Wehner's influence, came to be a heavy burden on Lübke, an honorable, very political president, whose ill health near the end of his term quite unjustly overshadowed his earlier effectiveness.

As early as the summer of 1967, almost two years before the election of Lübke's successor, Brandt, as head of the SPD, informed the leader of the CDU and Federal Chancellor Kiesinger that his party intended to nominate its own candidate for the presidency.

Speculation about who the candidate would be became rife. One name frequently mentioned was that of Georg Leber, who was highly regarded and rightly so, even by the Union. But there was growing internal resistance to his candidacy among many Social Democrats who felt he represented too clearly a sentiment for continuing the Grand Coalition.

I remember clearly having heard Gustav Heinemann mentioned early on during internal discussions. And before the SPD leadership could intimate as much, during a press conference in 1967 I expressed the supposition that the Social Democrats would agree on Heinemann because he was a viable candidate in these turbulent times. As I supposed, I was the first to publicly say as much. And when I spoke, I had not the slightest idea how the Union parties felt about Lübke's successor.

In the meantime the FDP began to stir. Given the opportunity as a small party to take the part of opposition all alone, it proceeded tactically against the government of the Grand Coalition, though with relatively little success. The public's focus was not on this minor party but on an opposition forming outside the government—the youth revolt. But the FDP was determined to remain part of the government even after the next elections. It wanted to be the group that tipped the scales in deciding with which of the two major parties, now drifting apart within their coalition, it would wield its power.

Walter Scheel had been elected to succeed Erich Mende as head of the FDP. Foremost among the difficulties facing him was a tendency, typical of his party, to waver between right and left. He quickly realized that the success of his leadership depended on eliminating the impression, often criticized, that liberals were indecisive and seesawed back and forth. Given this situation, Scheel demonstrated energy and courage.

In the spirit of the times and especially in light of the growing unrest among the young, he decided to fight for a change in the chancellorship in the fall 1969 Bundestag elections. Setting his sights on a Social-Liberal coalition, he recognized clearly that the election of Lübke's successor—which would occur shortly before the Bundestag elections—was the crucial factor in electing a new chancellor, since the number of FDP delegates in the Federal Assembly could make the difference.

Of course such considerations did not remain secret. Although the CDU had not set out to fight for the presidency in rivalry with its coalition partner, the SPD, those in the Union who hoped that the Grand Coalition would continue wanted at the very least to make an attempt to agree with the SPD on a joint candidate. Why not choose someone from the SPD, which had never had a federal president? The CDU would have preferred Georg Leber to Heinemann, whose prospects had by now risen sharply within the SPD but who made many Union politicians see red although in fact he was not very Red himself. They could not forgive him for his "treason" toward his former party, the CDU, and toward Adenauer. The Union leadership was therefore more inclined to put up its own candidate. And because the SPD had long since announced publicly its claim to the office, it became important to nominate someone who appeared highly electable to an adequate number of FDP delegates.

Presumably this was why in the summer of 1968 CDU general secretary, Bruno Heck, called on me to ask if I would let myself be nominated. I could not have been more surprised. Of course later in my political career there were occasions when I tried for a candidacy on my own—sometimes successfully and at other times losing—without knowing precisely each time whether I was responding to my party's wishes. But when Heck came to me with this proposal, I was speechless.

I had good reason to hesitate. I had never held public office. I lacked political and parliamentary experience. To the extent that I was known to the public at all, it was for my work in church affairs and writings on Eastern policy.

In addition, I was convinced that our two-party majority would be of decisive value in this election. Regardless of the effect it would have on the questions of a coalition following the Bundestag elections, I urged Heck to make common cause with the SPD. I was leaning toward Heinemann and soon advocated publicly that the CDU and the SPD agree on his candidacy.

At that time Heinemann was sixty-nine years old, twenty years my senior. I had come to know him pretty well through the mining industry in the Ruhr and especially from the synod of the Protestant Church. He was the prototypical democratic citizen. During the struggle between church and state during the Nazi years he had distinguished himself by his unyielding firmness. A successful leader in the steel industry, he became actively involved in local politics immediately after the war. Later, as federal minister of the interior, his quarrels with Adenauer primarily concerned questions of the two Germanys. I never found him easily approachable; he seemed to me taciturn and pigheaded. He had a keen intelligence and a warm sort of humor, though he liked to keep the latter hidden until after midnight. Many thought he was a Calvinist fanatic, but I believe this idea was unfair. In contrast to his widespread reputation, he generally behaved with moderation. But most important, he was independent. He recognized the need to agree on general guidelines within a party, but in borderline cases he always followed his conscience. In the extraordinarily difficult atmosphere of the late 1960s, a time defined by youth revolutions, his courage and readiness to work for agreement earned him high marks. This was shown particularly in his leading role as federal justice minister when the hotly debated emergency-powers act was successfully enacted in the spring of 1968, only a few days after the assassination attempt on Rudi Dutschke. In short, I considered Heinemann the right man for the critical task of integration, and I supported him both within the party and publicly.

But my efforts were in vain. Helmut Kohl, head of the party in my region, emphatically advised me to accept Heck's proposition for both personal and political reasons. He did not see my lack of political experience as a drawback. On the contrary, he believed that as an impartial outsider I was a better candidate than a hardened, labeled full-time professional. The head of government, Chancellor Kiesinger, also energetically urged me to accept, and the leader of the Bundestag section of our party, Rainer Barzel, did the same.

By now the subject had received widespread publicity. Soon there were opposing factions within the Union: one group argued that the experienced Gustav Heinemann should be opposed by a candidate with at least equal experience—Gerhard Schröder, longtime minister of the interior, foreign minister, and now defense minister. Thus Kiesinger's and Heck's initiative was opposed within the party, though no one doubted Schröder's political qualifications. He was, as he freely admitted, the prototype of a conservative, and he had played a decisive, at times leading, role in the Grand Coalition.

Now the FDP began to deal with the question—and of course I was not involved. But it became known that FDP leaders had at least twice clearly stated a preference for my candidacy over Schröder's. The FDP head of the parliamentary group in the Bundestag, Knut von Kühlmann-Stumm, wrote to tell me as much, and begged me to accept the candidacy. Josef Ertl and several others spoke with me to the same effect. Even Scheel, whose interests lay with the left, was most concerned that his bloc of delegates in the Federal Assembly remain intact because a breakup might be considered another sign of liberal weakness. He explained to Kiesinger that if I became a candidate, it would be practically impossible to commit his friends to Heinemann in a bloc.

The situation became difficult for me. I was just on the point of preparing myself slowly to declare my candidacy for a seat in the

Bundestag—that is, for the first time to take my place seriously and openly in party politics. My presidency of the Protestant Conference, which in 1965 I had considered an obstacle to running for political office, was scheduled to end before the 1969 elections. And here I was already in the middle of a maelstrom of conflicting interests and ulterior motives of the big political guns, for whom the election of a federal president was a particularly suitable field in which to maneuver. Without a doubt Heck's and Kohl's proposal was meant very seriously. And it was understandable and proper that Kiesinger should take a vital interest in the actions of the FDP. He was motivated not only by his well-known dislike of Schröder but also and more especially by hints that the next governing majority would lie with the SPD.

After another private conversation with Heinemann—the two of us were standing in an overcrowded local train from Bonn to Essen—I informed Heck that I was willing to abide by the party's decision on the candidacy.

What followed was entirely normal. An ad hoc electoral committee was formed that consisted of the executive committees of the CDU and the CSU as well as their entire parliamentary groups. The committee was to announce its decision between Schröder and myself on November 15, 1968. Besides the prime minister of Baden-Württemberg, Hans Filbinger, Franz Josef Strauss also became active in support of Schröder. Heck and Kiesinger remained in opposition. Years later Kiesinger still blamed himself for failing to combine his proposal for my candidacy with a vote of confidence in his own leadership of the party.

Shortly before the election it became obvious that Schröder would have a significant majority. A few hours before the decision was to be announced, Kohl advised me to withdraw before it was made public. But by now I was not prepared to shift with a change in the wind. I was convinced that it was a preferable public-relations move for the electoral committee to have an alternative rather than a simple, prearranged acclamation.

The process itself was short, clear, and painless: 65 votes for

Schröder, 20 votes for me. Scheel was relieved. By expending great energy, he succeeded in delivering his friends' votes almost unanimously for Heinemann. In the third vote Heinemann won by the extremely narrow margin of 512 votes to Schröder's 506. The SPD, and especially Brandt, celebrated Scheel as the author of what Heinemann three days after his election characterized as a "change of power," an expression that turned out to be appropriate though at the time it was almost universally criticized. Of course he was not referring to the power of the office; but admittedly, it would have been just as well if he had kept silent about the effects on the coming coalition negotiations.

For me the loss to Schröder was anything but a disaster. Undoubtedly his experience made the job much easier for him than it would have been for me. In truth I was fortunate to begin by living through a harsh political apprenticeship. Besides, I was much too young for that office. And to start a political career by losing an election—that first experience proved enormously valuable in the years to come.

The evening of the day the party decided on Schröder, a heartwarming scene unfolded before me at home. The proceedings had been shown on television. After the votes were counted, Kiesinger had positioned the two candidates on either side of him and—almost like a referee in a prize fight—raised Schröder's arm as he announced the outcome. When I arrived home and cheerfully began to tell about my encounter with Schröder, my youngest son, Fritz, eight years old at the time, grew outraged; he decreed that the name Schröder must never be mentioned again because he'd beaten Daddy. There was no calming the boy. Even though he had no idea what it was all about, he was determined to declare solidarity with his father.

Three years later another crucial election involved Schröder and myself, and this time I received twice his number of votes. This was the balloting for chairman of the party parliamentary group after Barzel's resignation. Though both of us—Schröder and myself—were beaten by the superior candidate Karl Carstens, Fritz was satisfied, because Schröder lagged behind me. He declared that we were allowed to talk about Schröder again.

It is repeatedly said that a political career loosens family bonds. Everyone knows about and understands such dangers. But this was not the case in our family. When I was employed in industry, we hardly ever talked at home about what might be interesting in my work. But when I entered politics, my children gained a practical idea of what Daddy did all day long and thus began to participate daily in my activities. For them to experience at home the ups and downs of the work that occupied their parents' generation brought us closer together and has kept us together.

The Bundestag Election

On September 28, 1969, elections were held to the sixth German Bundestag, elections that profoundly changed the history of the old Federal Republic.

Going strictly by the numbers, the final outcome made three different governmental coalitions possible: a renewal of the Grand Coalition, or an alliance of the FDP with one or another of the major parties. The situation was settled by the resoluteness of Willy Brandt, who from first to last set his sights on a Social-Liberal coalition against the advice of Wehner, Schmidt, and other prominent members of his party.

Brandt was fighting for his Eastern policy. From his term as governing mayor of West Berlin, he had a good impression of the FDP and a bad one of the CDU regarding this objective. Recalling the Grand Coalition, he still resented the Union's effort to put on the brakes and his extremely poor relationship with Kiesinger. He considered it unacceptable to continue this kind of collaboration. Finally, Heinemann's election to the federal presidency reinforced Brandt's liking and respect for the leader of the FDP, Scheel.

Both within his party and in Scheel's there were some unreliable supporters of the Eastern and economic policies dear to Brandt's heart. Nevertheless he forged ahead with forming the new coalition, at first with a majority of only 12 votes over the opposition Union. But he was determined to push through his Eastern policy, "if necessary, by merely one vote," as Egon Bahr quoted him.

The new elections saw the departure from the Bundestag of many leading figures of the postwar period, among them Heinrich Krone,

Eugen Gerstenmaier, Adolf Arndt, and the first woman in the government, Elisabeth Schwarzhaupt. Roughly 120 new delegates were elected, lowering the average age only slightly. The most prominent among them was Professor Walter Hallstein, then sixty-eight years old. He was joined by a group of outstanding specialists and academics: Paul Mikat, Horst Ehmke, and Ralf Dahrendorf. The novices also included Klaus von Dohnanyi, who soon raised the intellectual level of the Bundestag and became a particularly valuable person for me to talk to. I was almost fifty years old when I too was elected and started out on my political career.

In accordance with his agreement of 1965, Helmut Kohl had persuaded the delegates from the Rhineland-Palatinate section of the party to nominate me for a safe place on the list, behind Walter Hallstein and for the time being without a district of my own. For me it was the beginning of a twelve-year membership in the Bundestag.

No sooner did the parliament meet than the first discussion on German policy broke out. Characteristically it was a debate about naming the committee in charge of German policy. The Union made a motion that the title used up to this time, "Committee for Questions of a United Germany and Berlin," be retained. The governing coalition on the other hand wanted to change it to "Committee for Internal German Relations." Was the argument worthwhile? The Grand Coalition had, after all, collaborated pretty well in reference to German policy, especially Kiesinger and Barzel with the minister in charge, Herbert Wehner. Did this move signal a radical change of course? It is a well-known fact that questions of nomenclature are fraught with peril and can degenerate all too easily into bitter programmatic struggles. This peril was in the air now, since both major camps had strong wings with orthodox ideological positions. One side believed it important that the political vocabulary contain no hints that could be interpreted as admitting the mere existence of a German Democratic Republic; the other side, the peace faction, was not afraid to accept the fact that Germans were separated into two parts for the sake of their objectives.

The Union's new chairman of the parliamentary group was the same man who led the group during the time of the Grand Coalition, Rainer Barzel. When it came to policies about Germany, he had a great deal of experience and understood how to operate both with moderation and according to party principles. Since he knew about my long-standing connection with East-West questions in Germany, he wanted me to head the responsible committee. However, he arrived at this calculation without consulting the previous committee head, Johann Baptist Gradl. A brief tussle ended with Gradl's retaining his committee chairmanship and my becoming the parliamentary group's spokesman for German policy. Another consequence of this episode was that during all the years that followed, including all its problems, Gradl and I developed an invariably friendly and trusting relationship.

So I was to be a speaker, and during the very first debate of the new Bundestag I was called to the podium. With Barzel's approval I made every effort to maintain our bridges with the government camp in the area of German policy, even as I preserved the concept of unity as an objective for the present and the future—a course that was easily justified. Besides our elementary yearning for unity, we knew the importance of the way the two Germanys related to each other and to the wider world in the process of détente pervading all of Europe. The Federal Republic had become the eastern outpost of the West, while the German Democratic Republic was the western limit of the East. In spite of this twofold frontier position, Germany remained defined by its central location. The center was divided, but it remained the center, and as such it had interests and responsibilities throughout Europe. Since the thought of German reunification was unrealistic without a peaceful evolution on the Continent as a whole, there really was work to be done toward peace in both parts of Germany in a communal spirit, such as the Protestant Church had worked out in its documents.

As was to be expected, however, this particular dispute was settled by a majority against us. My maiden speech led to no more than "applause from all sides"—as the minutes recorded. The phrase "one

Germany" disappeared from the Bundestag's agenda in spite of my vote in opposition.

The dispute had been more than a mere formality; but it was over and done with. We immediately proceeded to the substance. The subsequent Eastern policy of the Brandt government took on such great importance not merely for Germany but for all of the international East-West conflict that the word *Ostpolitik*—"Eastern policy"—was adopted, sometimes without translation, into the vocabulary of other languages, especially in the United States, where it lives on as a typically German expression, like "sauerkraut," "weltschmerz," and "kindergarten."

Adenauer's historical achievement of firmly inserting the free part of Germany into the alliance of the Western democracies soon after the lost war was now followed by Brandt's equally significant action of finding a way to détente with the East for Germany itself. Based firmly on the West, Brandt's policies and actions led to important preconditions under which his fortunate successors would see a unified Germany and a united Europe.

Brandt looked to initiating direct treaty negotiations with Moscow as quickly as possible. The center of Eastern power would be the deciding factor in our eventual role when it came to the still open questions of relations with Poland, Czechoslovakia, and more important with the GDR and Berlin. Brandt wanted to avoid arousing the suspicion the Soviets had brought to previous encounters with former Foreign Minister Schröder when—for good reasons—he had established contact directly with the Warsaw Pact nations, bypassing Moscow.

Brandt dramatically smoothed the road to the East from the very beginning, with his inaugural address, by breaking the decades-long taboo that forbade any mention of the GDR in political speeches. But because he wanted to introduce the name as unobtrusively as possible, almost as an aside, he cloaked his core statement in an unassuming subordinate clause: "Even if two states exist in Germany, they are not foreign countries for each other." Thus for the first time in official West German wording East Germany as a separate German state saw the light of day. Brandt had voiced the most renowned subordinate clause in the history of German government declarations. Public agitation was almost boundless. But relief and agreement followed, not only in the Eastern bloc but also in the West.

Brandt further improved the climate with Moscow by signing the treaty on nonproliferation of atomic weapons in November 1969. With this stroke of the pen he put an end to a domestic controversy that had become meaningless in that he arrived at terms with the Soviet Union like those that had been arranged with the Western Alliance long before. Then he sent Egon Bahr to Moscow.

In retrospect it is difficult to fully comprehend the domestic and foreign-policy difficulties that had to be overcome in carrying out the Eastern policy. Let me cite a few of them, because from 1969 to the 1975 Helsinki Conference they represent probably the most dramatic and seriously conducted controversies in the history of the German Bundestags to that time.

It was also the most exciting chapter of all my time in parliament, since what was at stake were precisely the topics that had led me into active politics: most notably German policy and our relations with Poland in the spirit of the EKD memorandum, in which I had had a hand.

The first and foremost difficulty was that while East Germany was to be recognized as an independent state, the demand for a unified Germany was not to be abandoned. Formally Bonn was not authorized to negotiate the status of the GDR, since only the victorious powers, acting unanimously, were responsible for Germany as a whole and therefore also for relations between the two German states. Any direct negotiation between Bonn and Moscow was therefore sharply and mistrustfully scrutinized by the Western powers.

To call formally on the leaders in Moscow was politically unavoidable. But such a visit involved not only bilateral questions in the narrow sense but also topics relating to other nations, especially

Poland and the Oder-Neisse Line. The Poles immediately feared that the Russians and Germans would once more come to some kind of understanding regarding the borders of their country, which lies between Russia and Germany, over the heads of the Poles themselves. As a result Poland sought absolute security along its western border created at the end of the war. But the West German government could not and would not abandon at least the option of a peace treaty that depended on the future of German unity.

Achieving agreement on Berlin was of elementary significance and particularly difficult. For the future, new Berlin crises must be eliminated and various access routes must be secured and improved permanently. These measures were exclusively in the hands of the Four Powers.

Finally, Bonn was not prepared—and it was fully justified in this reluctance—to conclude any settlement with Moscow and Warsaw without an agreement on Berlin. Conversely, Moscow was not prepared to negotiate on Berlin only after the Bundestag had ratified a Soviet-German treaty.

Today, a quarter of a century later and after the successful reunification of Germany, we talk about all these complications as if they had been mere bagatelles, as if events had run a smooth course, the outcome of which was never in doubt, since it was politically inevitable. But at the time such ideas were not even remotely thinkable. The Eastern policy was a truly risky operation, unforeseeable to the very end.

Germany had started the war, invaded almost all of Europe, perpetrated deep injustices, and suffered injustice itself. Because of the partition imposed by the victors, a peace treaty, as was customary throughout history, had never been concluded. But questions concerning the consequences of the war—especially geographic results—that the Germans would eventually have to accept and be prepared to suffer were therefore also left formally open. Consequently our country for a long time sustained hopes of favorable changes in the de facto situation, especially the hope of displaced persons for a return to their ancestral homes, now ceded to Poland and Russia, or to the Sudetenland.

However, the victorious powers—and with them practically the whole world—had more or less come to accept the status quo established over the course of time without a peace treaty. German hopes were gradually transformed into illusions.

Of course the Soviet Union had not achieved all its desires. Its goal was to legitimize the international situation formally—that is, its actual huge increase in power in Central Europe.

In this situation the German government now seized the initiative. It began to throw off traditional chains, to accept the consequences of the war that were firmly in place, not to question the status quo, but without endangering its constitutional objective—that is, primarily the future of a unified Germany.

The job was also difficult because our Western allies were expected to see themselves as no longer alone in determining the direction of Europe's Eastern policy while the Germans, when it came to questions concerning Germany, acted independently and at almost breathtaking speed.

What Brandt's government expected from its citizens was no less daunting. Germans were now supposed to accept the fact that almost a quarter of Germany's prewar territory was lost for good. Until now no West German political leader had seriously been ready to take such a step. Concerning unification with East Germany, Germans were also supposed to understand and approve Egon Bahr's famous concept of "change through reconciliation." Brandt now added, "We must make today's facts our starting point if we want to change these facts"—a paradox not understood without some thought.

Negotiations began. The key figure on the German side was Egon Bahr. For many years he was Brandt's closest adviser on eastern and German policies. Their rare mutual confidence was demonstrated in the interplay of Brandt's instincts and Bahr's intelligence, a partnership that required few words. In its results neither of the two alone was half as effective without the other. When Bahr was sent out to negotiate, he had neither a political mandate nor experience in diplomacy. He negotiated as an official empowered with the highest possible authority, and of course he himself had the greatest influence on the extent of this authority. Besides the official levels of discussion he developed a mastery in quasi-conspiratorial contacts, shrouded in mystery, with highly placed officials of the other nation, people who could be trusted to keep silent.

He embraced the concept of "change through reconciliation" because he believed that the political, economic, and social superiority of the West would gradually prevail in relation to the East. He saw the Soviets as prisoners of a misguided and exhausted system. None of the actors in the Brandt government were as controversial as Bahr, and probably none was as interesting or as influential in his area. The Soviet foreign minister, Andrei Gromyko, known throughout the world as a laconic *nyet*-sayer, spent fifty-five hours in personal deliberations with Bahr—far more than with any other diplomat from abroad.

During Bahr's subsequent negotiations on a basic treaty with East Germany I regularly took part in his confidential briefings within the narrowest circle of the Bundestag. I am quite certain that he did not tell us everything he knew, and he talked in outlines, but what he did tell us was never less than true. His character no less than his intelligence kept him from making use of lies.

Those who criticized him for lacking a strong enough desire for the unity and freedom of all Germans did so without seeing him in action or understanding his ideas. Germany's self-determination was his central motive. Among the Western allies, not least Henry Kissinger, he was often regarded as a German nationalist to a downright dangerous extent. However, he had the rare good fortune of being assigned a task that allowed him to actually set in motion and change the relationships of his country.

On August 12, 1970, the Moscow Treaty was signed. Bonn resisted the Soviet demand that Germany formally renounce reunification. Conversely, Gromyko refused to include in the treaty a German right to unification. Instead the so-called Letter on German Unity, issued subsequently, stated that the treaty did not contradict the Federal Republic of Germany's objective "to work toward a condition of unity in Europe, in which the German people, in free self-determination, demand a return to unity."

The Warsaw Treaty was signed on December 7, 1970, and it included recognition of the Oder-Neisse Line. This was the most painful action of the federal government, stirring the people's feelings most deeply. Here, when it came to relations with Poland, the old German provinces, the monstrous war crimes, and the inhuman expulsions, much more was involved than mere political reason. The emotions of the people, the power of human morality, the heart of our neighbor were at stake.

When Brandt signed the treaty, he said, "My government accepts the results of history." The German Chancellor knelt at the memorial to the Warsaw ghetto. There may be some who say they would not have done so, but surely that eyewitness is right who wrote, "Then he knelt, the man who had no need to do so, for all those who did need to kneel but did not do so." It was an unprecedented event, an inconceivable moment.

Achieving favorable results with East Germany took a little longer. The heads of government began by holding two meetings, one in each German state. Brandt's visit in Erfurt ran a stirring course. The people, filled with renewed hope, cheered him along the way. They shouted "Willy, Willy" until Brandt's host, Willi Stoph, arrived. Then the shout changed to "Willy Brandt" to make it quite clear who was being cheered.

The treaty on travel, the first to be signed, brought a significant easing of restrictions. It was followed by the strangest of the Eastern treaties, the so-called Basic Treaty. I know of no other treaty that explicitly admits that the signatories are not in a position to solve the problem they clearly placed at the head of the agreement. The Basic Treaty's preamble states that agreement could be reached on many topics, almost all topics, but that one aspect was exempted—the basic questions, especially the national question. The central problem of citizenship also remained unresolved.

And yet both sides saw and took advantage of opportunities to realize their goals. East Berlin won recognition as an independent state with equal rights, and Bonn relinquished its claim to sole representation. At the same time the United Nations admitted both Germanys as member nations existing independently of each other. For the first time an American ambassador was accredited to East Germany—that too was a huge gain for the GDR. All in all, East Germany and East Berlin came away with a considerable and quite vital bag of prizes. The SED complained only that Germany was partitioned not merely into two states but also into two nations, one "socialist" and the other "capitalist."

The advantages to the Federal Republic lay in separate issues that touched the citizens of both states personally. An incalculably large number of people's lives were concretely and positively affected, for example in bringing families together, in the ability to cross the border on urgent family business, in minimal border difficulties, legal protection, sports, the media.

Finally the Berlin Agreement was added. While the negotiations were in the hands of the Four Powers, they did not have the crucial interest in them that Germans had. Of course the Western powers were inclined to the policy of détente, a situation that even Soviet suppression by force during the Prague Spring of 1968 could not alter. The French foreign minister, Michel Debré, an undiluted Gaullist, played down the uprising as a "traffic accident on the way to détente."

On the whole, Washington was relieved rather than disturbed by the change in the climate of Bonn's Eastern policy. But the United States was not willing to hand over the reins. Speaking to a high-level West German diplomat in 1970, Kissinger remarked, "I'll tell you one thing: when it comes to détente, we'll take care of it, not you." And of course he was right within the larger framework of East-West relations. But on questions concerning Germany and the situation of Berlin such an attitude was a fantasy; the initiative lay with Germany. It took a great effort to successfully persuade the Western powers to carry on negotiations on Berlin. Protracted and nerve-wracking disputes finally produced an extremely complex work of principal and subordinate agreements. The laying out of what we wanted and what we would accept took place in Bonn. The free part of Berlin felt that it could live quite well with the result. I tested its permanent effects personally when I was governing mayor of Berlin.

If we had to issue a certificate of paternity for the Berlin Agreement, traces of Kissinger, Gromyko, and Piotr Abrassimov, the Soviet "vice-regent" in the GDR, would certainly appear. But child-support payments for the offspring must surely be borne by Egon Bahr; it was his achievement for his and my city, for our capital.

Ratification of the Eastern Treaties
in the Bundestag

But the most difficult part, and the part most decisive for the German contribution to overall Eastern policy, had yet to be accomplished—the ratification of the Moscow and Warsaw treaties by the German Bundestag.

The mood in the country was generally favorable to a policy of peace and détente, but to voluntarily accept the formal renunciation of millions of Germans' ancestral homes on the far side of the Oder and the Neisse—that went beyond the strength of countless people. A deep conflict spread through the country, through generations, families, and friendships, a conflict between mind and heart, and of course it was reflected in the parties and their delegates. The resulting parliamentary debate was far from ordinary, without the usual rote speakers. Instead speeches resonated with human dedication and passion, weaving back and forth between confrontation and cooperation, practical seriousness and polemics, disappointment and confidence. Even twenty-five years later I can think of this time only with deep emotion.

A side effect of this profound confrontation was the dwindling majority of the governing coalition. We saw the first instances of so-called turncoats. Various SPD and FDP delegates refused to support Brandt's government. The situation in the Bundestag became entirely unpredictable.

The first parliamentary reading of the Eastern treaties took place in February 1972. At this time Barzel uttered his dicta "not now" and "not this way," expressing his own almost insolubly difficult situation. He had to experience the conflict that was defining the whole country in his own life. Together with Gerhard Schröder and myself, two other coalition speakers, he criticized not the Eastern objective but the government's method, which was full of ambiguities. Thus, for example, as I pointed out in the debate, President Georges Pompidou of France had recently declared that he would be pleased if the Federal Republic were to recognize East Germany, no matter what name it used to do so. The West German government challenged any such recognition even as it sought support and praise from abroad, especially from France. Barzel believed that the combination of treaties was still too unpolished. But more particularly, as chairman it was his job to hold the parliamentary group together. And there were many who rejected Willy Brandt's overall Eastern operation, some acting out of conviction, others out of anger at the methods and objectives.

On the other hand, Barzel had a very clear understanding of our situation. Foreign policy is the concern of the executive. The parliament may debate it, criticize it, and stimulate it, but it cannot itself act in the area of international agreements. In practice the only exceptions are international treaties requiring ratification. Their legitimacy depends on a vote by the legislature—but even so, this fact seems to delegate more power to the parliament than is actually involved: as soon as governments put their signatures on a treaty, it takes effect without foreign nations' waiting for parliamentary ratification.

All these considerations were present to an even greater degree when it came to these Eastern treaties. Though West Germany still had only limited sovereignty, it had waged East-West policy on a large scale and committed the Four Powers to the process. They went along, with or without inner reservations. Negotiations on the Berlin Agreement were in full swing. Preparations for the Conference on Security and Collaboration in Europe were under way in all countries. A negative vote in the Bundestag on the Eastern treaties would throw the Federal Republic into an unprecedented isolation that would have run strongly counter to our interests. Barzel was keenly aware of the situation. Though with a heavy heart, he, an East Prussian, realized that the Union could not justify the failure of the treaties; nevertheless, for the sake of the party parliamentary group, he tried to stall for time. What else could he do? His only alternative was resignation, a move that would only make the situation worse.

Barzel's job was not made any easier when Schröder, who since the 1969 election had kept silent as chair of the foreign-relations committee, made an impressive speech at the first reading to stress his recognition of the government's patriotism, which was no less than his own, but also to roundly reject the treaties.

I tried to help Barzel as best I could. Because I did not carry his full measure of responsibility, it was easier for me to go further than he could. I believed acceptance of the treaties was not only inevitable but also right, especially the Warsaw Treaty—and the Warsaw Treaty was not possible without the Moscow Treaty.

The crucial second and third readings were scheduled for May 1972. Before that date a highly suspenseful interlude intervened. The Baden-Württemberg regional election had lost the Social-Liberal coalition's majority in the upper house, the Bundesrat. By this time the Bundestag was at a stalemate between government and opposition. The leaders of the Union parties hoped for two further votes, and a call for a vote of no confidence against Brandt in favor of Barzel became irresistible. The CDU had already debated the move. Together with Hans Katzer and Gerhard Stoltenberg, I spoke against it, since I was convinced that, should the Union be successful, it would find itself in an untenable position, without clarity on Eastern policy in its own camp, with a growing mood among the people in favor of détente, with permanently unsettled majority conditions in parliament, and under the threat of inevitable isolation from other nations. As Schmidt, whom Barzel respected highly, reported, Barzel himself later told him that the situation was one the Union could barely control.

The great majority of the Union leadership now put its plan in action; the three of us opposed to it agreed to bow to the majority decision. On April 27, 1972, the no-confidence vote was proposed. In the subsequent debate Scheel gave a speech that could hardly be topped for sharpness and bitterness, apparently in certain expectation of the governing coalition's defeat. Since my opposition to the proposal within the party had become public knowledge, Barzel begged me to take part in the discussion. In doing so, I merely said that people who made use of an explicit constitutional right, such as a motion for a vote of no confidence, must not be judged harshly for that reason alone. No one could know what the vote would decide. Those unwilling to lose were acting as far from the spirit of our democracy as were those who avoided responsibility. The vote resulted in a defeat for Barzel—he missed winning by two votes. We never learned for certain whose they were.

The following three weeks involved us in a plot so thick it could hardly be unraveled and featured open battles and confidential meetings, bitter struggles, and reconciliations. Together with my close colleagues in the parliamentary group and friends Olaf von Wrangel and Walter L. Kiep, I tried to bridge the chasm. At odds with each other and yet still working jointly, the government and the opposition polished the resolution on German unity, which we hoped the Soviet Union would accept as written without objection. Ambassador Valentin Falin of the Soviet Union was drawn in as sort of an expert consultant—an almost unprecedented event, using the chief of mission of a foreign country as a specialist and go-between to help solve our domestic conflict. The statement's aim was to enable the opposition to approve the treaties, or at least that was Barzel's reasonable goal. But his situation grew increasingly delicate as the mood in the Union parliamentary group hardened. Strauss presented the greatest difficulties. Although at first he helped draft the resolution and was eager to support Barzel, he was persuaded by sentiment in his home party base to suddenly change course and lead his CSU to a negative vote.

The air was loaded with tension. Developments finally drove me into an extreme position as well. Because of the stalemate in the Bundestag, the government needed only a single additional vote from the ranks of the opposition to pass the treaties. Was that vote to be mine? I had absolutely no desire to play a lonely hero's role, but I was determined to do what I could to prevent the treaties' failure and keep at least the Warsaw Treaty afloat.

We had just survived the heated atmosphere in the Bundestag during Brandt's vote of no confidence. In the course of that plenary debate several SPD delegates had shaken their fists at me simply because I had chosen to speak. Only a little while later emotionally rousing scenes occurred within our own parliamentary group. There I explained and justified why, together with my colleagues Erik Blumenfeld and Winfried Pinger, I would vote in favor of the Warsaw Treaty. My announcement created a furor. I was clearly informed with considerable hostility and even rage to leave the parliamentary group and go to hell. Innumerable letters also accused me in unprintable terms of treason and other crimes.

Words spoken in the heat of battle must not be taken too seriously. But of course I had to face the fact that many people in my own ranks truly felt that I was not one of them. So I had to ask myself honestly whether I should resign.

It did not take me long to realize that my resignation would do no good to anyone. After all, the conflict was not about me but about the treaties. There must be some way to get them ratified without setting a spectacular personal drama in motion.

What followed was both bitter and inevitable. Toward the end of an hours-long debate within the parliamentary group Hallstein argued up and down against the treaties in a speech that seemed to go on forever. But since the most important thing was preserving the unanimity of the parliamentary group, he suggested that both those in favor and those opposed abstain from voting. Barzel had no choice but to go along with this suggestion. Abstention gave him his victory: The treaties could pass.

Hallstein was unjustly criticized for his actions. He alone had the dreadful task of keeping the floundering parliamentary group above water. His decision saved our country's domestic and foreign positions from a severe crisis—no small achievement—but in the end he put his own political future at risk.

The whole course of events left me wounded. Of course I too thought the treaties' success was our most important goal, and I had done my best to bring about their ratification. I was first to declare openly in the parliamentary group's plenary session that even if all the others were against the treaties, I would still vote for them. My statement ended the plans of opposition strategists who wanted to bring the entire resolution to a vote, but such a move required a unanimous vote of the party group. Nevertheless I found the entire proceedings deeply depressing. In a huge intraparty verbal battle on a crucial question affecting the life of Germany, the Union mountain had labored and brought forth a measly subsistence mouse. In one of the very few absolutely crucial decisions our country faced, half the members of the German Bundestag created the impression, by abstaining, that they did not care one way or another. That was and remains a failing, in my view. I did what I thought I had to do and all that I could do. But it was not enough.

The treaties were now ratified. All the capitals in the East but even more in the West felt relieved. Brandt was awarded the Nobel Peace Prize. And in the next Bundestag election he was rewarded with a comfortable majority for his coalition.

As a student in Göttingen, 1947

As a young soldier, in 1940

With his father, who was a witness at the Nuremberg trials, in 1948

At the Wailing Wall in Jerusalem, in 1986

With his wife and Shimon Peres, visiting a settlement

With Pope John Paul II at Villa Hammerschmidt, 1987

With Henry Kissinger, in 1987

With former Chancellor Helmut Kohl, in 1987. As the chancellor's and the president's offices were side by side, separated only by a wall, the two neighbors enjoyed many a confidential talk.

Walking with Erich Honecker, former president of East Germany, in the garden of the Villa Hammerschmidt during his first visit to West Germany, 1987. Two years later, the two Germanys were united.

Von Weizsäcker with former Israeli president Chaim Herzog during the first official German visit to Israel, in 1987. He relates, "Chaim Herzog took us under his wing, as if we were family." The *London Times* described Herzog as "A Lion in a World of Mice."

Ronald Reagan at Von Weizsäcker's official residence in Berlin, Schloss Bellevue, in 1988

Contemplating the Berlin Wall in the summer of 1989, in front of the famous
Brandenburg Gate. Six months later, the wall came down.

Von Weizsäcker with Willy Brandt, the mayor of Berlin when the Berlin Wall was
erected in 1961, and former chancellor of West Germany from 1969–1974.
They are at the Villa Hammerschmidt on Brandt's 75th birthday.

During a visit by then-U.S. President George Bush at the Villa Hammerschmidt in Bonn, in the summer of 1989. Bush proved to be a reliable friend of Germany's, which was appreciated all the more during the critical months of Germany's reunification.

After a tour of the city of Danzig, which once belonged to the German "Reich," Von Weizsäcker visits the Polish labor leader Lech Wałęsa in his office, 1990.

Czechoslovakian president Václav Havel is considered a very unconventional president. Here the two men are enjoying a spontaneous beer at a pub, after a stroll through the old town of Prague, 1990.

The Dalai Lama, head of the order of Tibetan Buddhists, during a visit to Germany in 1990, offers Von Weizsäcker a prayer scarf.

Queen Elizabeth visited newly unified Germany in 1992.
After touring Dresden, which had been destroyed by British bombs
during the war, they visited the baroque castle Augustburg.

With George Bush and Boris Yeltzin in Munich, in 1992

Von Weizsäcker's visit with Bill Clinton in the White House, in May 1993

Von Weizsäcker with the world-renowned and temperamental conductor of the Berlin
Philharmonic Orchestra, H. von Karajan, 1987

With his son and world champion G. Kasparov over a chess game, 1987

Receiving an honorary doctorate at Harvard University in 1987 and expressing his
gratitude on the behalf of all Europeans for the Marshall Plan, the extraordinary aid
program to rebuild post-war Europe that was unveiled forty years previously
in the same place by former U.S. Foreign Minister George Marshall.
Former House Speaker Tip O'Neill is sitting at the left of Von Weizsäcker.

With author Aleksandr Solzhenitsyn in 1993, who was on his way back to Russia after living in the United States

With Helmut Schmidt and Henry Kissinger, honoring famous publicist and friend Countess Marion Doenhoff, in 1989

With his granddaughter Sophie, 1987

Celebrating his reelection in 1990 with the entire family on
the lawn of the Villa Hammerschmidt

With Marianne in 1987, his wife then of thirty-three years

Summit Conference of the
CSCE in Helsinki

The multilateral keystone of Eastern policy, the Conference on Security and Collaboration in Europe (CSCE), took place some time later. In the summer of 1975 thirty-five heads of state and government met for the CSCE in Helsinki and passed the hopefully named Final Act.

This event brought the Soviet Union the universal confirmation it had wanted so long from the West and had already received bilaterally from Bonn: a promise of nonaggression and recognition of the status quo created by the end of the Second World War.

But the Final Act went far beyond the recognition of Soviet war conquests. To put it another way, the Act began to establish Continent-wide standards for the rights of humanity and minorities. These were included in the so-called Basket III of the Final Act, which contained these decisions.

Negotiations in the CSCE led to some strange results. For example, the Russians had cause to fear that in finally reaching the goal sought for so many years, they had achieved something quite different, something they had never intended. Meanwhile the West, which had fought so long against even the convocation of such a conference, in the end had reason to be delighted and grateful. Primarily the neutral nations contributed significantly to this success.

Even if the Helsinki Final Act contained little more than statements of intention not internationally reconcilable, Basket III was still the cornerstone for the expanding freedom movements in the Warsaw Pact nations. Without the Helsinki resolutions on freedom of speech, exchange of information, and easing of travel restrictions, Solidarnosc in Poland, Charta 77 in Prague, and dissident groups in East Germany could never have appeared in the way they later did. The process of gradual internal loosening now ran its course in the East. Though it brought sharply increasing gravity and dangers in East-West relations, after each setback the provisions of the Helsinki Final Act always set the new course. Thus the Helsinki Conference of 1975 was the climax of Eastern policy.

This time too the majority in the Union parliamentary group rose in opposition to the Final Act. During a parliamentary motion on the proposal—meaningless as far as the validity of the Final Act was concerned—most Union delegates voted against the motion. Because the executive committee of the World Council of Churches was meeting in Übersee at this time, I was absent, a fact that only increased my frustration.

Early in 1976 another vote was taken on a treaty that affected our Eastern policy. The document in question was an agreement between Poland and the Federal Republic that had far-reaching practical consequences. In the Bundestag I was the leader and spokesman for a minority in my parliamentary group that was in favor of the treaty. Together with Rainer Barzel, Walter Kiep, Norbert Blüm, and eleven other colleagues I voted yes. The majority of Union delegates once again—for the last time, as it were—was opposed. In the Bundesrat, whose vote would be decisive, Strauss had vigorously protested against the new agreement with Poland. But eventually the prime minister of Lower Saxony, Ernst Albrecht, won acceptance.

When the Union took over the government ten years after the dispute about the 1972 treaties, its earlier resistance to Brandt's Eastern policy was no longer an issue. The Union continued down the same road that Brandt and, after him, Helmut Schmidt had taken. A similar situation occurred at an earlier time, when Adenauer led our nation into the Western camp and his opposition, the SPD, which began with such vehement resistance, ten years later adopted the direction Adenauer had set. Fortunately the German foreign-policy situation is not suited to permanent internal conflict.

Foreign Policy in the Late 1970s

The leadership relations in Bonn changed both within the country and within the party. In 1973 Barzel resigned as chairman of the Union parliamentary group. The outward occasion was a vote on the Federal Republic's admission to the United Nations. A pivotal vote was involved in electing his successor. First Schröder asserted his claim to the position, but the labor members and the liberals in the group felt that he was too rigidly conservative. Then Hans Katzer asked me to become a candidate. My chances were slim, especially since Strauss with his CSU along with many others still suffering from enactment of the Eastern treaties had no desire to include me in their plans. But I agreed to accept. I always believed that people should run for office even if their chances of winning were not great, because democracy is nourished by giving voters choices, alternatives, especially within a large majority party composed of members from different constituencies. The newspapers saw me as the candidate of the left.

But then Kai Uwe von Hassel, a past president of the Bundestag, pulled his colleague from Schleswig-Holstein, Karl Carstens, out of the hat. Carstens, a former parliamentary secretary, most recently to Federal Chancellor Kiesinger, had just been reelected to the Bundestag. Immediately thereafter, during debate on the Basic Treaty with East Germany, he spoke impressively against the federal government's German policy. After the Union's resounding defeat in the last Bundestag election, his words were balm to the wounded spirits of the majority in the party parliamentary group. Welcomed with cheers, he was elected to the group chairmanship by a large majority. I ended up in the number two spot with a respectable number of votes. To my children's satisfaction I had at least managed to avenge my earlier defeat to Schröder. And I sincerely congratulated Carstens on his new office, which was hardly an enviable one. He carried out his job not with great inner inclination but with his characteristic acute sense of responsibility. Leading a large group and maintaining its cohesion can be a uniquely difficult job. This was all the more true in this case, since the Union had for the first time lost first place to the Social Democrats as the strongest party. Subsequently Carstens felt much relieved when he could trade in the group chairmanship—increasingly moving toward polemical battles—for the equalizing office of federal president.

Barzel remained federal party chairman. In 1970 when he was running for this office against Kohl, he suggested to me that I become general secretary of the CDU. If I had followed his advice, I would have had a good chance of winning for once. Until now, after all, I had a great deal of practice only in cheerfully accepting defeats. But this time I declined at once. I did not see myself as able to devise campaign strategies and attack other parties nonstop. Instead, at Barzel's request I became chairman of a committee on fundamental principles he had started. I will have more to say about this committee's work.

Personality problems also troubled the government camp. The great election victory of the Social-Liberal coalition was followed by a phase of its depletion, perhaps in part because the coalition had overestimated its capabilities. Brandt appeared tired. In the fall of 1973 the first open outburst was heard against him during the initial trip of a parliamentary delegation to the Soviet Union. The five of us were led by the president of the Bundestag, Annemarie Renger. The leaders of the SPD and FDP parliamentary groups, Herbert Wehner and Wolfgang Mischnik, along with the head of the CSU regional group, Richard Stücklen, and I made up the rest of the delegation.

Immediately after our arrival at the Moscow airport Wehner gave his first interview and spoke of Brandt in harshly critical terms. That evening in the German embassy Eugen Selbmann, his colleague on foreign policy, approached me looking very worried. He begged me to join the group of journalists Wehner had gathered around him to hear his notorious sayings: "The number one is removed, it prefers a bubble bath"; and further, "What the government lacks is a head." Selbmann hoped that Wehner would stop if I were part of the group. But we both severely underestimated Wehner.

Once during the trip I sat next to Wehner for three hours. When I asked him why he had chosen the Soviet Union of all places to criticize his chancellor so sharply, he replied that he had done the same at home more than once but had never found a willing ear. Brandt, he said, let matters slide, and such inaction was dangerous for Germany both at home and abroad. If there were strong reverberations to his remarks, two results were possible. Either Brandt would take up the reins and improve and everything would be well, or nothing would change, in which case he, Wehner, had done no harm.

We talked a long time about our families and our youth. He countered my account of a happy childhood in Berlin during the Weimar era by contrasting the protected childhood of a diplomat's son with his past as a young Communist sought by police.

For Wehner the trip brought a first important reunion with people and places from his mysterious Moscow past, which haunted him all his life. His experiences were as conflicting as the encounters the rest of us had had with him over the years. At Protestant conferences it was not unusual for him to remain fairly far in the background. On my fiftieth birthday in April 1970 he sent me a short handwritten letter "through all the turmoil"; the note was cordial and heartfelt, free of the routine clichés customarily found in political congratulatory prose.

In 1974 I saw a quite different Wehner. On May 6 Brandt resigned the chancellorship. Heinemann's successor as federal president was to be elected on May 15. Scheel was the candidate of the government coalition, which held a majority in the Federal Assembly. The Union party—including the CSU—nominated me. The following day, on May 16, the Bundestag would elect the new chancellor. Wehner, who had contributed significantly to Brandt's resignation and therefore caused strong resistance in his own ranks, was not entirely clear about who held the majority in the crucial election for chancellor. Thus he made every effort to ride out the presidential election of the previous day as a sort of dress rehearsal for the chancellor's election. To this end he went on the air to tell the voters in his coalition that if they did not vote for Scheel, they were behaving like the NPD (National Democratic Party of Germany). Did that mean that if I voted for the other candidate, I was committing an act of neo-Nazism? Wehner never answered my letter about this grotesque event. That was how he operated: he gave top priority to the cause of the moment, which in his case was always less political substance than raw power. Willing to use any means necessary for the sake of his cause, he never considered what his actions might do to the people in question. I encountered this trait when he became determined to secure Helmut Schmidt's election to the chancellorship.

In the Bundestag he was like a storm threatening to break at any moment. Thin-skinned and because of his mysterious past vulnerable all his life, he literally hoped that mean-spirited hecklers would attack him so that he could demolish them with his lightning bolts. When he was speaking in the plenary chamber, if someone so much as looked at him intensely but innocently enough, he would nail that person with his verbal hammer. Although not the best debater in parliament, no one else electrified the house as much as he did. For years he was the most important delegate in the Bundestag, this man of intense sensitivity and steely hardness, a unique figure and quite surely not a traitor to his country.

The trip to Moscow showed us that the Soviets were serious about détente. But at the same time we realized how difficult it still was for Russians and Germans to understand each other. I remember our walk through the Piskarevskoye Cemetery in Leningrad (now once again called St. Petersburg), which contains 650,000 graves, most of civilians who had lost their lives to force of arms, cold, and starvation during the Nazis' nearly three-year siege of the city. The monument is inscribed, "Let everyone know: no one is forgotten, and nothing is forgotten." The spokesman of the memorial site used the most cutting words to describe the battles for the city. He showed us the positions from which the "Huns" had attacked the city's defenders.

That night a ceremonial banquet for us was hosted by Leningrad's party secretary. His address struck the same note. This time it was my turn to reply. I could not resist noting frankly that as a young infantryman I had been one of those "Huns" fighting for the other side; I still recognized many of the place names. We had been fully aware of the suffering on all fronts but especially in this city. And now we were here to do our part to make certain that future generations would never have to repeat our experiences. My confession upset our ambassador, but after initial silence the Russians demonstrated one of the true qualities of their nature. The result was a more open and almost warm human atmosphere.

When I called on the minister responsible for religious questions, we learned that we might have met once before—facing each other in trench warfare in the same front-line sector at the same time.

Once I secretly absented myself from the delegation program. My splendid colleague Jürgen Heidborn, who spoke Russian, had found out Andrei Sakharov's Moscow address. I called on him and found him living in close quarters with relatives, his freedom severely limited. He was filled with both bitterness and hope. Of course I worried about getting caught during my unsanctioned adventure. But apparently no one discovered my visit, because on the following day the propaganda minister, Leonid Samyatin, told me that Western rumors about Sakharov's restricted circumstances were all lies and that he was living in complete freedom outside Moscow in a beautiful villa of his own.

On another occasion (when I left the delegation early during an operatic performance) I visited a magical marionette theater that had a reputation for dissidence. I was caught in the act and taken back to the opera literally under police escort.

Our laundry was also handled in the Moscow state guesthouse. I had stupidly left my best cufflinks in a shirt, and when the shirt was returned, the links were missing. I asked housekeeping to look for them, without success. Then I pleaded with the manager of the house to check—again in vain. I explained to him that the cufflinks were a present from my wife and that I would not leave without them. At first nothing happened. The following day our delegation was granted an audience by Prime Minister Nikolai Podgornyi. We were just assembling outside the audience chamber in the Kremlin and the door was about to open when suddenly from behind someone pushed an envelope containing some hard object into my hand. It was my cufflinks. Apparently I had raised the fear—of course quite groundless—that I would tell Podgornyi about my loss. Even with my joy at having the cufflinks returned, my conscience was troubled, since the entire incident was the result of my negligence. I never learned what consequences followed.

Though all our discussions were serious and informative, I could not count on the Russians to keep appointments. Once the German ambassador invited a group of high-ranking Russian officials to join Frau Renger and her delegation at dinner. But when she came to the table, our president found herself without either of the men slated to flank her. I too sat beside other than the planned Russians. Ambassador Heinrich Sahm merely sighed and commented that this was fairly standard procedure here: people did not reply to invitations, and those who did reply did not show up. Those who did show up had not been invited.

A large German press corps traveled with us. Of all the reporters, Friedrich Nowottny caught the brass ring: He had Soviet television open its Leningrad studio, where he put on a live broadcast with the whole delegation as a "Report from Bonn." Our hosts' amazement knew no end.

All of us had a memorable time in the Soviet Union on that trip. Though we were forced to face dark moments from the past, we also found many opportunities for new beginnings.

Of my subsequent trips to the Soviet Union, one in particular stands out: Kohl's first trip, when he was the Union candidate for the chancellor's office in September 1975. Our Bundestag colleague Werner Marx and I traveled with him. For Kohl the trip turned into a test of both domestic and foreign policy.

Admittedly the first problem was purely technical. After paying a call on Vadim Sagladin, the head of the foreign office in Soviet Communist Party headquarters, we were riding down in an ancient elevator, the kind installed within a curving staircase and open on all sides. But our ride was short: the elevator stopped halfway down, and for forty-five minutes we could only stand and watch as functionaries of the Soviet empire plodded up and down the stairs without paying any attention to us. We were already picturing the headlines in the German tabloids about our sad fate when a workman finally came to fix the problem. We learned an important lesson: A country can become a pioneer in space travel without requiring smoothly functioning elevators in its political headquarters.

A more serious test came later. While we were visiting the city of Kama 800 kilometers east of Moscow, *Pravda* printed a malicious, inflammatory article against Franz Josef Strauss. How should we react? Of course the Russians were fully aware of the tensions between Kohl and Strauss. Should we threaten to leave immediately, as some of the German press traveling with us suggested? Such a course would make it very easy for the Soviet leaders to declare the visit by the brand-new candidate a failure. But to respond too mildly would create new difficulties with the CSU at home—difficulties Kohl would be hard put to overcome. Kohl passed the test with flying colors: he called off some of the planned activities until our hosts intervened with clarification and good sense. As would be shown later, the trip was valuable to all involved.

Our other major destination during the 1970s was the United States. We felt closely allied though we were separated by an ocean. At the time legislators from both nations worked closely together. We knew each other in person much better than we do today. Of course there were good reasons for such teamwork, since in spite of détente the end of the Cold War was not yet in sight. We therefore needed close agreement on actions and words in the Western Alliance.

At first the superpowers were reasonably satisfied with the Helsinki Final Act, but for different, in part conflicting, reasons. Moscow considered the oddly named Basket I as a kind of substitute peace treaty—that is, a multilateral recognition by all European nations as well as the United States and Canada of its dominant position in Central and Eastern Europe. For the West, Basket III was central, since it contained the first definite steps toward freedom of movement, human rights, and democratization in these countries. As previously mentioned, these provisions were not legally binding. But they did constitute a jointly written and signed text that had to be reprinted in the newspapers even of the Eastern bloc nations. Freedom-loving people in the Soviet sphere of power could now invoke these clauses with their promises of free speech, free travel, and free exchange of ideas and information when they petitioned their rulers. This opportunity in itself was not, of course, sufficient to bring about political freedom, but given the prevailing conditions, it represented an enormously, fundamentally new situation.

Between the two there was Basket II, with its call for far-reaching collaboration in all fields of science and technology, economy and culture. This provision would show whether East and West were really willing and able to coexist peacefully. For the Soviet Union, which had introduced the concept of peaceful coexistence, it meant international class struggle without war, while we in the West understood it to mean something quite different—a coexistence that was not only peaceful but also capable of opening up systems.

It was generally recognized that the Soviet Union had striven for recognition of the status quo. Had we in the West agreed to this demand? But what specifically had we agreed to? The distinction had to be made: Basket I meant renouncing all force and recognition of the status quo's existing frontiers, combined with the right of peaceful, negotiated change. But Basket III made it impossible to grant recognition to the system practiced by the other side—its domestic, ideological, economic, and human-rights principles and practices.

The central question was whether we could achieve a coexistence that would be peaceful and open up systems. In the long range, opening up the system could mean only one thing: altering the system. Today we know this change finally came about. But in the 1970s no one knew whether the attempt would succeed.

These questions were at the center of our running transatlantic discussions. At first, of course, the dreams of the Helsinki Conference were overshadowed by new international crises not arising from the East-West conflict.

The United States blew hot and cold on Europe in unpredictable ways. The Vietnam war and its agonizing costs caused worldwide inflation. The monetary system of Bretton Woods, which had prevailed for nearly three decades, collapsed.

In connection with the Israeli Yom Kippur War the Arab nations caused the oil crisis, aggravated during the subsequent revolution in Iran and the war between Iran and Iraq. Wild increases in oil prices and currency speculation resulted. The dollar began its roller-coaster ride. After the exchange rate had remained steady at 4.20 DM to the dollar for a relatively long time, it sank to 1.70 DM. German industry, which depended heavily on export, had to struggle against inflation and deficits in the balance of trade. This situation introduced our worst recession of the postwar period.

Precisely because these new international crises diverted attention from an active Eastern policy and disturbed transatlantic relations, our contacts took on increased importance. Progress was complicated even more by the high turnover in the United States presidency: from Nixon through Ford and Carter to Reagan, four presidents in eight years with strongly differing political agendas.

In addition, as happens so often in Washington, differences of opinion and power struggles between the legislative and the executive branches of government prevailed. During meetings in the White

House and in the State Department I was asked many times to repeat an opinion I had just uttered as soon as I could to prominent members of Congress, to persuade them to listen to reason in foreign-policy concerns. But now and then I was given the same mission in the opposite direction.

Understandably United States congressmen concentrate primarily on domestic issues, especially those affecting their states or electoral districts. At times I became aware of how narrow this focus is when I encountered astonishing one-sidedness. I recall having one discussion somewhat later in Washington, when I was governing mayor of Berlin, with two United States senators. They took a lively interest in the sale of wheat to the Soviet Union and had only good things to say about the Soviet leaders. At the same time both were visibly amazed to learn from me that United States soldiers were stationed in Berlin, for very good reasons.

We should also remember that United States politicians cannot really improve their chances of reelection by becoming experts in foreign affairs. The United States' worldwide responsibilities and global affairs find a minimum of interest among the citizens of that vast land. Once I spent two weeks at a course in the Colorado mountains. Every day I read the only available newspaper, the *Denver Post*, by our standards a large and good regional paper. During the entire two weeks I found only one report on European concerns—an article about an exorcism in Würzburg.

But such individual cases cannot dominate our overall view. On the whole I found the level of information and responsibility concerning foreign affairs impressively high in the foreign-relations committees in the House and the Senate—unfortunately a higher level then than now.

Helmut Kohl gained a similar impression when he joined me on his first trip as leader of the opposition to call on President Jimmy Carter. Good relations with the newly elected president of the United States were important for all of Europe and not easily obtained. Carter, with his new human-rights policy, which diverged from that of previous administrations, tried to achieve international peace, while the Soviet Union, with its revived aggressive arms buildup, would not allow it. Kohl's personality and arguments found a ready response both in the White House and on Capitol Hill. He also cultivated cordial personal relationships with leading members of Congress—relationships that turned out to be extraordinarily valuable to Kohl as chancellor.

Shortly before, I had traveled to the United States as part of a delegation that included all the different parties in the Bundestag. Bundestag President Renger once again headed our company in a fair and circumspect manner. This time she had an easier time with the tour group than she had had with Wehner on our trip to Moscow. This visit was defined by friendship on both sides. I especially recall an amusing incident staged by Hermann Höcherl, the former federal minister of the interior, renowned for his intelligence, sense of humor, and extraordinary girth, which made it difficult for him to buy clothes. To add to his wardrobe, he planned to visit one of the largest and best-known men's clothing stores in the United States, Brooks Brothers in New York, and asked me to come along as consultant and interpreter. We started our search on the top floor of the store, unfortunately without success. On the floor below we obstinately shopped for almost an hour—still without finding anything suitable. We left the next floor with empty hands as well, and so on until we reached the ground floor. There we were met by an ashen-faced manager. After bowing slightly, he explained in tones of deep depression that in all his years he had never seen anything like it—being unable to satisfy a customer. Talkative in a most un-American way, he begged our forgiveness, close to tears. Höchel thanked him graciously and left the store, beaming. As the first person to disprove the company's infallibility, Höchel and his figure had been victorious!

Chancellor Schmidt seized the initiative in all foreign and security policies. He rigorously followed NATO's Harmel Doctrine—the indivisible link of Western defensive preparedness and détente policy. As early as 1975 he had created one of the necessary preconditions for the success of the Helsinki summit by reaching an agreement with Poland's party leader, Edward Gierek, on the difficult bilateral questions that remained to be settled.

At the same time, however, Schmidt was no less true to Alliance policy. Almost as if to test his position, the Soviets gave him ample reason to call on Allied resolve. In mid-decade Brezhnev began to exploit the Western euphoria about détente to engage in rearmament. He produced and stationed new, highly effective intermediate-range ballistic missiles—the famous SS-20s—in the western sectors of the Warsaw Pact nations. Though their range was too short to reach the United States, they could hit almost every point in Europe. The Soviet arms-control agreement with the United States did not prohibit this action, but for Western Europe, and especially for the German Federal Republic, the situation was intolerable—a condition the United States at first had trouble understanding. The Americans spoke of "theater weapons," a concept we found unacceptable. When Carter did not appear to understand our position at once, Schmidt gave a speech in London that soon became famous. He demanded that the SS-20s be withdrawn; otherwise, comparable rearmament with NATO's tactical nuclear weapons would become imperative.

The tone between Schmidt and Carstens was fairly gruff. During this time West Germany maintained a relatively uneasy relationship with the United States. Finally, in 1979, the chancellor's agenda was accepted in an agreement with United States, British, and French leaders. NATO's so-called double-track resolution was established.

This resolution later caused Schmidt problems in his own country, since the stationing of new missiles was resisted by all European NATO nations. New peace movements arose, strongest in West Germany, and despite being called peace movements, their confrontations with government organizations were more turbulent than peaceful. Schmidt could not work out the antagonistic tendencies within his own party in such a way as to prevail. But all this happened much later. For the moment it was the chancellor who set the international tone.

Together with President Valéry Giscard d'Estaing of France he

originated the world economic summit, a conference of the leading
Western industrial nations. Conceived originally as a confidential and
private discussion, it later degenerated into a gigantic media spectacle,
though today such a form may be suited to integrating Russia more
easily into the international community. Schmidt also stirred up the
European Community. In 1979, together with Paris, he used the monetary situation of 1972 to create the European currency system, with
the objective of establishing a stable currency zone within the Community. This process was subsequently confirmed at Maastricht.
Helmut Schmidt was at the top of his international esteem.

Domestic Policy in the Schmidt Era

D omestically the situation also stabilized in favor of the great Social-Liberal coalition. In the fall of 1976 Kohl won a large number of votes in the Bundestag, the second-largest number in the history of the Union. The contentious Chancellor Schmidt did not pay sufficient attention to inflation, and his policy on pensions also came under vehement attack. Soon after the election, however, the economy took an upward turn.

The 1970s were defined in the Federal Republic by a very active party democracy. Even though the generation of '68 had begun by creating disturbances in all areas outside of government, the majority eventually began to work for change through established institutions. The party that benefited most from the influx was the SPD. Citizen participation in elections to the Bundestag hit an all-time high during this decade, with a turnout of more than 90 percent of eligible voters. The established parties of the Federal Republic—Union, SPD, and FDP—together received over 98 percent of all votes cast. The number of Union party members rose to unprecedented heights, only to fall again later.

Work on party programs reached a peak. The SPD worked out the so-called Economic-Political Orientation Framework 85, to which Helmut Schmidt contributed significantly. In the Union, Barzel established the Commission on Basics, which soon developed into the Commission on a Basic Program. As chairman of the commission, I acquired a second field of political interest, alongside my work with German and Eastern policies. This work was both stimulating and difficult.

I found it invigorating that notable people outside the inner circle were finally taking an optimistic interest in the programs of the political parties. This new attention was demonstrated in numerous significant contributions made by often highly qualified economists and sociologists, historians and political scientists, physicians and lawyers, biologists, theologians, and even a few artists, such as Oswald von Nell-Breuning, Wilhelm Krelle, Ulrich Scheuner, and Joseph Beuys.

A controversy between the SPD and the CDU developed into a worthwhile discussion on basics. Both parties were committed to the fundamental values of liberty, justice, and solidarity. The SPD could claim to be the first German party to adopt these principles, though the advantage was not very impressive, since these concepts were derived from Christian doctrine and had been secularized by the French Revolution.

The controversy centered on the question of solidarity. In the era of industrialization, solidarity had been the legitimate badge of the labor movement and was successful in the long run. It was the struggle of all who were equal against those who were unequal, to establish basic human working and living conditions.

In the meantime, however, because other, newer oppositions and conflicts had come to dominate, the interpretation of solidarity was now the object of deep division between the SPD and the Union. The SPD Orientation Framework 85 described solidarity in almost unaltered terms as a community engaged in a struggle against others. The document went on to state baldly that solidarity between rich and poor, powerful and powerless, educated and ignorant was impossible. To dispute this thesis only demonstrated the political opponents' fundamental misunderstanding.

But what is a policy of global evolution if it is not solidarity among entities of unequal power? Is the demand for a liberal policy concerning asylum and aliens anything but solidarity among rich and poor? Who, if not the educated classes, has the primary responsibility for cohesion and social peace in a society of inequality?

Admittedly it is unbelievably difficult to establish solidarity "from above" toward those who are weak and those who require help. However, it must at least be an objective made explicit in the program, so as to keep wealth, power, and knowledge from working solely to secure and increase the advantages of those who already possess them.

This was the issue about which we quarreled at the time. Lively discussions broke out within the CDU as well. Heiner Geissler supported conscientious and concrete answers to what he called "the new social question." New social services were introduced. Kurt Biedenkopf, mindful of the state's exceedingly large contribution to the social product, used his analytical strengths, keen mind, and courageous independence to unleash a necessary debate in favor of political basic principles and against distribution policies. A dispute broke out over the ideal of quality of life—was it a privilege or must it be earned? For years there was no unity on educational reform, with disagreement focusing on whether equal opportunity or fair opportunity was paramount.

Intellectual structures and principles must be measured against realistic possibilities. The language of political parties specifies that they must demonstrate their usefulness in the constant struggle for power. Though it is important for parties to identify motivating concepts and "claim" them at the proper time, this purpose is seldom successfully accomplished. Because in the Commission we had the luxury of merely thinking about the program, without constantly keeping the next election in mind, our procedures earned us more respect than influence in the party, especially as the CDU, unlike the SPD, was not an aging youth movement but a modern election machine. For ten years I won the greatest number of votes for chairman at the party conferences. But one journalist described the unequal share in power by writing, "Biedenkopf [at the time general secretary] manages, Weizsäcker thinks, Kohl steers." That, at least as far as it concerned Biedenkopf, was an understatement; the basis of his actions was and still is his pleasure in independent thinking.

The call for traditional values, which waxes and wanes, is stronger today than in the 1970s. The market economy has become almost globally established. With the aim of maximizing gains, frontiers that stand open everywhere are now crossed. Thirty years ago our coalition failed not least because of the unemployment figures, which were only one-tenth of today's. In every country, especially in the reforming nations previously under Communist rule, there is a call for an active, ethical capitalism that was a central element for the founders of market economics, especially Adam Smith and subsequently Alexis de Tocqueville. A search followed for the renewal of a social market economy, for the viability of the ideas framed by its intellectual teachers Walter Eucken or Wilhelm Röpke, whose best-known book was characteristically entitled *Jenseits von Angebot und Nachfrage* (Beyond Supply and Demand).

One motive for the renewed call for values, heard even within the parties, was voiced in a demand for moral capitalism. Drawing on my own experience in the debate over basic values in the 1970s, I want to call attention to the lack of clarity and usefulness that an overly abstract discussion of the topic produces. It does not cost a great deal to invoke liberty, justice, and solidarity, and the result is equally cheap. There is one thing that capitalism and democratic constitutions share: Both live by preconditions they are unable to create themselves. They create opportunities, and they protect the citizen from government encroachment; but they cannot conjure up the citizens' liveliness any more than they can arouse their sense of duty and their decency. That is why the discussion of obligations or, following the classical and Christian model, virtues, is far more urgent. It is closer to the core of the answers we seek than a survey of values. Even then it was an alarming sign that Chancellor Schmidt, when he listed such virtues and stressed their central importance, was lured into abandoning his ranks and advocating secondary virtues that had allegedly sacrificed their value after being misapplied in authoritarian systems.

For good constitutional reasons we could not supplement the magisterial catalog of basic rights in our constitution with a catalog of basic duties. The state cannot prescribe peoples' lives. In the long run, however, our liberal democracy and free market can survive only if we

understand and practice the humanistic virtues and duties that responsibly paved the way to our current freedom. These remain the central
topics for all parties.

The 1970 discussions on programs resulted in a relatively viable
consensus on the foundations of state and society. They did not, however, significantly influence the tone of parliamentary debates and
campaigns. As long as Brandt was chancellor, the political dispute ran
a fairly moderate course. Once he attacked me because I—admittedly
not showing much good sense—spoke of the closed ideology of neo-
Marxism. He believed that as far as my remark was a direct criticism of
the SPD, it was an instance of tilting at windmills. But the fact that I
had gained some prominence in the opposition as a Don Quixote, he
claimed, was no accident but a result of that party's leadership figures
being cut on the jib of Sancho Panza. I could not let this unexpected
praise pass, since if I were doomed to lifelong banishment on a desert
island and allowed to bring the products of only one writer, I'd pack
the collected works of William Shakespeare before I'd pick Cervantes.
So I sent Brandt an edition of *Don Quixote* and told him I hoped he
would take pleasure in the incomparable strength of this hero, who
always contributed unequally more to humanity's change for the better
than we politicians managed to do. I hope that he forgave me my
momentary enthusiasm.

When Helmut Schmidt became chancellor, the atmosphere in
the parliament became more caustic. The keen mind and sharp tongue
that marked his speeches contributed to turning the Bundestag into a
true national forum, at least for a time. His public addresses also
showed his strong but controlled temper. As happens to the best of us,
at times his arguments went wide of the mark, as when he declared
that the SPD more closely embodied the Sermon on the Mount than
did the Union—though surely members of all parties found it equally
difficult to approach this ideal. But in truth he had a strong interest in
the basic political-ethical questions, often transcending party.

When he spoke about morality, duty, and responsibility, he usually warned against expecting intellectual leadership in political mat-

ters. Nevertheless he acknowledged that attribute—as was only right—in the clear awareness of the difference between a politician's patronizing sermons, which are inappropriate, and the necessity of having basic convictions, expressing them, and practicing them. He was able to tutor professional thinkers in practicality—as when, aware of his own fallibility, he put American pragmatism at the service of the ethics of Immanuel Kant and Hans Jonas.

Schmidt was exceptional both in his domestic and international economic skills and in his expertise in matters outside politics. His strategic thinking was marked by the care he took with details, his respect for minutiae, as he moved toward his larger aims. In his dealings with experienced and responsible colleagues he was more alert and patient than in the inevitable small talk of the world at large—and why not? It was not so easy to find a way to engage him personally, but when you did break through, the experience was all the more worthwhile.

In the decisive verbal battles about the chancellor's budget his favorite opponent was Franz Josef Strauss. On those occasions Schmidt made every effort to play the "first speaker of the opposition," as he called Strauss, off against the "second speaker of the opposition," meaning me. At that time Strauss had developed the "Sonthofen" strategy, demanding that the Union parliamentary group engage in absolute opposition. He was interested not in proposing helpful alternatives but in driving the government into bankruptcy. Of course this strategy led to vehement protest, even within the CDU.

At the time Strauss was on the warpath in every direction. After Kohl had lost the Bundestag election in 1976 but done extremely well for himself, Strauss used a session in Wildbad to dissolve the association of the CDU and CSU parliamentary groups in the Bundestag. Of course that decision was short-lived, since too many CSU district delegates—legitimately guarding their self-interests—realized that they would be left out in the cold at home if the CDU's "invasion" of the Free State of Bavaria, which we had announced, were to come about.

This contretemps was followed by an even more difficult phase. Strauss campaigned to be the party's candidate for chancellor in 1980 and won. So far he was within his legitimate rights. But now he wanted to see a war, waged with clubs, of "liberty versus socialism"—touching the limits of the admissible, since the phrase was supposed to represent a universal choice. Was he referring to the actual existing socialism in East Germany, which must be countered with the longing for freedom? Or did he seriously mean that democratic socialism did not include liberty? The latter concept was grotesque and unbelievable, even if the SPD could not avoid the question of whether its governmental policy of the "protected" citizen did not limit his power to be independent and thus the full use of his liberty. Strauss called himself the German Margaret Thatcher.

Together with others I had worked in vain for the candidacy of Lower Saxony's prime minister, Ernst Albrecht, whom I had come to admire in the Commission on a Basic Program and whose courage I had seen in action during the difficult ratification debates over the Polish treaties in the Bundestag in 1976. The campaign was unpleasant. We made it relatively easy for Schmidt, compensating him for the fact that his own party had by now begun to rebel against him.

My relationship with Strauss improved when I came to Berlin and he started his own constructive Eastern and German policy. He could be irresistibly charming when he wanted. It was a pleasure to listen to him explain his general views. In responding to a widely publicized questionnaire, he listed Old Shatterhand and young Werther as his favorite fictional heroes, the nightingale as his favorite bird, and good nature as his best character trait. When asked what he would like to have been, he answered: a professor of history or the German chancellor in 1932.

Conversation with him was always fruitful, even though it might test you sorely. In general he was known not only for his phenomenal memory but also for unusually thorough preparation. Twice during a discussion with him I saw him pull out a file containing all my latest public pronouncements, which he now used to subject me to a little interrogation. He greeted clear responses with pleasure and brought the breadth of his mind to every exchange of opinion. His historical insights and universal views helped Bavaria gain new, lasting respect around the globe.

To Berlin

In the spring of 1978 Kohl surprised me with an offer to become the Union's leading candidate for the office of governing mayor in the Berlin elections of 1979. He had thought the matter through carefully. Too much time in opposition had badly weakened the Berlin CDU, though Peter Lorenz, its head for twelve years, had done relatively well in the last elections to the house of representatives. His decency and unselfishness had created an atmosphere of trust and humaneness. He never tried to shift problems or reproaches onto the backs of others, though there were many of them. In the service of his job he had risked the utmost against terrorism: his life. When Helmut Kohl sounded him out about bringing in reinforcements from Bonn for the upcoming Berlin elections, he agreed at once.

At the time I was vice chairman of the Union's parliamentary group. The suggestion that I move to Berlin was in line with the CDU's overall strategy since its electoral defeat in 1969. The party's objective was to use new successes in regional elections to pave the way to a return to federal leadership. Gerhard Stoltenberg had gone to Schleswig-Holstein, where he was now prime minister. Ernst Albrecht had assumed the same office in Lower Saxony. Walter Wallmann, also one of the outstanding figures in our Bundestag party group, campaigned successfully for the office of municipal head in Frankfurt on the Main. Walter L. Kiep took over the party leadership in Hamburg. Why should Berlin of all places be left in the hands of the Social Democrats, who had governed there for decades without serious opposition?

Kohl had two reasons to select me for Berlin. One obviously was my work in the Bundestag—that is, my Eastern and German policies; if they were to be understood and refined, Berlin was the ideal location. Kohl was more secretive about the second reason, even when speaking with me, but everyone knew what it was. His mind was on the next election to the federal presidency, planned for 1979. Though Kohl had supported my candidacy for this office as early as 1969 and five years later I had again been the Union candidate, it was a secret to no one, least of all to me, that Strauss and his CSU had anyone but me in mind as a viable Union candidate. Furthermore, his CSU was part of the Union that held an absolute majority in the Federal Assembly. At that time Strauss was still ill disposed toward me because I had advocated the Polish treaties. He wanted to steer the candidacy to Bundestag President Carstens, who maintained a confidential relationship with the Bavarians.

No serious dispute broke out on this question, least of all on my part. Though for a time there was speculation that Kohl's objective was a second term for sitting President Walter Scheel, to smooth the way for a subsequent renewed coalition of the CDU and the FDP, I never heard anything about this plan. Nor did I expect that Kohl, who was having a hard enough time with the CSU in any case, would willingly engage Strauss in a conflict for my sake. By offering me the job, he freed himself of a potentially troublesome problem in a way perfected in all party leadership groups—that is, by unerring shunting in the personnel switch yards. And that is exactly how the media saw the situation. The publisher of the *Frankfurter Allgemeine Zeitung*, Fritz Ulrich Fack, emphatically praised Kohl's successful "Berlin coup." Fack's fellow publisher Johann Georg Reissmüller added that this proposal let Kohl "painlessly" dissolve the "paralyzing consultant dualism" between the hard-liners in Eastern policies and myself within his parliamentary group.

All of this was to the point, and in the end it was to my good fortune. Like Kohl, I too had great respect for Karl Carstens the politician and the man, having worked with him for many years on the foreign-policy sections of our party program. Furthermore my work as federal president would be much more difficult because I lacked experience in an executive political office. Therefore no problems between Kohl and myself could arise because he wanted to nominate Carstens.

The thought of going to Berlin intrigued me at once. Even though I had spent the last thirty years living on the banks of the Rhine and had a wonderful home with my wife and our four children in Bonn, my older, deeper roots in Berlin had never withered. It was the city of my childhood and my time as a soldier. Before the war ended, I had spent a few frightening hours in the cellar of my parents' home, which had been badly damaged in the firebombing. After the war my activities in the Protestant Church brought me to the divided city well over 150 times, especially into the Soviet-occupied sector. My activities focused on taking concrete everyday experiences of East and West Berliners and applying them to the general aims of East-West policy. I was as familiar with the city's character, which frowned on any displays of warmth and kindness, as I was with the Berliners' compelling urge to save themselves from the psychiatrist's couch with their untiring, self-directed ironic grumbling. I understood this aspect much better than all the previous governing mayors. Only Peter Lorenz outdid me, with his deeply authentic Berlin accent.

Nevertheless my decision was anything but simple. For decades the political parties in Berlin had seen a steady exodus of their most talented members to Bonn, with only minimal movement in the opposite direction. Shortly after I did so, Hans-Jochen Vogel also left Bonn and resettled in Berlin where he received a telegram from Axel Springer, a local voter, welcoming him at a time when candidates had to be beaten like dogs to chase them to Berlin. That was the situation at the time. Nor were the parties exceptionally attractive to Berlin's younger generation. They had become shopworn either from overlong responsibility for governing or fruitless opposition. In my own party, besides the selfless and magnanimous Peter Lorenz, one group appeared to be made of concrete. Some of its members spent more time parceling out the more interesting offices among themselves than dealing with what I considered necessary German and Eastern policies. But of course they were far superior to me in knowing and understanding local politics.

Only six months remained before the June 1979 election, far too short a time for a completely green candidate from elsewhere to campaign, especially since federal conditions favored the Social-Democratic coalition. And though I had taken part in many campaign rallies, I had never before stood at the head of a whole regional assembly as a candidate for the top governmental post.

In short the hurdles were high, but as it turned out, not too high. After an exceedingly friendly consultation with Peter Lorenz I agreed to run, and I have never had reason to regret my decision.

Two Election Campaigns
in the Divided City

Now I was facing a storm of new demands, a situation that could not have suited me better. Mental planning for long-range programs had to give way to dealing with day-to-day affairs. There was nothing wrong with looking for consensus; but my primary concern was to wage the good fight, and so I entered on an apprenticeship that, though hard, taught me a great deal. Since aside from a few tasks on behalf of the church, politics had by now become my full-time career, this learning experience was somewhat like liberation from theory.

The situation in the city was difficult. The Basic Treaty with East Germany and the Four Power Agreement had secured for West Berlin certain links and routes to the outside world and allowed us to include them in our calculations, and the Helsinki Final Act improved the situation. Little by little West Berliners stopped thinking of themselves as defenders of an embattled frontier outpost and began to wish for a good time. While such a shift in mood was only too understandable, it also promoted a predisposition to provincialism and mediocrity alongside a never-ending demand for grants, glossed over or even eclipsed by the display of Queen Nefertiti's head in the Egyptian Museum, by von Karajan on the podium of the Philharmonic, and by Peter Stein at the old Schaubühne theater.

In its role of permanent regent, the SPD was not in the best shape. In 1977, after ten years as governing mayor, Klaus Schütz had been forced to resign. The party broke into two warring factions, one preferring Dietrich Stobbe and the other supporting Hans-Jürgen Wischnewski as the best candidate to succeed Schütz. Stobbe won by a vote of 17 to 15. He himself admitted that he was the head of a divided metropolitan party. Stobbe was acutely aware that even though the party's bloom was off the rose and it was getting along on membership-book management, the party had captured the district. Though such an outcome is not inevitable, it usually is the principal risk when the voters cannot change power for a long period.

Stobbe chose to concentrate on community affairs and called his program "A turn toward municipal policy." When my move to Berlin became known to SPD leaders in Berlin, Stobbe stated publicly that the city would profit from my presence. He welcomed me with great warmth and called me "a figure of light," whatever that might mean, whose hands had not yet become soiled in the political morass of the metropolis.

Of course my election campaign did not take a back seat to other duties. I enjoyed it especially because rallies of cheering supporters and speeches to the converted were kept to a minimum, replaced by countless street-corner debates, widespread canvassing, and technical meetings on specific topics. The best part was always the Berliners' completely direct, heartily bold, and frank manner.

Nevertheless Berliners were not a very active political group. The common practice was to complain of the shopworn SPD; certainly there was nothing new about that. Voters had become used to the situation without giving any thought to doing something about it. The CDU's reputation was not very solid either. Though some of its objectives on education reform were welcomed, it was considered fairly reactionary in all other respects. For example, it had just opposed Willy Brandt's Eastern policy in Berlin as well as in Bonn without encountering a strong response from the people.

The president of the house of delegates, Heinrich Lummer, who was very influential in the party and whose views were far to the right, had used my arrival in Berlin to air the idea of a fourth party of his followers. This announcement abruptly plunged me into my first and sharpest intraparty mediation. I thought the idea nonsensical and sure to fatally damage any chance the CDU might have in the election.

Though Lummer vigorously disagreed with me, he followed my directive. Later, when he served as senator for domestic affairs and as my deputy in the Berlin government, we crossed swords more than once even as we worked harmoniously together. Lummer and I held different opinions on many, though not all, important issues, and he always honored guidelines and kept appointments.

The Berlin section of the CDU also kept aloof from contemporary trends in culture and art. When my wife and I visited the Schaubühne theater for the first time to see a play by Botho Strauss, we were greeted by strange looks all around. Why were we here, we were asked. No CDU politician had ever shown his face at the Schaubühne before.

Except for Axel Springer's newspapers, the media, especially the electronic media, were fairly unanimously opposed to a change of ruling parties. During the final television debate I sat alone, facing not only the speakers for the other three parties—that is, the SPD, the FDP, and the Alternative List—but also the moderator of the SFB (Sender Freies Berlin—Free Berlin Television). The most objective and fairest exchanges were the verbal duels with my real opponent, Governing Mayor Stobbe.

Trade unions and staff and management councils were particularly influential in the city, almost exclusively favoring the SPD. Public agencies were overstaffed, and public employees enjoyed generous benefits. More than one young worker trained by Siemens—the largest private employer in Berlin—offered a permanent place with the firm preferred to work for the municipal sanitation department, with its easier hours and better health benefits. One newspaper asked satirically why the head of human resources in the public sector could not serve directly as CEO of the corporation called Berlin.

At a large campaign rally of all staff councils and trade union functionaries Chancellor Helmut Schmidt declared that though the CDU candidate, Weizsäcker, was a very nice man, he did not represent his organization, being neither fish nor fowl but chopped meat. Great outrage in the ranks of the CDU! How could we defend ourselves against such slurs? My colleague and close friend Norbert Kazcmarek, a calm and witty man, showed the way. The following day I declared that the only kind of chopped meat Berliners recognized was meatballs, which they certainly preferred over hamburgers. (We all knew that Schmidt had grown up in Hamburg and maintained a home there.)

An election campaign conjures up a number of new experiences. At one meeting I was interrogated by two hundred architects. What, they wanted to know, did I think of the residential high-rise building on Schlangenbader Street that had a branch of city highway running through its extensive basement? Pleased at the choice of topic, I answered that if I were a sly little devil who wanted a special project to plague the people, I'd think up just this kind of subterranean autobahn, where trucks would spend zestful nights speeding under the beds of hardworking Berliners who badly needed their sleep. In response one gentleman rose and identified himself as the little devil I admired; he was the architect of both the building and the road.

Sometimes events were more athletic. Each afternoon for a week the party hosted a seniors' ball in a large hall to help us win the female vote. But here the role of the candidate was not aggressive: Each dance was ladies' choice, cutting in allowed. Once I believed that I might actually be close to breasting the election tape, since in the space of ten minutes I waltzed with twenty-five different ladies full of grand-motherly vivacity. I also saw myself forced to escort the last of them back to her table, to mollify her husband.

But all good things come to an end, and the election took place in June 1979. Though in contrast to the general national trend, which did not favor the CDU, the party showed a slight gain over previous elections, and the Social-Liberal coalition prevailed once more. The usual interpretation was put on the election results by the victors; everybody had won.

Nevertheless, Stobbe's situation soon grew more precarious. In spite of Schmidt's clear victory over Strauss in the Bundestag elections of 1980, the Berlin SPD was in turmoil. Stobbe rebelled by restructuring the senate in a way that reinforced the administration. Peter Glotz, newly appointed senator for science and research, made especially significant contributions. To this day Berlin profits from his appointments to university posts and from the science lectures he established. But the public was more affected by economic reverses and collapses, especially the bankruptcy of the construction and party lion, Dietrich Garski, which was a great loss to the province of Berlin. Constantly expanding problems also plagued residence policy, especially the many empty apartments in municipally owned housing combined with an increasing housing shortage that resulted in disturbances and illegal squatting.

Besides the CDU, the opposition included the Alternative List, which at the time was half Maoist, half Green. It too did not shy away from extraparliamentary demonstrations and occasional riots. In the plenary chamber of the house of representatives the desk of the head of each party parliamentary group was equipped with a telephone. I recall more than one situation in which the leadership of the Alternative List used a double strategy: even while waging verbal battles against all the other parties in parliament, they wielded their telephones to direct the street marches leading to the gates of city hall as a way to put pressure on delegates from outside the government chambers.

Thus the CDU and the Alternatives had little in common except one thing: We were united in pressing for a new election at the earliest date. In this fight a stipulation of the Berlin regional constitution offered a complicated but effective tool. If one-fifth of registered voters agreed to hold a referendum on new elections before the current legislative term ran its course, such a plebiscite must be held. If at least half of all registered voters cast their ballots in the plebiscite and a majority favored dissolution of the house of representatives, new elections must be held as soon as possible.

The provision had never been tested in practice. But now, under my leadership, the CDU took this path against the outraged protests of the SPD. The ruling coalition did not stop us, however, since we were simply utilizing a popular constitutional initiative, even if it went beyond accepted common practice. The Alternative List joined our cause almost at once.

We quickly realized that the first step—gathering enough signatures to guarantee a referendum—could be accomplished. We urged voters to stop allowing the parties to make all the decisions, letting themselves live as nullities buried in Article 20 of the Basic Law that established parties, and to take matters into their own hands. Our appeal generated a strong response.

Once again Stobbe rebelled, and on January 15, 1981, he stepped on the dais of the house of delegates to propose still newer names for his senate. But all the SPD candidates he proposed did not get the necessary majority on a parliamentary ballot. Stobbe, undermined by some in his own party, resigned that same day.

Critical blows rained down from all sides. Peter Glotz, recently named federal manager of the SPD and thereby escaping the ship of senate just before it went down, merely noted in lapidary terms, "The ritual sacrifice of a bellwether is hardly enough." But what should happen next? That consideration set the blood of the federal SPD boiling. The very next day Hans-Jochen Vogel was named to succeed Stobbe, and only a week after Stobbe's fall Vogel was elected to the post of governing mayor by an impressive new senate team. On a single ballot he garnered more votes than his coalition held in the house. The SPD had managed to hold on to "its" Berlin one more time.

Wielding great authority and his inimitable energy, Vogel went to work. In a short time he won back a sizable amount of the good feeling his party had recently lost. To benefit as fully as possible from this trend, he did not wait for us to arrive at the second stage of our new-election missile, the referendum. He seized the initiative and made arrangements to set an early date for new elections on May 10, 1981, only three months after becoming mayor.

We were campaigning once again. By now I had mastered this activity and—as I would never have believed possible—found it a very pleasurable occupation. This time, however, a problematic aspect intervened: my personal relationship with Vogel. We did not see eye to eye on all issues, but we did agree on many matters important to Berlin, especially international questions concerning the city and the office. I had great respect for his character and work, and I was drawn to his personality. I had no doubt that his presence was a huge win for Berlin. He also treated me, his adversary, with candor and warmth. We developed an unrestricted friendship that lasted long past both our days in Berlin and grew deeper over the years in a way that is rare among older people.

Our friendship began during that campaign, and we repeatedly had to remind ourselves that our unswerving devotion to democratic principles required us to debate as antagonists. We managed pretty well but did not always elicit applause from the hard-liners in our respective parties for our way of campaigning, especially when the campaign was accompanied by scurrilous doggerel.

No matter how indefatigably and thoroughly Vogel worked, his problems continued to increase and feelings about the senate worsened again. The biggest problems were the empty apartments and consequent squatting. To solve the housing question, Vogel developed the so-called Berlin Line, a package of measures to legalize, decriminalize, or clear illegally occupied houses. But none of his initiatives could prevent the number of squats from increasing, from about 30 when he assumed office to 169 at his resignation. His campaign slogan, to the effect that the city no longer needed a change of parties because he, along with his new senate, incorporated the necessary changes, became somewhat less convincing.

The last straw happened on Palm Sunday of 1981. While Vogel was away from the city on official business, instances of ugly destruction and violence occurred—a crowd of rowdies shattered store windows and broke shop accessories along a mile of West Berlin's most elegant street, the Kurfürstendamm. Pictures of this violence captured the public imagination, and the resulting disgust did not change materially from that Sunday to election day, four weeks later.

The election took place on May 10. Though the CDU did not win an absolute majority—such an outcome could hardly be expected realistically in Berlin—we did get 48 percent of the vote, more than ever before and roughly 10 percent more than the standard Berlin party, the SPD. The FDP, traditionally torn by internal strife, barely managed to scrape together enough votes to make it into the house of representatives. The relatively largest gain was won by the Alternative List, which garnered more than 7 percent to become the third-strongest party. According to a supposition I had harbored throughout the campaign, the SPD itself was somewhat complicit in the AL's gain. Though Hans-Jochen Vogel had always explicitly rejected violent social protest, he had also shown great understanding of the desire by many, especially younger, people to lead their lives and coexistence according to new and different standards. This understanding might be greatly to his credit, but it reinforced the view of a significant number of voters that their course was correct. Vogel even confirmed it, didn't he, and if an alternative way of life was possible, why not vote for the Alternative List? Anything but that old warhorse, the SPD.

Thus after many, many years the Social Democrats were banished into the opposition. Even if the CDU with its 48 percent could not alone elect the senate, there was no longer any doubt that only the CDU could assume the governing role. After some shilly-shallying, five of the seven FDP delegates provided the absolute majority needed for the senate candidates I proposed and for me personally. This vote, however, did not obligate them to enter into a coalition with us. We were often called the minority senate, a term I always found amusing since we had all been elected by an absolute majority of the house. How was that a minority?

By whatever name, we now set to work on the other side of the table. I personally had no experience in governing. But the office of governing mayor is so unique that even Stobbe had rightly noted that all previous holders of the position had campaigned for the office without previous experience, including Ernst Reuter and Willy Brandt.

At a time when the city, the country, and all of Europe were divided into individual sovereignties, there was no more interesting and varied job in all of Germany. Activities ran the gamut, from settling a heated spat over renaming a 100-meter-long alley in the Wilmersdorf section to dealing with the enormous tensions of the East-West conflict, for which Berlin was a particularly responsive sounding board and in which all the mayors of the capitals of the Western Powers were regularly consulted.

Berlin as a whole was under the command of the four victorious powers in the Second World War—the United States, the Soviet Union, France, and Great Britain. In West Berlin the three Western Allies held the supreme power. Once a month the governing mayor called on the three municipal commandants and their political-diplomatic deputies. The mayor rendered his report and counsel was given, always in a fully cordial atmosphere. The most comfortable residence with the handsomest gardens and the best tea were owned by—who else?—the British. More than once I told them that it was no trouble for us to put up with this remnant of an occupation government more than thirty years after the end of the war. These four were the only occupying powers I knew that stayed in the occupied territory for as long as the local populace wanted them to. Of course we were pleased with their presence, and we were perhaps the only population ever to be grateful to their occupiers.

After all, the Western Powers had safeguarded our freedom and continued to protect it. We had a good, often truly warm, relationship. Time and again we saw representatives of the three Western Powers in Berlin who were reluctant to go on to their next post, and we too were sad whenever a change of personnel occurred, because each time we were losing a new friend. I never felt that any of the protecting powers tried to influence the policies of the governing mayor.

The contradiction, given classic wording in the Four Power Agreement, which dictated that the western sectors of the city were not part of the Federal Republic and existed outside the governance of that state at the same time that the links—or according to the Soviet interpretation, relations—between the Federal Republic and Berlin were to be "kept up and developed," worked out well in practice. On the one hand we were governed by Bonn like any of the West German provinces, but with the special bonuses of Berlin Aid and Berlin Advancement. Just over 50 percent of our budget was financed by the federal government, and tax abatements provided jobs. On the other hand we remained officially independent. Any laws enacted by the Bundestag and the Bundesrat were not binding on Berlin unless the house of delegates passed separate resolutions to validate them.

Of course there were limits to this unique status, but it could be useful to politics and policies. We were both more dependent and more independent than governments in other provinces, all of whom sat in the Bundesrat along with us. A governing mayor would do well to model himself on a child who takes his request to the parent more likely to grant it, depending on what it is—one day the federal agencies, another the sovereign Three Powers.

We were also close participants in German foreign policy. Soon after my election I called on Ronald Reagan, François Mitterand, and Margaret Thatcher. President Mitterand, as it so happened, in beating out Giscard d'Estaing, was elected the same day I was and consequently stole my thunder, even in the German media, as the triumphant winner of an election. These leaders all showed a lively interest in the mood and political direction of West Berlin, that perennial barometer of East-West weather. My political exchanges with many world leaders grew into good, close personal friendships. Mitterand's interest in the history of Prussia and Berlin far exceeded that of any of his predecessors. George Bush, then vice president of the United States, and I quickly became close. Lord Carrington, the British foreign minister, and I also formed close and cordial ties. I happened to be visiting him when Argentina surprised Great Britain by occupying the Falkland Islands and the British public requested a reprimand of its government for not being sufficiently alert. Though Carrington had done nothing wrong, he announced his resignation at once in order to lift the burden from his colleagues and Mrs. Thatcher. When I left my Berlin position, he made me a gift of tin soldiers representing the Grenadier Guards, his regiment, which in 1815 had joined with my traditional Potsdam regiment at Waterloo to defeat Napoleon.

Governing Mayor

Of course my work was not primarily in the great big world, it began at home. My first test came in naming a senate. I had to make good on my campaign promises: not to substitute rule of one party by another, and not to make the senate the monopoly of party politicians, especially those living in Berlin, but to bring new vigor to Berlin by using outsiders and creating the best possible mix.

I was pleasantly surprised and gratified to see that my invitations issued throughout West Germany found a favorable response. It also helped that the Berlin CDU was willing to cede some of its advantages in favor of newly attracted colleagues from the West. Six of the twelve senate members came from outside Berlin: Norbert Blüm for federal affairs; Hanna-Renate Laurien for education, youth, and sports; Elmar Pieroth for commerce; Ulf Fink for health, social policy, and the family; Rupert Scholz, at the time unaffiliated with any party, for justice; and Wilhelm Kewenig for culture and science. I also proposed to mix tested as well as new names for the members from Berlin itself: Heinrich Lummer became senator for domestic affairs; Gerhard Kunz took over finance; Edmund Wronski covered labor and management; and then, surprising everyone, I assigned municipal development and the environment to Volker Hassemer, a virtual unknown.

All in all I had high expectations for the established Berlin CDU groups. Under the leadership of their managing regional chairman and head of the parliamentary party group, Eberhard Diepgen, the party willingly set out in a new direction. Only one very brief rebellion occurred when Elmar Pieroth did not gain the required number of

votes on the secret ballot in the prescribed senatorial election, allegedly defeated by rumors of a "Rhineland-Palatinate mafia" in my "im-
ported" candidates. But at the exact moment the president of parliament announced that Elmar Pieroth had failed to win sufficient votes, I
announced that the new candidate would be Elmar Pieroth, and he was
easily elected on a second ballot.

My senate was now up and running. Soon the Federal Republic
gave its approval, and even several national papers praised it as the
best regional government to date. In any case it proved itself seawor-
thy, and I enjoyed our collaborative efforts enormously. But without
the experienced, intelligent, and unconditionally reliable help of Eberhard Diepgen, especially in the ranks of the Berlin party, my job would
have been much more difficult at first.

After I had held the office a while, the media decided that I had
changed from a philosopher to a tribune of the people. They were
wrong on both counts. The only truth was that I felt totally fulfilled
giving advice to others and being forced to practice what I had previously only preached. This was especially true regarding the central
topic in Berlin—the consequences and future of the city's division in
the continuing Cold War. In the late 1970s East-West animosity entered on a new, more chilling phase, which included new Soviet
medium-range missiles and NATO's double-track resolution that resulted in rearmament. When the Soviet Union started its war in Afghanistan, which was as senseless as it was inhumane, global contacts
came to a standstill.

The next collapse occurred in Poland, where the Solidarnosc
movement—thanks to the courage of its leaders, who always scrupu-
lously invoked the CSCE Final Act—unleashed a veritable dynamic of
opposition. The Polish leadership, both loyally Communist and na-
tionalistically Polish, could find no other path between the Scylla of
the hated Russians and the Charybdis of the feared freedom movement
at home than imposing martial law. A nadir such as the East-West
conflict had not seen in twenty years set in.

The Moscow leadership was somewhat superannuated in both its power and its thinking. The new United States president, Ronald Reagan, struck a sharp note when he spoke of the Soviet Union as "the Evil Empire." In the United States' strategic planning there was talk of a "decapitation of the Soviet Union." It was a question of whether a stability-maintaining nuclear balance of horror should be kept unchanged or whether the so-called SDI—Strategic Defense Initiative, nicknamed Star Wars in the United States—should be added. This new device, it was hoped, would allow the United States to ward off a Russian nuclear attack without being prevented from carrying out its own attacks against the Soviet Union. In a word: the practicability of atomic warfare was to be restored.

Most Europeans believed that this plan was technically, strategically, politically, and humanely half-baked. The suspicion of a breakup within NATO arose. Voices in the United States muttered that Europeans, and especially West Germans, either had the souls of shopkeepers because they were so fond of trading with the East or were simply cowards, easily intimidated by Moscow. The United States also called Bonn's continuing dealings with the other Germany "self-Finlandization" on the part of the Federal Republic—that is, voluntary acceptance of dependency on Moscow. I always considered this a fairly ignorant disparagement of the impressively brave Finns, and considering our central position on the Continent a shortsighted and mistaken viewpoint. But it was a typical expression of the moods and tensions of that time.

In truth both federal chancellors of that period, Helmut Schmidt and, beginning in October 1981, Helmut Kohl, were steadfastly loyal to the Alliance and never entertained the thought of leaving NATO. This loyalty was one reason why Schmidt lost the majority of his party group and thus the chancellorship, and similarly why Kohl won a majority of voters for his coalition in the Bundestag election in the spring of 1983. But both chancellors also made every effort without hesitation and in the end successfully to limit damage to the East-West relationship—that is, to prevent détente from being sacrificed to a new arms race—by helping to nurture relations between the two Germanys and between Poland and the Soviet Union.

It was, of course, essential to Germany's welfare to promote mutually beneficial political and social relations between the two German states, not least in Berlin itself. Easing suffering and lightening burdens, however, always had to be done without compromising the fundamental goal of reunification. How that end was accomplished is a question that still arouses much controversy even in the most recent scholarly investigations.

When it came to politics, Martin Luther said, Germans, like drunken peasants, tend to fall off the horse either to the left or the right. In reality most in demand was our ability to balance security and détente, maintain confrontation on the principles and cooperation in practice, and advance concrete steps to aid Germans in the GDR—who could not be approached except with the collaboration of their rulers—and the future goal of unification, even if no one knew when, how, and if it could be attained. All these issues had to be kept in mind when I pursued the objectives of my own activities in Berlin and offered my contributions on the federal level to German and Eastern policies, especially in extensive debates in the Bundestag.

Let us recall once more Egon Bahr's dialectic, as clever as it was controversial, of bringing about change by means of reconciliation. Destabilization of the East German regime, he argued, could occur only if it was preceded by stability. Temporary recognition of the status quo must be the precondition for its gradual abolition. This argument was both hard to comprehend and imbued with great risk. Were we agreed on what *status quo* meant—the borders, the states, the alliances? Or would the term include current political and ideological systems? No, no, surely not the latter. Instead, we needed to transform the Soviet concept of "free coexistence" into a form of coexistence that opened their systems, and in the end changed them.

The answers to such questions were relatively easy when applied to Poland. Poland was a nation, and we must respect its borders, including the Oder and the Neisse. Poland's system, on the other hand, especially given the martial law imposed to stem the Solidarnosc movement, was a program we need never accept.

The situation was more complicated in regard to East Germany. Unlike other Communist parties within the Warsaw Pact, the SED was faced with a special problem: the German alternative to the GDR—the Federal Republic. Therefore the SED was all the more eager to distance itself from its earlier commitment to form a unified German nation. To stress the point, it even deleted two lines from the East German national anthem that referred to a single German fatherland.

Later on, the SED leaders went further, ending the distinction between the state within its borders on the one hand and its political system on the other. Until late in 1989 they clung to the theory that the GDR was conceivable only as an antifascist, socialist state—"the socialist alternative to the Federal Republic," as the leading SED party ideologist, Otto Reinhold, put it. He amplified his meaning by noting, "For what significance could there be for a capitalist GDR alongside a capitalist Federal Republic? None at all, of course." The message thus addressed to West Germany was crystal clear: If you try to fiddle with our system, you're fiddling with our state.

What conclusions was the West to draw from this stance? We wanted and needed social improvements in both Germanys—ease of travel, reunited families, material aid. However, West Germany could not unilaterally enforce these changes; we had to negotiate them with East Berlin. We knew and had tested the fact over and over that the more the negotiating climate between East and West Germany was disturbed, the less fruitful were our discussions. Was that a reason for us to free the SED from the fear that we were trying to infiltrate its system? Surely that reassurance would strengthen the system instead of changing it, as we intended.

So many questions. Were we too casually helping to stabilize a government that was inimical to human rights? Conversely, were we within our rights as outsiders to further—even demand—the right to rebel of a population that was oppressed and spied on by a dictatorship?

When Willy Brandt went to Erfurt in 1970 and the people wistfully cheered him as he stood on the balcony outside the railroad station, he had no choice but to calm the crowd rather than to further inflame emotions. "I'm going right back to the West," he said to his companion. "They can't."

It requires great inner control and moral effort to hold back in such a situation, to keep all feelings in check, to respond to crowds without endangering them by inciting them further—to communicate by small signals, as it were. I don't mean to equate the significance of my own experiences with Brandt's, but I too have been touched by the same feelings on almost every one of my visits to East Berlin. When, for example, I went to Hedwig Cathedral for a ceremony conducted by the head of the East German Conference of Bishops, the splendid Cardinal Alfred Bengsch, I was almost literally suffocated along the way by the expressed feelings and hopes of the loudly shouting and cheering East Berliners.

To what extent, then, must we accept reality and where must we confront it boldly? We cannot and must not ever give up the idealism and morality of freedom. But we must also require such idealism only of ourselves, not of others; those who choose not to accept it must pay the price without expecting us to share it.

I must refer once more to the NATO double-track resolution. Stationing United States' cruise and Pershing missiles in West Germany created a number of problems for several European NATO members. The roads to the missiles' positions had to be cleared with police force. It required courage to publicly advocate rearmament. Even at public functions, where a certain measure of tolerance and neutrality are called for, the atmosphere grew heated. At the Protestant Conference in Hamburg in 1981, for example, which took place in a huge hall and was attended by more than five thousand participants, I was on the podium when SPD minister of defense, Hans Apel, was forced to explain and defend the double-track resolution under a hail of eggs and tomatoes.

At that time West Berlin also emphatically demanded that the Harmel Doctrine be followed not only in part but on both tracks. The resulting tension had to be countered by any means; in my opinion we had no option but to hold out against Soviet attempts at blackmail. In spite of the urgent necessity for détente, that policy could succeed for the West only if the gentlemen in the Kremlin had no doubt about our determination and ability to defend ourselves. We would have lost precisely this ability without NATO's effective antidote to the new medium-range missiles. We would have lost our credibility.

Nor, working out of Berlin, could I allow the tender young plant of détente to dry up. I experienced this conflict with particular poignancy in 1983 in Luther's city of Wittenberg. The occasion was the five hundredth birthday of the Reformer. Reacting to my invitation from the Church, the Politburo of the SED discussed in a session— giving me too much credit—whether the invitation could be revoked. Finally I was given permission to speak in the church and subsequently to address more than ten thousand East Germans gathered in the market square. It was a first of its kind. Manfred Stolpe, often unfairly criticized, managed to gain acceptance for this coup as well as so many others against the rulers of the socialism that prevailed in the real world. He was acting in the interest of a united Germany.

I found Wittenberg no easy task. On the one hand our East German hosts' warmth and sense of solidarity with their West German guests was overwhelming. We were both grappling with complex, difficult problems. There was no argument that we were jointly eager to strengthen the peace. Never again would war emanate from Germany—we were completely agreed on that. But how could we secure this peace? "Make peace without arms" the banners announced, and Wittenberg also publicized the biblical command "swords into plowshares." I was an eyewitness when Father Schorlemmer, standing over an open fire in the rear courtyard of the Melanchthon House, tried to smelt a sword into a peaceful agricultural tool. His action was directed primarily against the leaders of the GDR, who had always, with NATO in mind, demanded peace without Western weapons. But Schorlemmer was also thinking of Western rearmament.

For my part I felt I could not and must not keep silent about the reasons I considered the double-track resolution—that is, this type of rearmament if the SS-20s were to remain—to be essential, exactly because peace must never mean submission. These discussions were the most committed and fairest in which I participated during those years. The Wittenberg audience—perhaps not surprisingly, given that conditions in a dictatorship made it so much easier than those of a free democratic *bellum contra omnes*—was much more disciplined than the crowds that had attended the Hamburg Conference. In the end the hot topic in the market square among the thousands of participants was not so much the arms race as this overwhelming manifestation of German unity.

At that time Germans working on all fronts to further rapprochement between East and West saw a motley mixture of successes and setbacks. Trade between East and West Germany increased. The autobahn from Hamburg to Berlin was built. The Teltow Canal for shipping to Berlin was opened, markedly cutting transit time. Some, though not enough, defusing measures were also enacted for the so-called border regime at the Wall and barbed wire.

Even though financial contributions from West Germany to East Germany were often objects of criticism, they became increasingly important to the GDR's economic and social survival. The total amount became an indispensable element in the SED's financial planning, a factor of qualitatively altering weight, a political instrument for the West, and therefore a factor bracketing East and West. Franz Josef Strauss, who after his 1980 electoral defeat concentrated his activities entirely on his home province of Bavaria, soon acknowledged the benefits of this unifying financial aid and participated actively in credit transactions with East Germany. Though many in his home province resented this reversal, it was immensely useful to West Germany as a whole. East Germany's need for hard currency, to a degree satisfied by this aid, cannot have prolonged the life of the SED. Our primary purpose was to make a show of generosity. Spending funds to that end was not open to debate, it was a necessity. All government agencies, the Chancellor, and federal ministers in Bonn rightly participated in the effort. If there was talk later on of obscene trading in human lives, such statements showed a stupendous ignorance of the political and ethical objectives that ruled the West at that time.

One of my tasks was to be as active as possible from my Berlin vantage point in shaping public opinion throughout West Germany in regard to our German policy. Time and again we had to deal with the apparent contradiction between peace and unification. On the edges of the controversial double-track resolution, some leading German politicians declared both at home and in the United States that the military balance between East and West was a crucial condition in keeping peace, though at the same time the balance was a fundamental cause behind the continued division of Germany. During a debate in the Bundestag on June 17, 1980, I asked what this position meant. Was a peace policy identical with the division policy? Were peace and division necessary to each other? Would an imbalance promote reunification? If someone supported abolishing the dividing trenches and walls, did that make him guilty of endangering the peace? This seemed a dangerous fallacy to me.

Of course even we who lived in Berlin were not prophets. We knew no more than our colleagues in Bonn about what measures might persuade the Soviet Union to permit peaceful German unification. But we did learn daily object lessons in partition. And as Berliners it was our special task to keep the subject alive in Bundestag discussions and throughout Germany. We lived with the Wall, this pile of stones and symbol of partition. And we could see clearly that day by day the painful and harsh injustice of this symbol became a greater burden on the East German government.

Those who built the Wall had intended to end "voting with your feet" by East Germans' emigration to the West, thus stabilizing their own political system. The East German population would over time learn to accept partition and separation. But the longer the Wall stood, the more obvious it became that it missed its mark. On the contrary, it became a daily reminder that the question it was meant to answer once and for all remained open, a visible structure symbolizing the solidarity it was intended to erase from everyone's mind. Had it been otherwise, the Wall wouldn't have been necessary.

When we took foreign visitors to the center of the city where the sectors were separated, they could see for themselves what we felt: As long as the Brandenburg Gate remained closed, the German question remained open. Erich Honecker was finding it increasingly difficult to explain to visitors to East Berlin why he was inviting them to view the Wall. When President Kaunda of Zambia heard Honecker call the Wall a monument to socialist liberation, Kaunda openly expressed deep astonishment at this repulsive, inhuman structure. Early on, even Khrushchev characterized the Wall as ugly, though temporarily unavoidable.

The Wall, which cut the metropolis in two at its center, marked the border. But the city center was not suitable for a border. One fact was impossible to ignore: that from a historical perspective the Wall could not be permanent, even without knowing what consequences it would have for both states. This was my simple message and admonition from Berlin to many doubters in the West and reflected our immediate sentiment in Berlin. We did not need to wage a religious war among ourselves, since the inconclusiveness of the German question was what we felt daily. We became increasingly convinced that a divided Berlin united Germans more than it separated them. In spite of all efforts, Berlin was a source of hope.

It was well known that the leaders in Moscow and East Berlin had always wanted to turn West Berlin into a so-called independent political entity. Though this aim was contrary to the Four Power Agreement on Berlin, West Berlin leaders had to be careful not to feed this Eastern trend. For example, the Soviet ambassador in East Germany, Piotr Abrassimov, repeatedly invited me to Moscow. I was willing to go but only on condition that in Moscow I would be looked after and escorted by members of the West German embassy, like any other German statesman, precisely because we did not accept the theory of West Berlin as an independent political district. As a result I could not travel to Moscow.

On the other hand, it was the duty and custom of my predecessors and my own Berlin senate to negotiate with East German representatives about the border regime and assorted measures to ease travel restrictions. To emphasize our demands to further improve the lives of the populace on both sides, I decided in September 1983 to call on the general secretary of the SED, Erich Honecker, in East Berlin. This visit was a complete novelty. Some commentators expressed the fear that this would reinforce the idea of West Berlin as an independent political sector. One undersecretary in the Bonn foreign office sent me the longest telegram I'd received in my whole life, intended to make me realize the risk of such a venture. But he was attaching too much gravity to my tiny step. Of course I had no intention of altering the status quo and could not even if I wanted to. I informed Kohl, chancellor for barely a year, of my intention and discussed the visit with the United States envoy in Berlin, who at that time represented the three protecting powers. He too raised no objections.

Our meeting place was Niederschönhaus Castle in the Pankow district of East Berlin, where Frederick the Great had banished Queen Elisabeth Christine, the wife he did not love. After the Second World War, Wilhelm Pieck used it as the residence for the president of East Germany. Later it became a government guest house, and after reunification it became the site of the round table for all political parties.

It was my first meeting with Honecker. There was no sense that I had entered the lion's den, except that I knew how much suffering and injustice were connected with his party's rule. After meeting him, I could not guess what personal traits qualified him to move to the head of his system. He appeared unpolemical and not hostile, but he was detached and anything but humorous. There was no electricity between us. On the whole our conversation was businesslike. We wasted no time reciting our well-known and radically opposite positions. I pressed for concrete improvements in travel and visiting arrangements, but I was able to win only very modest concessions. The to-do about the icebreaking event soon died down, as was appropriate.

Besides practical everyday disputes, historical-intellectual confrontations were also part of the permanent program. To enhance East Germany's image as a separate German nation, the SED used far more than merely its party ideology. More and more it tried to strengthen its quest for a "socialist national consciousness" by laying claim to German history. Honecker had the famous statue of Frederick the Great on horseback brought back from Rauch and set up on Unter den Linden again. His party was no longer content to evoke the instigators of the Peasants' War as the class-struggle precursors of the GDR; Johann Sebastian Bach from the baroque era, the archconservative Field Marshal Yorck from the wars of liberation, and even Goethe, that admirer of Napoleon, were given a place in the genealogy of East Germany.

A special effort was made to celebrate Martin Luther's five hundredth birthday. Honecker called him one of history's most significant humanists and national revolutionaries. Luther was added to the gallery of ancestors of the socialist nation.

But I did not believe that such goings-on should cause the West to sneer and leave it at that. It was more important to engage seriously in a peaceful dialogue based on historical roots. Did we have anything to fear in this area? If they invoked Bach, they could surely grow only by measuring themselves against his intellectual-artistic standard. The same was true for Goethe's humanism and Yorck's deep-seated patriotism. And Martin Luther? Intense preoccupation with him during the jubilee year could do no harm. This, in my opinion, was true both within Germany and beyond the ecclesiastical lines of separation. The ecumenical nature of the celebrations for the Confessio Augustana in Augsburg at the same time seemed to me proof of that theory. In the end it was impossible to escape what Luther had really preached, which was not revolution but forgiveness of the sinner for no reason other than grace—and this applied to Eastern as well as Western sinners.

We in West Germany had to demonstrate that this attempt to appropriate German national history as a sectarian claim would not advance any cause. Of course, with our Western consciousness we had to be very careful, down to the language we used. What would the Germans in the GDR think if we called them our brothers and sisters while the sports reporters in all the media spoke of a game of "Germany versus the GDR"?

Why should we be frightened by Honecker's historical calling forth not only of insurrectionists Thomas Münzer and Karl Marx but also, beyond Martin Luther, Frederick the Great, the Prussian reformers, and even Queen Luise? Politicians always try to promote their own cause when soliciting history. He who has the history, the saying goes, may also have the future. For us Germans who were living in a partitioned land this preoccupation with history in reality displayed many signs of our solidarity. We saw no reason to consider the SED's growing interest in historical events and figures as proving their justification of permanent separation.

Thus German and Eastern policies in its historical, political, and human dimension remained the focal points of my tasks as governing mayor of Berlin.

Berlin Domestic Policy

Everyday life in Berlin, always crammed with work, was by preference filled with problems concerning the city itself and our collaboration in the senate. Thanks to differences of opinion and temperament, senate business proceeded in a lively and always orderly manner that was, to use the phrase diplomats are so fond of, "result-oriented."

Few debates concerned fundamental issues, though at times these appeared to be more essential than day-to-day disputes. I am reminded of a confrontation, never resolved, with Scholz concerning the relationship between justice and mercy. Because of my lifelong interest in the evolution of clemency in a secular constitutional state, and because cases of clemency must never be dealt with routinely, I was looking for clarification. Because in Berlin clemency for any crime except a minor misdemeanor is the collective responsibility of the senate, we found ourselves more than once embroiled in open, passionate debates that wrought havoc with our agenda. As minister for justice, Scholz legitimately felt that he alone could determine clemency, and that he must do so by weighing each instance in measurable and comparable legal terms—with the consequence that legalization of clemency was increasing. I was bothered even by the word *clemency*; of course I was aware that common parlance, which spoke of "mercy before justice," did not express the values of our constitutional state, when it would be more accurate today to speak of "mercy after justice." Mercy can have its chance once the rule of law has been complied with. A general amnesty is no substitute for a prescribed legal proceeding, does not annul a verdict, and is not the same as rehabilitation.

Today we deal neither with the Christian concept of clemency nor its practice by an absolute ruler. In his day Immanuel Kant called merciful clemency "of all the sovereign's rights the most slippery." He was thinking of the dangers of arbitrariness, now foreign to us—we live in a constitutional state. How does this fact affect mercy? Has it become unnecessary, even foreign to the system, under the rule of democratically applied justice? Is clemency's only role at most a reflection of abstract general rules, almost legally prescribed, perhaps to be applied only by the same courts that pronounced the verdict? It was exactly this trend that to me appeared to be more danger than blessing. Gustav Radbruch, the great jurist during the first half of this century who is repeatedly invoked to this day by our federal constitutional court, calls clemency "the lawless miracle within the world of judicial law"—a miracle based on the "unconcealed recognition of the dubiousness of all law." As a pioneer of the constitutional state Radbruch was a model. He was all the more impressive in that he did not overlook human limitations affecting the free actions of lawmakers and judges.

The law is an important standard for clemency but not the only one. Clemency heeds the law without being subject to it. To confer or withhold it is among the most difficult of decisions. Even in the secular constitutional state clemency can be justified not by guidelines but only within the consciences of those with the power to grant it. Therefore mercy and law remain connected in a necessary relationship of tension. The viewpoints in the senate debate between Scholz and myself never changed. I have always remained grateful to Scholz for his solid, shrewd, and fair arguments, especially later, when I had to deal with the most troublesome clemency decisions for former Red Army Faction terrorists.

From the first, questions of law captured most of our attention in the senate. The core problem was illegally occupied housing. There was no question that the building and housing policies themselves, given the persistent need for housing, created ever new unoccupied apartments through protracted proceedings, and these were so outrageous as to practically invite illegal occupation. These empty spaces became illegal spaces.

In my first address I respectfully mentioned my predecessor's line regarding Berlin, but I also announced that even though I fully understood the reasons why we were in the current situation, our highest priority was to restore judicial peace—that is, peace through law, not peace alongside the law.

Expressing such constitutional verities had become a bitter necessity in Berlin. Soon after my election I visited a school in the Reinickendorf district. I asked a large class of eleven-year-olds what they would like to discuss. One boy stood, and as if recalling a well-known song, announced with a beaming face, "Where justice becomes injustice, resistance becomes our duty." When I asked what he had in mind, he answered just as cheerfully that he didn't know. None of the others knew. The teacher came to their aid by explaining to me that the district had just gone through a month-long debate about the route for a new autobahn. He and some of his students had fought in vain for one particular route and lost at every step along the way, even in the final two law courts. The outcome was an injustice, and that was why resistance became a duty.

I never forgot that morning. What will become of our constitutional state if teachers indoctrinate the students entrusted to their care with slogans the children cannot understand, much less evaluate? At first it is a game, then it becomes real—real because there is ignorance of the work and the meaning of justice. Teachers do a good job when they teach students, not blind obedience, but how to develop their critical intelligence and courage to resist. It is essential that teachers explain to students how much effort and sacrifice it took to establish our democratic legal system and that justice and law require constant attention to keep the government from engaging in arbitrary behavior and to keep the weak from being crushed by the strong.

At the time I took office, such apparently trivial ideas were in the balance. With his belief about the route of the autobahn in

Reinickendorf, the teacher may have reflected a higher justice, as did many a squatter. The social tensions, shortage of available apartments, search by many for new and unique ways of life, and conflicts between young and old—all deeply disrupted the life of the city. But these circumstances hardly made respect for the rules of human intercourse irrelevant. The constitutional state, after all, could not be sent on vacation until all these conflicts between generations could be resolved. Thus our crucial mission was to make clear the beneficial effect the law could have on peace. This objective could be attained only through the cautious and unwavering application of the law.

The occupied houses were the most important tests of this theory. The work was complicated. The debates, both in public and in lengthy internal senate sessions, seemed endless. Some models of so-called sweat equity made a strong impression. In these instances groups of squatters personally performed necessary repairs. Building Senator Ulrich Rastemborsky worked with devotion and courage to find legitimate solutions for the occupied dwellings.

At the same time we made it clear that every home previously empty and now newly occupied must be cleared that very day. In cases that had seemed to resist solution for far too long we pressed for speedy abandonment. I and the new senate were in office a bare three months when we organized the first compulsory clearing of eight occupied houses. This action was within the law, covered by the "Berlin directive" that my senate had inherited from its predecessor. However, it was heavily burdened by the fatal accident of a young West German run over by a bus of the Berlin line that was going in reverse through the agitating rioters.

As a result demonstrations and riots broke out anew. The newly unleashed crisis interrupted the many discussions and negotiations designed to bring about legally viable agreements. In this situation I invited representatives of the parties, churches, associations, and other groups to a large roundtable meeting. Of course no one else could or should relieve the senate of its duty to determine a course of action.

But the chances of achieving an urgently needed peace in the city were nonexistent if all segments of the population did not share in the discussions and subsequent responsibility.

There was wide divergence in positions. For example, even Berlin's Protestant bishop, Martin Kruse, whom I respected absolutely and with whom I shared a deep friendship, caused a problem. In a pastoral letter he took the side of the minorities and demanded further changes in the law "to provide those seeking a different way of life with the necessary space to develop their needs and to maintain it." He also advocated the view that the squatters' beliefs "might be closer to the biblical conception than is the normal self-centered idea of the affluent society."

In numerous cases he was quite right. But those of us working in the senate could not change the law, we could only apply it peaceably. This end required a sincere public discussion that explored the deeper causes of the tensions within our society. That was the purpose of the roundtable, which passed the test in a most impressive manner. No one refused the invitation. Bishop Kruse as well as the longtime head of the Jewish community, Heinz Galinski, attended, as did the Catholic vicar general, the presidents of the chamber of handicrafts, the unions, the chamber of industry and trade, and the tenants' association. All contributed to defusing the explosive situation so that it was resolved into a moderate atmosphere. Never before had I experienced so much work and willingness to share responsibility cutting through all levels of society. Gradually the mood in the city improved significantly. Not all obstacles to a peaceful settlement had been removed, but step by step such an outcome became a stronger possibility. By the time I left office, only one-tenth of the 169 illegally occupied houses remained.

The second serious internal problem for Berlin was the employment situation. We could not seem to climb out of years of recession. The percentage of unemployed in the city was considerably higher than the average in the Federal Republic. The second-largest private employer, with ten thousand workers, AEG, was on the verge of bankruptcy, or at least of shutting down its Berlin factories. When I addressed a labor meeting in the Wedding district attended by more than two thousand workers, I found it difficult to explain the daily struggles to keep the factory open, especially because management had not seen fit to send a single representative. I barely managed to get past the looming disaster.

Part of the tradition of previous policy in West Berlin was to relieve the labor glut by repeatedly creating new positions in the public sector, though sufficient need was not always proven. However, since the Berlin budget was always legitimately and increasingly rigorously controlled by Bonn's budget office and finance minister, we had to decide on cost-cutting measures, some of which were, of course, long overdue. I could hardly believe my ears when the colleague in charge of transportation suggested a resolution whereby passes for public transportation would no longer be issued to students attending the university for more than nine years.

At the time, out of two million inhabitants about 150,000 were on public assistance. Following Senator Ulf Fink's suggestion, we tried to introduce unprecedented new measures to reduce this number. We offered decent jobs; those who refused them without good reason had to bear the consequences of losing benefits. We managed to raise the number of job-training slots to forty thousand and markedly increased the state budget's contribution.

The senate's progressive efforts to combine city planning with environmental protection and human services into a single agency—heretofore assigned to two different, often conflicting, departments—resulted in the creation of the senate administration for municipal development and environmental protection. The inspiring work of Senator Volker Hassemer in this office bears fruit to this day.

As is inevitable, a certain amount of partisan conflict ruffled the parliament, but time and again we also saw constructive collaboration. My own department, the senate chancellery, employed about six hundred people, almost all of whom, I was told at the outset, were registered in one or another of the parties that made up our Social-Liberal ruling coalition. Party-membership government is without a doubt a widespread evil and it had certainly not bypassed the Berlin senate chancellery. And yet I had neither the intention nor the slightest reason to take an interest in my coworkers' personal involvement in political parties. In the course of their work none of them ever lacked the loyalty or essential willingness to conduct an open, critically constructive consultation.

I was also thankful that party squabbles did not affect one topic of particular importance in the city—our relations with the many foreigners living among us. I created the office of a specialist for aliens in the senate and was fortunate enough to have Barbara John accept my invitation to take on this difficult task. With good sense and compassion she has now practiced her job for over fifteen years and has become a model for the entire federal area, contributing substantially to Berlin's traditional reputation that in good times the city is open to immigrants from all over the world.

Turks formed the largest of these groups. They had taken over whole neighborhoods, and their children constituted the majority in many schools. German parents were heard to complain frequently about this situation. In the Kreuzberg district I visited one school where the parents' organization complained to me that Turkish children had trouble keeping up with the class and therefore lowered the level of instruction. Three years later, when I paid a return visit to the same school, the parents still had a complaint, but this time it was that the Turkish children seized all the academic prizes just because they worked hard in school and had help from their parents with homework. I do not believe that the parents were aware of the revelation they were making.

In fact, the Turks of Berlin shaped my ideas regarding the urgent need of reform of German naturalization laws, which were enacted before the First World War, when no one could have foreseen current realities. Over the years the *ius sanguinis* lost its validity as against the *ius soli*. Do we really want the third generation of foreign-born offspring to face difficulties in acquiring German citizenship? For them it would not be a return home but an emigration if they went back to the land of their forefathers, and they would have little cause to do so.

In this context another consideration is dual citizenship. Time and again I saw that Turkish young people wanted to become Germans, while their parents and grandparents had no such desire. But these same young people were reluctant to give up their Turkish citizenship, out of respect for their elders and to maintain close family ties. Quite a few other civilized countries offer dual citizenship, but we hide behind pretexts concerning military service, rights of inheritance, and similar excuses. As a result needless tensions arise within Turkish families. Is this necessary? Don't we all in any case develop a kind of pyramid of identities—a communal self, a national self, and a European self? And isn't dual citizenship far better than using naturalization laws to keep up razor-sharp national distinctions that are only remnants of the nineteenth century?

Once I took a longish trip to Anatolia, where I was given a warm welcome as mayor of the largest Turkish city outside Turkey. Only the German ambassador in Ankara seemed worried; he thought that my open policy for the Turks in Berlin was dangerous—history would be overturned and Vienna's heroic resistance to the Turks three hundred years ago at Kahlenberg would be made a mockery. Thanks to my policy in a hundred years Berlin would cease to be a Christian city and become a Muslim one. I invited the diplomat to come to Berlin and see for himself that most of our Turkish young people are already more like young Germans—whose Christian fervor is not all that strong— than foreigners loyal to the religious traditions of their families. Of course it was important to wait and see how re-Islamization of original Kemalist Turks in their homeland affected Turks living abroad. In Germany, and especially in Berlin, however, evolution into a common secularization was the most probable outcome.

The more common conflict in Turkish families was not between the young Turks and the young Germans, who went to school together, trained for jobs side by side, and in most cases ended up being friendly workmates. It was, instead, often difficult for Turkish fathers when they saw their daughters growing in ways that did not reflect ancestral tradition and echoing German girls' desires for education and careers.

The famous Harvard professor Samuel P. Huntington has predicted the "clash of civilizations," which he sees as the cause of future wars. His theories are as stimulating as they are questionable. We will have to deal with them intensely. Of course it makes a difference if they are seen in the global perspective or applied to a concrete surveyable society. What I saw in Berlin during the 1980s, in any case, strongly contradicts Huntington's abstract prophecies of a clash of cultures, which at most are only likely to stir up ancient fears of whatever is alien.

Non-Germans created a fair share of our problems. For example, irresponsible international traffic in illegal immigrants brought in a large number of undocumented aliens seeking asylum, who arrived through Schönefeld airport in East Germany. Foreign residents in Berlin resisted the influx of new immigrants because they were reluctant to share their "property" further. While at that time Croatians had a tendency to vociferously act out Yugoslavia's internal conflicts on our soil, relations between Kurds and Turks were as peaceful as those between Greeks and Turks.

On the whole we lived together peaceably. For the most part "multicultural" turned into "intercultural." Each clan cultivated its own cultural traditions, but all groups visited each others' neighborhoods, often sharing in celebrations, and began to enrich their lives by sharing in the traditions and ways of life of other nationalities.

Culturally we Germans are no better or worse than any other nation. We have made unique contributions. Our farmhouses, our music with its great lieder composers, the museum-quality variety of our breads, our philosophy, and many other traditions have often been praised as cultural advances for all humanity. But when it comes to unqualified hospitality to foreigners, we in Berlin and elsewhere in Germany can learn valuable lessons from our Turkish and Greek neighbors. Sometimes on summer weekends I took a walk in the Tiergarten between the Reichstag and Bellevue Castle. Every square inch of lawn in this huge municipal park was claimed by Turkish families, though these improvised campsites where children played and mothers cooked were not always welcomed by the authorities. Visitors were greeted by cheerful pictures of human companionship, but that was not all: People at each of these outdoor kitchens invited passersby to sit down and share a tasty meal. The pleasure the Turks take in the happiness of their guests is overwhelming and irresistible. Friends and total strangers alike found it impossible to resist their warm invitations.

Germans and Turks encountered each other not only at work but also at numerous intercultural sports events. Whenever an international match in the Olympia Stadium took place between the Federal Republic and Turkey, it seemed to the visiting team almost like a home game. In the divided city West Berlin won only rarely, especially when the game was soccer. The city had a hard time competing with the Federal Republic's best sport. Our excitement and happiness was all the greater when in 1982 the traditional Berlin club Hertha BSC managed to move up in the federal league. I can recall only one instance during my term as mayor when my security officer showed extreme excitement, and that was in the first few minutes after the closing whistle that made all the difference in the advancement of the Hertha team at the Olympia Stadium. Of course no one was out to harm me. I was a happy participant at the center of a crush of thousands of Berliners tipsy with joy, and I have to admit that it was almost life-threatening.

In these Berlin years the arts also brought us many great events as well as almost insoluble problems. Once during my term the famous Schiller Theater was looking for a new manager. For years after the senate made its selection, I had to listen to the reproaches of Claus Peymann, manager of Vienna's Burgtheater, because he was passed over the leadership of what at the time was the greatest German theater. I think he was right, as the public excitement he repeatedly causes in Vienna would seem to confirm.

At the Schaubühne, Peter Stein devoted himself, with great success, to staging the revolt of the generation of '68. Each year the Theater Weeks organized by Ulrich Eckardt, still the ingenious leader of the Berliner Festspiele, brought Berliners the best productions from other theaters throughout the city, thus providing the public with a constant education in discernment.

Götz Friedrich, who assumed his mission as director of the Deutsche Oper the same year I became mayor, gave me fascinating, exciting, and sometimes controversial nights. It was difficult as well as a privilege for the senate to do all that is humanly possible to provide a stage like the Deutsche Oper with the means to mount its productions. The commitment to art is surely based on more than the personal desires of one governing mayor who likes music, the opera, and theater. Time and again, near and far, I saw the value of every kind of theatrical performance in promoting the city and our entire country. The theater remains one of our most important cultural ambassadors and is indispensable to enhancing our reputation.

Of course some dynamic theater managers suffered from the crisis in contemporary dramatic literature. The paucity of new playwrights complicated their job, which is to use the theater as an audible participant giving voice to the vital questions of the day. Though they have Thomas Bernhard, Botho Strauss, and a few other contemporary playwrights, they are more addicted to Shakespeare and the nineteenth century. Inventively staging the old warhorses is an understandable but somewhat trite effort. As a result some directors turned more actively to opera management, with varying results. Stagings of *The Marriage of Figaro* have repeatedly stressed social tensions and injustices so clearly that the question arises whether Mozart should not retroactively rewrite his music to make it fit the director's vision more closely.

Verdi provides tempting opportunities as well. One such performance of *La Forza del destino* staged at the Deutsche Oper under the direction of Hans Neuenfels featured austere and artistically outstanding staging but was larded with aggressive polemics. When in one scene the Spanish monks entered in a simulated armored car waving banners bearing the slogan "La bella guerra" and began to beat the daylights out of disabled war veterans in the crowd, my wife at my side could not help but utter a soft "Boo." Gentle as it was, the exclamation could be heard all around us, and the following day the front page of the most widely read Berlin newspaper ran the banner headline, "Frau Weizsäcker's solitary boo," with the subtitle "The Governing Mayor whispers soothing words into his wife's ear." But that was not what happened. In spite of my unchanging respect for Neuenfels, I was not, contrary to what my wife believed, upset at her reaction, I was proud of her. On the whole she was not alone in her protest. At times the action onstage was accompanied by such an uproar in the audience that the curtain was very nearly rung down. The vehemently encouraging and condemning catcalls from the audience more or less balanced each other out. But that's the way it is, and why should it be different? Surely the theater is not meant to lull us to sleep but is designed to encourage us to participate. I could easily understand when some time later my Austrian presidential counterpart grew upset over a production of Thomas Bernhard's *Heldenplatz* at Vienna's Burgtheater. But such outrage does not alter the quality and meaning of this play along with Peymann's staging.

Keeping the theaters financially alive was always hard. As soon as someone said the word "theater," the defensive responses echoed from every direction: check the government grants. But what do we mean by grants? Support for a basically impractical enterprise that cannot keep its head above water without aid? Even Adam Smith recognized the value and limits of the market: It serves the well-being of nations but cannot fund unprofitable or marginally profitable social and intellectual ventures that are nevertheless essential. What is the meaning of "grants" then?

Does public education thrive on grants? Do we build parking lots or sewage-treatment plants with grants? Do we fund our probate judges and mayors with grant money? No one would ever think of calling funds budgeted for such purposes grants. These are indispensables—but so is the theater.

Is the theater pure luxury? In that case a mayor is an equal luxury.

Which of the two can we more easily do without? The answer is a matter of opinion. In my view we need both, but we do not need a false concept of grants.

The theater entertains in order to help people deal with life. As children all of us play. Some might think that the best part of theater is over when childhood is behind us and the time of play is past. But listening and playing remain. This drive gives us the strength to do more than look at our image in the mirror; it allows us to step outside ourselves, to acquire the distance to meet the person we are, to understand our problems, options, and developments, to transform ourselves.

Is it pure sentimentality to speak of this life-giving source in such tones? The first vital nonessentials to return to the gruesome war ruins of Berlin were makeshift stages, and hungry crowds streamed in. The Ruhr festival sprang up immediately after the war because the best Hamburg actors were looking for warming coals, and the miners and their families were looking for entertainment. The populace of Nackenheim in Rhein-Hesse played out their own pranks and love affairs, using the roles of their ancestors, whom Carl Zuckmayer immortalized with such ravishing realism in his *Der fröhliche Weinberg*.

Bernhard Minetti played Quangel the workman in the dramatization of Hans Fallada's novel *Jeder stirbt für sich allein* (Everybody Dies Alone). No other personal experience, memoir, or work of contemporary history better demonstrates on such a deep level what went on in the hearts of alert human beings in the time of war and injustice like this conscientious, almost wordless creature into whom the great actor transformed himself. That is what happens when art begins to take charge of people's lives, as pitilessly, as lovingly, as vital as only art can be.

Of course theaters, often seeing themselves as contradictions, must be able to tolerate contradictions of all kinds. Writing good plays and staging them is no easy task, especially today. Since all of us stutter, it is not surprising that some playwrights and directors stutter as well. It is an accepted duty of the theaters to give an accounting of the ways they use the public's money, and they must include every penny granted by the state. The audit office must also keep as close an eye on theater managements as it does on the senate chancellery. There too funds are occasionally squandered, even though such instances do not turn the senate chancellery into a dispensable luxury institution. It is difficult to justify to the public why culture and art are required as daily necessities. But they play an indispensable role, first on a human level and then in commercial and political areas. Anyone who shares in the responsibility for Berlin should never lose sight of that fact.

The Philharmonic Orchestra, which has a worldwide reputation, stands at the center of the Berlin music world. Whenever I attended a concert in the hall designed by Scharoun and heard this orchestra under its permanent conductor, Herbert von Karajan, I often felt that I was at the very center of the universe or, virtually the same thing, lost to the world. However I could not escape the realities of working with this great artist, a circumstance that Karajan himself helped create. Once he and his orchestra quarreled over hiring the clarinetist Sabine Meyer, and soon the whole city knew about the clash. Even I—the wholly innocent governing mayor, who by virtue of his position represented the employer when it came to Karajan's Berlin mission—was made to feel the wrath of the conductor, who thundered like a Greek god. If the orchestra resisted the hiring, he said, he would invite the clarinetist to be the soloist at a concert, in which case the press would praise his protégée to the skies and call her superior to the orchestra, making her uncollegial colleagues green with envy. But from its inception the Philharmonic had been an artistic democracy where no one could perform unless voted in by all the musicians. Orchestra members were not disputing Meyer's musical qualifications but felt that she was better suited to a career as a soloist than as a member of an ensemble. A sign of the orchestra's outstanding rank is the fact that for its first hundred years it had only four permanent conductors—giving each an average tenure of twenty-five years—and that many instrumentalists stayed with the orchestra for as long or longer.

Next to the renowned yearly film festival, the pictorial arts exercised a traditional Berlin magnetism even in the divided city. For many, a trip to Berlin was worth it if only to see the collections and exhibits. At the core are the displayed treasures that form the basis of the Prussian cultural heritage as well as the city's castles and parks. During my time as mayor the Karl Bröhan foundation established a museum named after him for art nouveau, art deco, and functionalism—a museum unique in Germany.

Repeatedly we had to deal with involving the younger generation in preserving our heritage. Unverifiable estimates placed the number of young artists working in Berlin in the early 1980s at about ten thousand. Most of them earned their living from non-art-related activities but found Berlin to be the indispensable ambiance for artistic inspiration.

Among the most famous holdings in Berlin is the collection of significant works by Jean Antoine Watteau started in the reign of Frederick the Great. One of the most frequently admired paintings is the *Embarkation to Cytheria*, which the leading Berlin art historian Otto von Simson claims to be arguably the most beautiful and important painting produced in the eighteenth century. At this time it was still in the possession of the house of Hohenzollern, and there was a plan to sell it abroad—a heavy blow to Berlin. But how could we raise the 15,000,000 DM required to keep it here? Thanks to a collaborative effort with the past master of the German banking system Hermann Josef Abs, we managed it. He made himself solely responsible for raising one-third of the amount from private sources, and this sum along with funds from the regional and federal governments allowed the city to retain possession of this work of art, which is truly irreplaceable. Like almost no one else, Abs with this and similar initiatives became the patron of many German cultural assets. Now everyone who visits the collection at Charlottenburg Castle in Berlin enjoys the fruits of his endeavors.

Science, research, and education also play a leading role in Berlin, just as they did during my term as mayor. Though there was some turbulence at the universities, their academic functions were not disrupted in the long term. Before the election I attended a discussion of German policy held in the largest lecture hall of the Free University. A tumult, apparently well rehearsed, broke out in the crowded hall, and one of the most peculiar brawls I have ever witnessed developed. Almost without a sound large groups tried to shove each other outside. For forty-five minutes this indescribable pushing and heaving went on without arguments but with raw physical force, but resulting in only a few minor cuts and scrapes. The most severe injury happened to one of my particularly brave academic coworkers, who almost lost his right index finger when an opponent nearly bit it off. Finally about 150 rowdies were thrown out, leaving the next two hours for a highly informative general discussion.

Berlin's scholars pursued their interests but only rarely contributed to discussing city problems. The imaginative, liberal, and scrupulous manner of our senator for science, Wilhelm Kewenig, continued the work of Peter Glotz and other valued predecessors.

I especially treasured my contacts with individual professors. Among them was my old and close personal friend from the time in Nuremberg, Hellmut Becker, head of the Max Planck Institute for Educational Research. In the months immediately after the war at Kressbronn on Lake Constance, he and his wife, Antoinette, gave me a series of private adult-education courses, especially in literature and the social sciences. For him, the son of the Prussian minister of culture C. H. Becker, who is remembered for his work in educational policy, I was a test case for his subsequent work as president of the German public-school association. Whenever he scolded me, he claimed to be acting on pedagogic grounds and doing what was best for me.

The Institute for Educational Research he established and led pointed the Max Planck Society in new directions. Its influence in the always highly controversial field of education policy was stronger than that of any other German research center. In the late 1960s Becker, working with the historian Karl Dietrich Erdmann in the educational council, performed what may have been the first effective planning of any value in the postwar period. These men taught us to think in dialogues. Stark political contrasts were forced to capitulate before the intensity and quality of their methods.

Becker was dedicated to the indispensable cultural substance of politics and the political power of culture. He was partial to jurisprudence, medicine, and pedagogy—the "hypothesis-intensive fields" (Wolf Lepenies). Becker proved his friendship for me especially with his intelligent and honest candor when advising me in personal as well as political matters.

Election to the Federal Presidency

And so 1983 drew to a close. During the year Federal President Carstens, to everyone's surprise, announced that he was not willing to serve a second term. At once the media began to speculate about a possible successor. More and more specifically they dropped my name and urged me to take a stand. But I could not and would not answer a question that had not been put to me by anyone with the authority to ask it.

The Union parties had an absolute majority in the Federal Assembly. Thus their nomination of a candidate was enough to decide the outcome of the eventual election. And so it became the task of the party executives to decide whose name they wanted to put forward. But since no word was forthcoming from these sources, I kept silent as well. Only once did I respond to a particularly persistent reporter by noting that until now everyone in my position had gone to heaven or to Bonn; I was still debating which of these to choose, or at least in which order.

In reality it was a very difficult decision, and not only for me. There was no mystery about the delay. Obviously Kohl's first concern was not for the office of the head of state but for the good of his party. He wanted to see the results of upcoming local elections in Hessen and Bremen. After both had gone more badly for the CDU than expected, he was all the more worried about the chances of the Berlin party in the next round of elections. He therefore had good reason to delay and in the meantime look for alternatives to fill the office of the presidency.

Public discussion, however, continued unabated. In general my administration as acting mayor of Berlin was judged favorably. All my "eastern blunders" had substantially raised my standing in the Union parties. That fact, however, worked itself out in contradictory ways. One faction, mostly Berliners, wanted me to remain in the divided city for that very reason. However, others from all parts of the country saw my role in Berlin as the precise recommendation for the office of federal president.

While the media overwhelmingly agitated for my nomination to succeed Carstens, some in the Springer press organization and especially the *Frankfurter Allgemeine Zeitung (FAZ)* ran several articles arguing for me to remain in Berlin. The debate culminated in the feature section of the *FAZ* in one spectacular article. For a change it was not signed by the editor or editors; three asterisks represented the authors. The article began by praising me at length because I had altered the climate of Berlin and given the city back its confidence in itself. Then the long introduction was quickly followed by the death blow: If I retreated now, I would be denying my true purpose. I regretted the anonymity of this criticism appearing in the guise of praise. Nevertheless the article was a serious call to me in a difficult personal decision.

I had put down deep roots in Berlin. The city, especially the people in East and West Berlin, demanded my full attention and fulfilled me completely. In the face of repeated newspaper rumors I had no wish to be a part of any future federal government. I was eager to work in and for Berlin in the long run. And I said as much publicly. I knew if I retreated from the office of mayor, it would cause disappointments even among close friends within and outside the circle of politics.

Nevertheless, taking the long view, I felt myself pointed in another direction but toward the same objective. The situation in my Berlin area of responsibility was now more or less ordered. The most important job had been successfully accomplished—that is, to raise the atmosphere in the city from its depths. What remained crucial was to bring out and give weight to the experiences and future tasks of Berlin in the larger framework of German policies both within the

Federal Republic and in relation to the East. That the federal constitutional organizations could be especially effective in this area was not in question, as all who sought to give me advice and I fully realized. President Carstens, speaking with Kohl and me, took the same view. He also pointed out the positive effect on Germans in the GDR should I succeed him. The SPD and FDP announced that if I were nominated, they would not run any candidates against me. Personally I was quite certain that in changing jobs I would see the problems to be solved in Germany with a Berlin heart and mind.

But the top echelons of the party made no public announcement. Kohl still held off. Gradually his hesitation threatened to degenerate into disarray. Once again the Union aroused the suspicion that it was juggling the office of federal president in favor of other questions more important to the party.

In this situation the Bavarian prime minister set out on a long-planned trip to Berlin. Without alerting me beforehand, he announced at the end of a press conference, "There's got to be an end to this game." Strauss, who liked to speak of himself as the last Prussian, declared in favor of my nomination to the federal presidency and promised the votes of the CSU. As had happened five years earlier in Carstens' election, he was once again the first to take the public initiative.

A few days later Kohl, referring to the previous Bavarian vote and after consulting his committees and holding a long conversation with me, let it be known that the Union would nominate me for the post of federal president.

I resigned my office as mayor of Berlin in February 1984. At the suggestion of the Berlin CDU, the legislature elected Eberhard Diepgen to succeed me. On May 23 of that same year the Federal Assembly elected me by 832 out of 1040 votes to be the sixth president of the Federal Republic of Germany. On July 1, 1984, I was inaugurated into my new office.

Berliners always had reason to realize that I remained one of them even after becoming president, and the same was true even of those of my friends who began by being disappointed at my decision.

The Office

B ut what was this office that I was assuming? A heated dispute on this point occurred during the constitutional convention at Lake Herrenchiem in 1948. A sizable minority had advocated assigning the powers of the head of state to a troika. For good reasons, however, this faction did not prevail. For how can serious responsibility be shouldered collectively? The suggestion was boiled down to declare the office superfluous altogether—just as a far-left group had demanded in the Weimar National Assembly and as some right-wing constitutionalists had occasionally advocated quite recently.

In the end a compromise was reached to create an office with fewer explicit powers than the presidency had enjoyed in the Weimar Republic. However, it still had the central mission to embody a nonpartisan constant middle ground free of quotidian confrontational struggles of factions and interests, to see to social integration, and to represent the nation in dealings with other countries.

From the outset the parties vigorously sought the office; at no time did an outsider have a real chance. Not only the elected presidents but also, as a rule, the defeated candidates were experienced and prominent politicians, such as Kurt Schumacher running against Theodor Heuss, Carlo Schmid against Heinrich Lübke, and Gerhard Schröder against Gustav Heinemann. Allegedly even Konrad Adenauer had striven for the office, though he labored under the illusion that he could be president while remaining chancellor.

Though the image of the president drawn by the constitution remained vague, in practice a clear idea of the office developed quickly and has remained largely unchanged to this day. The officeholder is meant to act independently and in a nonpartisan way but is also expected to form opinions. The president is not accountable to the parliament and especially not to the government. Only the Federal Supreme Court has the right to correct his actions and omissions or, in an extreme case, to remove him from office.

After a number of scholarly disputes concerning the correct interpretation, today there are few serious constitutional quarrels concerning the president's powers. He exercises a formal and material right of discovery, to make certain that new laws ready for his signature agree with the constitution. His public statements do not require the government's approval. That is one difference from constitutional monarchies. He has the power to advise and, should the occasion warrant, even express opinions that deviate from the government's position. But in his mission to represent the Federal Republic in international relations it remains his primary duty to guarantee that the country speaks with one voice to other nations. The president works most intently in the area of foreign policy. German governments practically never disputed the extent of his authority to represent the country in the international sphere—unlike recent events in Austria, in a more or less comparable situation.

In this general framework the person determines the office. The person of the president sends out the impulses with all their human differences. Every officeholder concentrates on the aspects he cares most about, and each must deal with particular problems during his time in office. For Heuss the central issue was making certain that democracy became rooted in Germany; Lübke took persuasive steps to assure help and balance between north and south; Heinemann was concerned with "more democracy"; Scheel saw his priorities in Europe; and Carstens conferred validity and status to every part of our country with wide-ranging travel that served to unite our people.

In the executive branch the most important weapon a politician has is action. Since the time of Heuss speeches have made up the federal president's primary actions. In their application he will get his bearings from general experience, his own convictions, and views in the community. He will respect but also challenge them. He may very well care about making the first move. He will take his bearing from Max Weber's definition of politics: the strong, slow drilling of hard boards with passion and judgment. The constitution has nothing else in mind, and that is how it works out in practice.

Concentrating on Foreign Policy

I assumed office at a time of considerable social upheaval. An unusually prolonged labor dispute—which, measured by the number of lost work days, was the harshest in the country's history—had still not been settled. A short while later the government coalition passed new legislation making it more difficult to call a strike, a move that did not please the unions.

Anxiety also characterized the mood within the political parties. Shortly before, the SPD's internal conflicts had caused it to fall from grace. The party now looked for a way to make good its losses, without much success. The FDP had forced a change of government in the middle of a legislative term; as a result it had again "fallen over" and needed to win new voters to make up for the loss of old adherents. But how?

Though the Union party led the governing coalition, initially it had little luck in establishing the intellectual-moral change it had promised during the campaign. The Flick Affair—allegations of illegal political contributions and corruption—surfaced. Coalition leaders submitted the draft of a "Law to Regulate Tax Questions in Party Financing" as an attempt at general amnesty for sins of campaign funding; but the effort met with resistance from, among others, the then president of the federal constitutional court, Ernst Benda. On the day of my election by the Federal Assembly, Kohl announced that the project was being dropped.

The victim in the next affair was NATO's deputy supreme allied commander in Europe, General Günter Kiessling, who was cleared of malicious and never proven suspicion only after a long period of accusation and defense. All in all the popular attitude about politics had worsened. There was talk of "party indifference" when I assumed my duties in the Villa Hammerschmidt.

My immediate response to the situation was to hold back. In his "Views of a Critical Conservative," George Bernard Shaw admonishes us to be cautious in forming opinions: "Humanity, which for the largest part is incapable of engaging in politics, considers it an easy and suitable substitute to insult the politics of others." Whether this acute satirist correctly characterized our generation's discernment and whether he would have considered the attitudes described here as unfounded is, of course, a matter of opinion. Whatever the case, occasions for public pessimism come and go. I did not think it appropriate to address this state of affairs in my maiden speech in the Bundestag. Instead I talked about the ongoing labor dispute with its persistent and grave evils: neither side had paid attention to the needs of a third sector—the many people looking for jobs. Labor conditions in the present had been established without any thought for the future. Few long-term perspectives could be discerned, let alone our principal political mission—how to create a life worth living for future generations.

My second topic, directed to Germans in the GDR, was designed to call attention to our position in the West. Precisely because they wished to promote our solidarity, people who suffered as much as they did from the separation hoped that West Germany could exert enough influence to maintain peace in all of Europe. In speaking on this subject, I touched on my principal concern during my first few years in office. When Karl Carstens handed me the office he had held in such exemplary fashion, he gave me selfless and intelligent advice, particularly regarding foreign relations.

Because close collaboration with the foreign office was essential, I immediately asked for such a link, and during the ten years of my presidency this connection never faltered. This relationship was first and especially due to Hans-Dietrich Genscher, who served as foreign

minister during most of my time in office, until he was succeeded in
1992 by Klaus Kinkel, who was equally reliable. Genscher made certain that I was kept completely informed at all times. Over time we
developed a running consultation and, most important, accord on foreign policy—an accord constantly tested. One recent period was unusually difficult for him as head of the FDP when he steered his party
through the change in coalition with the Union. However, he earned
the thanks of our entire country by making certain that when the
government changed from Schmidt to Kohl continuity in foreign affairs prevailed.

While Genscher was frequently criticized for being hard to read,
like a sphinx, my experiences with him were just the opposite. In
conversation, on travels, and during all our contacts at home and
abroad I saw him tenaciously pursue a clear course. He acted on the
premise that our newfound importance as Germans obligated us to be
especially cautious. Our actions did not affect us alone; German history has never belonged to us alone and will never be ours alone. To
the extent that we wield any power, it is important that we exercise it
responsibly. Trivial as it may sound, this idea remains our vital national
objective, although there are times when we unfortunately violate it.

Genscher's brilliance, which allowed him to react with lightning
speed, his stupendous memory, and confident handling of a large and
highly qualified staff were all impressive. But most important was his
inner compass to determine what was good for Germans in the world
and for the world in dealing with Germans. Of course he rightly did
not always tell everything he knew, especially about others. In my
opinion this discretion is one of his good qualities, and many of his
contemporaries may heave a sigh of relief at the protection Genscher's
discretion affords them.

Another asset was his propensity to always think and act in the
interests of both parts of Germany. This statesman, who left Halle for
the West when very young, never lost his empathy for those who did
not get out. He understood why and in what ways most of them tried

to lead a decent life under the stifling conditions in East Germany. That was also why he subsequently did not expect any of them to rewrite their own past.

I also enjoyed an open, close, and productive collaboration with the chancellor's office, which controlled relations within Germany. Despite the many differences in the programs and language of the Bundestag parties, in practice chancellery ministers Philipp Jenninger, Wolfgang Schäuble, and Rudolf Seiters made certain that a responsible political continuity profited our compatriots in the GDR on the road to reunification.

In my post I was fortunate to have two of our best foreign-service officials heading the president's office during my two five-year terms. In my first term Klaus Blech, our ambassador in Tokyo, held the position, while the second term brought me Andreas Meyer-Landrut, our Moscow ambassador. I had known both of them when I served on the foreign-service committee of the Bundestag. They had always intelligently and knowledgeably kept the delegates informed about conditions in their diplomatic posts though not without guarding the slight advantage of superior bureaucratic knowledge, to safeguard it from manipulation by party politics. Their worldly experience and independent thinking combined in an exemplary manner the supraparty, responsibly critical operative function of the diplomat with loyalty to political leaders.

Collaboration with them was for me—and I believe everyone on my staff—a joy, not least thanks to their upbeat personalities and senses of humor. I learned a great deal from each—of course, often quite different things. Blech knew more about Heidegger and Japanese cuisine, while Meyer-Landrut had more knowledge about the history and customs of Slavic peoples and horsemanship. Each had his own way of dealing with the never-ending stacks of paper. Meyer-Landrut allowed no document to rest on his desk for longer than five minutes. Conversely, if we were looking high and low for an important file, chances were that we would find it in Blech's office, where it was properly guarded.

Peter Schönfeld was head of my personal office. He too came from the foreign office and spoke French and English better than any of us. His altruism and loyalty, sense of style and tactfulness deepened the confidence in our duties on which a sensitive public office relies.

I enjoyed an enormously valuable ongoing exchange of ideas with the Institute for Science and Politics in Ebenhausen near Munich, which my old friend Klaus Ritter, along with Arnold Bergsträsser, a social scientist from Freiburg, had founded during the 1960s. Using the Rand Corporation in the United States as their model, they developed it into the most important German center for the systematic analysis of foreign and security policy. With its contributions to research, which benefited from a lively exchange with all international political-science groups, it served as a consultant to the party groups in the Bundestag as well as agencies of the federal government.

The institute performed the necessary and long overdue task of sweeping away widespread German prejudices to the effect that academic freedom was compromised by pragmatic collaboration with politics and that neither parliaments nor government agencies needed abstract and systematic scholarship. In the course of time the Institute became internationally recognized for its outstanding contributions to political consultation. It performed an invaluable service in aiding East-West relations, especially in exchanges with Soviet political scientists, whose thinking was generally far ahead of their own political leaders. The fact that the Institute depended on the chancellery budget for financing never affected its complete independence in political questions.

These were the years when the East-West conflict approached its crucial turning point. The two opposing systems and alliances still competed against each other, but their relations had deteriorated into a nuclear "stalemate system" (Stanley Hoffmann). The fact that each superpower had a secure second-strike capacity safeguarded their striking power even as it diminished the influence of their weapons as instruments to solve pending problems, much less bring about power-political changes. The search for other ways to escape the impasse continued.

Within each treaty alliance member nations had different concerns. Within the Warsaw Pact displeasure with the concept of an "Eastern bloc" grew stronger among Moscow's partner nations. Increasingly these countries tried to interpret their tasks in national terms and resolve them individually without confrontation with the outside world. Nevertheless the Soviet Union continued to impose discipline on its member nations, which could not act outside these constraints.

The main problems facing the Soviet Union were steadily growing economic arrears and the loss of international competitiveness. Since its principal tactic, rearmament, provided security but was useful only to a limited extent in the arena of power politics, the overall weaknesses of the Soviet system became increasingly obvious. The gospel of salvation implicit in its dogma could win no further advantages in the world. Their ideology dwindled more and more into an unconvincing rhetoric of sovereignty. What remained were natural resources and the always-high abilities of its people. But while the countries continued to be dominated by a system that cut itself off from the outside world and actually feared open exchange, these advantages could not make themselves felt. Economically the Soviet Union could barely meet its own needs, let alone compete successfully in the global economy. Its predominant provincialism undermined the country's claim of being a world power. A nation that walls itself off falls behind. There can be no world power without a world.

Thus the most urgent problem for the Soviet Union was modernization, which required an opening to the West. Could such an opening be managed in a way that preserved the system? Or were there irreconcilable differences between the capacity to reform and the stability of the system? This crucial question was becoming paramount.

The reaction in the Western camp reflected its pluralistic nature. The United States government, left more or less alone to handle the "stalemate," at first continued to steer a course for containment. Reagan wanted to bring Moscow to its knees primarily through the arms race.

The European NATO partners were nevertheless reluctant to break off relations with the Eastern bloc, with Germany foremost in this effort. The West German government had persuasively advocated rearmament as the way to restore the weapons balance now tipped in favor of the Soviets with their medium-range missiles. At the same time we were planning for constructive progress in our policies with the East and the other Germany. We were concerned with improving the lives of inhabitants in both parts of Germany by markedly enlarging the holes beginning to appear in the iron curtain between the two states. If détente broke down altogether, Germans would suffer the greatest damage.

Beyond these considerations the Western core idea in the Helsinki Final Act of 1975 now proved its worth: coexistence and cooperation, designed to break systems open. Economic collaboration, credits, budgetary aid, and an exchange of experts were designed to bring about an "increase in connective tissue and frontier-crossing mobility" (Klaus Ritter) and thus not only open but also change the Eastern system. Hand in hand with these goals the liberal aims announced in Basket III of Helsinki became increasingly important to the Eastern governments.

The May 8, 1985, Speech

In the mid-1980s the widespread sound of creaking could be heard as changes began to shake the structure of the ossifying East-West conflict. None of us knew what the future held, but this hopeful tension grew, and with it international attention on Germany's behavior, resolve, and sensitivity.

These new trends appeared during my first term as president, and soon I faced difficult challenges. The mood in the federal republic was somewhat edgy. For example, the Association of Silesians invited Helmut Kohl to its annual meeting, which had as its theme "Silesia Is Ours." Was that the new future of our past? Were we now to rescind the binding effect of the Eastern treaties concerning Poland's western borders, to which the Bundestag had already agreed? The Chancellor, accepting the invitation, was placed in a precarious position and made every effort to get the slogan changed.

Another problem concerned the fortieth anniversary of the end of the war May 8, 1985, which coincided with President Reagan's projected visit to Germany. The chancellery and White House had considered celebrating the anniversary with an address by Reagan in the Bundestag to highlight the legitimacy of West Germany as a partner in the Free World. It was not meant to call attention to the past. But in accordance with the constitutional offices and in response to my express request, it was decided to commemorate the anniversary by ourselves in the Bundestag, without the help of friends from abroad.

Reagan therefore moved his visit up by a few days. After attending some official events in Bonn, he inspected the concentration camp site at Bergen-Belsen and then, accompanied by Kohl, visited the military cemetery in Bitburg. This itinerary evoked vehement protests in the United States because after he had agreed to the schedule, it was learned that members of the SS were also buried in this cemetery. None of the planners of this visit had any nefarious purpose in mind. And a cemetery is surely a suitable site for marking an end to discord and persecution. But the full gamut of sensitivities in dealing with the past came to the surface.

Mindful of this background, we assembled in the parliament on May 8, 1985. Bundestag President Jenninger gave a dignified speech. Then it was my job to recall the end of the war, with its causes and consequences. There were no new insights in what I had to say. All my predecessors, beginning with Theodor Heuss, had addressed the past in blunt terms. It will always remain what it was.

But time does not stand still, and hindsight, with its new perspectives, can alter emphases. That understanding gave the most meaning to the commemoration.

Four decades had passed over our country since the end of the war, a long time in the lives of people and nations, as history has taught over and over again. No wonder then that religion—especially Judaism and Christianity—assign deep significance to that number of years. According to the Old Testament, Israelites had to wander the desert for forty years before being allowed into the Promised Land. Though biblical tales are not comparable to the present, we too asked ourselves fresh questions after forty years. As new generations arise, will the past be forgotten? Is a dark period coming to an end, giving us confidence in a rosy future?

It was strange: We were moving toward a point where epochs intersect, where a deep internal connection across the bridge of time emerges. The idea of a different future came into view, attainable only if we retained a clear awareness of the past, which the future is replacing and in which it is rooted.

These outlines of new, momentous movements emerging in East-West relations brought such thoughts to light. As we steered toward new shores, we felt a newly awakened desire to understand the past and its consequences, both in our own country and among our neighbors.

How do we interpret our past? And who are the interpreters? As a rule, once a war is over, the victors give their one-sided answer and record it, including their assignment of responsibility for the war. This interpretation is generally recorded in the form of peace treaties, with fatal consequences. In our century Versailles in 1919 was the classic example, which placed a heavy burden on the Weimar Republic, a burden the new government could not remove to its bitter end. This burden allowed Hitler, the destroyer of our first republic, to make the correction of the unaccepted past an item on the agenda with which he conjured up the National Socialist inferno and the eventual collapse of the Reich.

The Second World War did not end in a peace treaty; the victorious powers subdued us in different ways. Germans were separated into a divided country and made pawns in the Cold War. Each German state became a useful, even indispensable, member of its camp. The respective alliance partners were fully occupied with their postwar needs. Retrospective thoughts of the last war with Germany had apparently lost all reality. Instead the separation of Germany appeared within the context of a divided Continent as a fixed element in the international equation.

But now the two camps in the East-West conflict were increasingly experiencing changes. Forgotten or displaced questions, only apparently grown obsolete, arose anew, primary among them the question of Germany's future—in short, the open question. And as if by spontaneous action, the vistas of things to come, though still blurred, were combined with historical retrospectives and sensitivities. What new reality would now grow in Germany? What ideas would Germans develop about their identity, their nation, their patriotism, their tasks? How could their understanding of the past serve as a foundation for the future?

It was no longer up to the other powers to answer such questions. What mattered was our own German image of our origins, no longer obscured or forced on us by a victor, on which to build our future. This was the topic of my speech. Aware that I had to speak for all of us, it was important that I link respect for people's infinitely difficult lots with unmistakably clear statements on the whole subject. I found my themes not in abstract contemporary analyses but in the concrete experiences of my own generation. These included the four major events in our lives as a nation: the end of the Weimar Republic, National Socialism and war, separation and Cold War, and the hope of reunification through a policy founded in history and morality.

In my speech I quoted a line from a religion that was not mine, a piece of old Jewish wisdom: "The desire to forget prolongs the exile, and the secret of salvation is remembrance." We cannot save ourselves, nor can we undo what has been done. We have lived through unfathomable and abysmal events and taken part in them. But one thing we can and must do: look at our past steadily, recognize its truth. We owe it to ourselves and to future generations.

This was the most political and personal speech of my presidency. Its importance could be seen in the response it evoked in my country and abroad, a response that has not yet abated. To prepare for my address, I talked to all sorts of people and worked hard, most intensively with Michael Engelhardt, a diplomat in our foreign service recommended to me by Walter Scheel; thanks to his complete independence of mind and keenly conscientious discernment, he had become an indispensable coworker. All the same it never occurred to me that the speech would be reprinted so widely and translated into so many languages. The strongest echo came from the many discussions and correspondence I had with students and young people. Altogether, even if at times it was controversial, the lively reaction was an encouraging sign of things to come.

Travels Abroad

My priorities now focused on relations with our most important neighbors in the West and East—first France and the Netherlands, then Poland and the Czech Republic, all leading up to the Soviet Union. In all these contacts my job was to relate the past to our future.

My first visit would have to be to France—that was not in question. In the course of history our two countries had always measured themselves against each other. What characterized our previous relations had been, not the erroneous concept of a hereditary enmity, but the idea of neighborliness in the dialectic of attachment and aloofness—until the tendency to see the neighbor as the negation of one's own being and fight him gained the deadly upper hand. Only after the inferno burned both nations did the moral strength of the peoples flourish, until they finally and irrevocably found a common way. Even before the end of the war Jean Monnet had pointed us in the right direction.

The old ideological roots of closeness quickly developed new vitality. During my visit to Paris I recalled the words of the French poet and diplomat Paul Claudel, which he wrote soon after the Second World War: *"L'Allemagne, cette immense coulière, cette immense vallée, n'a pas été faite pour diviser les peuples mais pour les rassembler."* In 1981 one Frenchman, Pierre Bertaux, speaking at our Prussia exhibition in Berlin, could open his remarks with the words, "Why is a foreigner speaking here? In Berlin a Frenchman is not a foreigner. In this city, where at one time every third Berliner came from France, a Frenchman has a certain right to feel at home."

My host, François Mitterand, exhibited similar sentiments. De Gaulle and Adenauer had both moved within the confines of the Rhine, their sentiments far from Berlin. Mitterand on the other hand liked nothing better than to talk with me about Prussia. The fact that France had not understood the Prussian reforms of the Napoleonic period and learned nothing from them, so he told me, was partially to blame for France's weaknesses throughout the nineteenth century. In our many meetings he repeatedly assured me that nothing had been further from Prussian nature than Hitler.

But now, of course we were no longer dealing with Prussia but with Europe. In regard to the European Community, Mitterand and I tried to promote advancement, not without a certain amount of impatience. "Together we'll manage it. But we are in a phase when destiny is has not yet made up its mind," he said.

Mitterand was a host of overwhelming courtesy. He loved giving presents that, though not lavish, were obviously selected with the recipient in mind. Once he handed me a thin volume of Rainer Maria Rilke's *Marienleben*; it was a rare edition included in the Künstler-Götz exclusive series, of which only thirty copies had been illustrated and bound by art nouveau artists. Mitterand had found it at a secondhand book dealer along the Seine and thought of me. I hardly ever saw him agitated by pressure. He enjoyed appearing as if he had all the time in the world. He grew most animated when talking about the connections among culture, history, and actual political perspectives.

In later years I invited him to Weimar and the Wartburg. First he earnestly assured me, while standing directly under the Goethe-Schiller monument outside the National Theater, that with all due respect for pickled boar—the specialty of the Palatinate—he much preferred Thuringian bratwurst. Then he became a fascinated and curious sightseer, and that evening he thanked me for finally giving him a chance to see with his own eyes the two desks at which Luther and Goethe respectively had created the German language and therefore German culture. Then he joked that until that day we had only sailed him up and down the Rhine, thus familiarizing him with French culture. Nor did he hold back when the subject was France's contribution to European culture. Once in the Villa Hammerschmidt I showed him an early work by the great painter Max Ernst, who came from Brühl near Cologne. Mitterand immediately praised me for decorating my residence with works of French artists. Mitterand saw Ernst's moving to France not for political reasons but for the sake of a woman as a special reverence for his country.

I requested that my state visit include a meeting with students and was invited to the Lycée Louis Le Grand, one of the most respected French secondary schools, which lists among its illustrious graduates Molière and Voltaire, Victor Hugo and Jean-Paul Sartre, Valéry Giscard d'Estaing and Jacques Chirac. These brilliant young French people seemed completely relaxed but not particularly intensely involved with their German coevals. After high school they plan to attend a university, as do German students, preferably in the United States. When they return, the language they speak across the Rhine is usually English. Our conversation nevertheless centered on the future of Europe, and even these elite students expressed amazement that their German counterparts were so concerned with damage to forests and concentrated their interest on the eastern part of the Continent instead of looking southward.

In fact, when it came to Eastern policy there was not sufficient collaboration between Paris and Bonn, though the French were more responsible for this situation than we were since they retained a certain reluctance to accept our policy about a partitioned Germany. While they saw some merit in the objective of humane relief through negotiations with the rulers in East Berlin, they took a dim view of German reunification. France had been on the winners' side at the end of the Second World War but lost influence in the context of the global power structure. Perhaps because France, even more than Great Britain, had been forced to relinquish its role as a world power, that nation now carefully nurtured the few trappings of world power that remained. These included the guardianship of Francophone families in the former colonies, the force de frappe, permanent membership in the United Nations Security Council, and most especially French participation in Four Power rule—that is, the "rights and responsibilities" for Berlin and Germany as a whole, that phrase they loved to repeat in their international penthouse high above German soil.

All the areas of direct consultation between Paris and Bonn as well as our shared duties in the EC (European Community) proceeded smoothly and briskly. Adenauer, Robert Schuman, and de Gaulle had laid the groundwork. The friendship between Giscard d'Estaing and Helmut Schmidt moved matters forward even further, especially in economic and currency policies. The meeting of François Mitterand and Helmut Kohl in Verdun was an honest expression of the wish to confront the past together. But Paris—and every political party in France—never forgot its slight advantage in the sovereignty for all of Germany.

My state visit to the Netherlands, a great center of the European spirit, also occurred during my first year in office. West German relations with Holland were closer than with any other neighboring nation. Our scientific and artistic exchanges flourished, and trade bloomed in both directions. Countless Germans visited the cultural sites, the beaches, and the department stores in the Netherlands. Conversely, long lines of cars carrying Dutch vacationers thronged our autobahns. Contact could hardly have been tighter, yet relations were never quite free of tension. For example, fairly loaded atmosphere could be felt, though quite harmlessly, whenever our soccer teams played each other. In general, the past as it related to our two nations had clearly not been overcome. It had, as it were, been handed down undigested.

When I spoke to a randomly selected group of first-year university students in Amsterdam, one young woman spoke accusingly: "You Germans treat the Turks today the way the Nazis treated the Jews." She spoke drily, as if describing a natural state, without emotion or visible insight into the vitality of history. I invited the entire group to come on a week's visit to Bonn so that they might work out an understanding with young Germans of the same age. Fortunately the encounter went well.

My visit to the Netherlands also gave me clearer insights into the actual workings of our two countries. The Dutch engage in little glorification of the state and therefore also show little contempt for it. Instead they have a marked proclivity for popular initiatives and social protests. The purpose of redistributing standard employment, self-employment, and leisure time; forming bonds with people from other nations; conquering the cruel misuse of drugs—the Netherlands is an exemplary laboratory for all these experiments. The Dutch take the constitutional state seriously but are even more serious about having a state ruled by justice. The people are not complacent but driven by conscience, and this characteristic is evident in their great moral power, which does not shrink from zealotry. At times the Dutch give the impression that even the Catholics among them are Calvinists.

During this visit the speech I had given three weeks earlier, on May 8, played an important role. At the state banquet Queen Beatrix began by giving a precise, highly interesting, moving, and very personal speech. Immediately after my reply, her husband, Prince Claus, abruptly jumped to his feet to everyone's surprise. He asked forgiveness for this breach of protocol and, reaching across the table, handed me a copy of my speech that he had translated into Dutch. This intelligent, empathetic, and enormously decent prince consort from Germany, who had had a difficult time in the Netherlands at first, wanted to give the entire table a sign of the ties between his old and new homes. It was an unforgettable moment, and it took great pains to keep the Dutch prime minister, Ruud Lubbers, from leading a cheer for the prince, who had turned our evening into a significant historical moment in the dialogue between our two European nations.

This visit was soon followed by a trip to Norway. In hardly any other country did the German invasion during the Second World War cause so much horror and unleash so much pain, since these two nations had heretofore been free of political conflicts and were very close intellectually and culturally. This free exchange of culture and art even helped the artists find their way into the larger world. In the field of romantic painting Johann Christian Dahl and Caspar David Friedrich were examples of this process. Edvard Munch paved the way for the characteristically German art of outstanding expressionists. In Norwegian world literature Henrik Ibsen and Knut Hamsun in particular became virtually part of our own literature.

In 1986 former King Olaf V was our host. As crown prince, he had been named Norwegian commander-in-chief in the midst of war. He had an animated and warm nature. As a young man he had distinguished himself at the Holmenkollen run in ski jumping, and now that he was over eighty, he still took part in sports competitions. His eyes twinkled with good humor and wit. He liked to say nothing at all, and he interrupted his taciturnity only occasionally with short volleys of affectionate repartee. Whenever he appeared in public, his people gave him an enthusiastic reception. Every Norwegian knew about the great moral uprightness and courage with which Olaf had distinguished himself during the war.

How he treated me now was characteristic of him. He invited me on an excursion into the countryside to a small town over a hundred kilometers north of Oslo. He gave no reason for the invitation. Apparently I was supposed to believe that he was going to give me a restorative sight of Norway's beautiful, calm natural wonders.

The trip turned out quite differently. We drove to Elverum near the Swedish border, where in April 1940 his father, King Haakon, had taken up temporary quarters after the Germans invaded Norway. It was here that Haakon received the ultimate demand from the German government that he install a Norwegian puppet government under the leadership of Vidkun Quisling. In the presence of his son Olaf, then the crown prince, he replied with a simple, straightforward "no." He was speaking for the entire nation. Later, in his honor, the Norwegians erected their historic freedom obelisk in Elverum and named the monument "The King's No."

Forty-three years had passed. The crown prince who had been

king, now eighty-three years old, was my host. When we arrived in Elverum, he led me to the monument, saying, "Here my father uttered the King's No. Here I want to say to you and to your country the King's Yes." A magnanimous, modest man had spoken as simply and self-confidently as his father. It was one of those solemn moments for which we remain grateful all our lives.

The Norwegian prime minister, Gro Harlem Brundtland, also contributed substantially to the good feeling between our countries. She traveled to the far north with us, to Tromsø, where together we visited the site that commemorated the sinking of the German warship *Tirpitz.* Mrs. Brundtland talked about NATO's problems with the Soviet Union on its northern flank.

She used her energy, courage, and warmth to promote the cause of Europe among her compatriots and the cause of the world's southern hemisphere among the Europeans. Her work earned her increasing international respect, not only for Norway but for all of Europe.

Her husband, an astute political analyst, also came along on the trip north. The couple's views allowed them to make up a kind of political and family grand coalition. When Mrs. Brundtland was asked by her predecessor to run for the office of prime minister, she replied that because of her children, she would have to talk to her husband before deciding. When she asked him if he could take over responsibility for the children and the house, he asked for time to think it over. The following morning he said that he was willing, but only if she promised not to interfere in the housework any more than he—politically further to the right than she was—would try to influence her office. They told us this story as we traveled north. Obviously they made a great success of their bargain.

An exchange of official visits with Israel, a central objective of my administration, followed. Though relations between our countries had steadily improved—Adenauer, Brandt, and Kohl had been warmly received in Jerusalem—there had not yet been an exchange of state visits on both Israeli and German soil. Now I was invited to take part in such a reciprocal affair.

I had traveled to Israel several times before. I had looked up my old school friend from Berlin, Gerhard Nassau, in Safed and the kibbutzim in which our children had spent many weeks working and making friends. In 1973 Hans-Jochen Vogel, Carlo Schmid, and I had represented West Germany at Israeli prime minister David Ben-Gurion's funeral. I shall never forget the image of Golda Meir, whose imposing figure stood on the square outside the Knesset motionless and quite alone during the three-hour ceremony. She resembled an Old Testament statue hewn of granite, immovable like her nation's will to survive. On the flight back to Germany we were celebrating Carlo Schmid's birthday when we heard an earsplitting noise; an Italian fighter plane came within a hair of ramming us over the Adriatic.

I made another trip to try to assuage the feud between Israeli Prime Minister Menachem Begin and Chancellor Schmidt, which both heads of government waged with the unyielding rigidity characteristic of each. Though Begin listened to me courteously, he turned a deaf ear to my plea—a fact that did not diminish my respect for him, though I was careful to conceal my feelings from Schmidt.

Our close friends Yohanan Meroz, the former Israeli ambassador to Bonn, and his wife, Yael, lived in Jerusalem. Teddy Kollek, that model for every mayor in the world, had been my companion on many a walk through his ancient city. The past and present conjured up indescribable difficulties for him. He never allowed himself to avoid a tense situation, renounced all forms of violence, and lived his beliefs absolutely and without sentimentality. Always impatient, always on the move, always uneasy, with all his wit he inspired confidence in the strictest sense wherever he appeared. To stroll through the city with him in shirtsleeves, to see the wholly unaffected, naturally cordial response he received from people of every origin and religion was, quite simply, very encouraging.

This state visit did not involve any negotiations. It was enough that the visit occurred at all, having been preceded in Israel by a number of protests to show how far this official visit was from the ordinary. So now a clearly marked German Luftwaffe plane landed at the Jerusalem airport, escorted by Israeli fighter planes. On the tarmac stood the president, the prime minister, and the speaker of the Knesset to welcome the German guest with a twenty-one-gun salute and the German anthem, in which the Israelis could make out only the words "Deutschland, Deutschland über alles." On every face you could read the feeling that moved them at this moment.

President Chaim Herzog immediately took us under his wing. He and his warmhearted wife, Aura, treated us like guests of the family, with whom you could talk about everything and anything without mincing words. Herzog was born in Ireland, had gone to school in Palestine, was an officer in the British army during the war, and was in the frontline regiment that liberated the survivors of the Bergen-Belsen concentration camp. Then he became one of the pioneers in establishing the state of Israel—a proven fighter and diplomat, statesman and author, a "lion of a statesman in a world of mice," as the London Times called him, without spelling out who they meant by "mice."

Herzog spoke bluntly when he complained bitterly to me about the Federal Republic's plans to build an arms factory in Saudi Arabia. He was equally harsh in accusing the senate of Hebrew University in Jerusalem of hypocrisy because they regularly accepted financial aid from Germany but for reasons of historical principle refused to grant any German visitor an honorary degree. To Herzog's and my great pleasure, the Martin Buber Institute of the University, which had originally proposed the degree, instead gave me a gift: a first edition of the book of Isaiah, translated into German by Buber and Franz Rosenzweig, with Buber's handwritten marginal notations.

The central event of my trip was the visit to the Holocaust memorial, Yad Vashem. I had been there several times during earlier trips to Israel. As a silent monument it reminds us of a horror unparalleled in human history. No one who has been to Yad Vashem can ever forget.

We held political discussions with the government and the parliamentary leaders in the Knesset. This visit took place years before Israel set out on the peace process with Arafat and the Arabs later agreed to in Oslo. But Shimon Peres, then prime minister of a large coalition government, pursued that objective with his analytical acumen and untiring political tenacity. The two of us traveled to the Negev Desert to Sde Boqer, where Ben-Gurion had lived and where he is buried. Looking out over the unforgiving mountain chains bare of trees and bushes, far down toward the Dead Sea, the visitor senses something of the implacable harshness with which the prophets addressed their people. But he also begins to understand what it means to draw new life from the stony desert.

"Jerusalem is builded as a city that is compact together," the psalmist tells us. And so we came together during this official visit. The Protestant provost of the Church of the Redeemer, built in the late nineteenth century, invited us to the Old City. The mufti of Jerusalem received us on the Temple Mount and delivered a thoroughly moderate address. Meeting with the Benedictine monks on Mount Zion, we held a discussion on religion with students and professors of the theological faculty of the Dormitio Abbey. We all came to the same conclusion: Anyone attempting to be a Christian will fail if he knows nothing about the god of the Jews. Outside we were greeted by a crowd of German tourists singing the Doxology.

A discussion with young Israelis was next on the program, starting with the keynote by twenty-nine-year-old Yael Gouri, whose family had died in the Holocaust and who was tenaciously researching the responsibility of German soldiers in the war. She could never bring herself to set foot on German soil, she said. It was mainly Friedbert Pflüger, speaker in the federal president's office, who responded to the young woman. He had an unusual awareness of the opportunities for understanding open to the next generation across the borders. During the harshest confrontations at German colleges he was head of the organization of Christian-Democratic students, and as such showed much courage, acumen, and skill in conducting dialogues. While studying in the United States, he had concentrated on Jimmy Carter's human-rights policy. After years of collaboration in Berlin he had become an indispensable aide in the office of the president, as he was now in Jerusalem. With his unique commitment, he wrestled with the young woman over her and our ideas. The following day he persuaded her to fly back to Germany with us to gather her own impressions, and she was unsparing of herself and us. All the young Germans she met learned along with her.

Chaim Herzog and I developed a personal friendship that grew deeper until his death. In 1987 he came on a state visit to Germany, marking the first time an Israeli head of state set foot on German soil. Herzog had to overcome strong opposition in the Knesset before he was able to make the trip. We drove to Bergen-Belsen; he spoke the truth: "The only ones who can forgive are dead, and the living have no right to forget."

We visited the Jewish cemetery in Worms, the oldest in Europe, and, in the same city, the Rashi House, a memorial to Rabbi Shlomo Yitzaki, probably the foremost commentator on the Bible and the Talmud. Herzog also honored German resistance to Hitler in the prison in the Plötzsee district of Berlin.

Meeting with Gorbachev in Moscow

In the meantime great progress was in the offing for East-West relations. In the spring of 1985 Mikhail Sergeyevich Gorbachev became general secretary of the Communist Party of the Soviet Union. It is entirely due to him that the Soviet Union seriously pursued major reforms. Gorbachev realized that the high priority of rearmament could no longer provide his domain with greater world power but instead only dangerously aggravate the troublesome domestic economic situation. He believed it had finally become urgently necessary to open his nation up to the rest of the world.

Glasnost and perestroika were intended to allow the Soviet Union to compete globally. Gorbachev prescribed these reforms for his country in the conviction that he could establish them and still preserve the principles of the Soviet system. He even hoped that he might for the first time establish the true nature of the system.

As events ran their course, however, his error became evident: There was no way out. The longer the system remained closed off the more quickly it would be stifled, but opening it inevitably led to its destruction.

Nevertheless fundamental historical renewal processes are linked with Gorbachev's name. He became, in short, the key figure behind these revolutionary changes by almost entirely peaceful means. One of his most important achievements was abolishing the Brezhnev Doctrine, which recognized only limited sovereignty for the various socialist states and granted a general right of intervention to Moscow. According to Gorbachev's shocking measures every socialist nation was now to freely determine its own future. The spokesman for foreign policy in Moscow, Gennadi Gerasimov, coined the name "Sinatra Doctrine" for the General Secretary's measures, after the song "My Way," identified with its singer, Frank Sinatra. The end of this era was marked by the dissolution of the Soviet empire and the peaceful change of power in Hungary, Poland, Czechoslovakia, and East Germany.

At first progress was slow. In foreign policy Gorbachev concentrated primarily on relations with the other superpower. He agitated to reduce the arms race by massive disarmament all the way to zero solutions. He began by giving unilateral concessions to put pressure on the West, and not without success. At his 1986 meeting with President Reagan in Reykjavik matters advanced more quickly and unpredictably than seemed reasonable to advisers of the United States president.

Gorbachev was more cautious in establishing links with Western Europe. He explored among the capitals. For a while British prime minister Margaret Thatcher believed that he had chosen her to mediate with the entire European community. Without a doubt she had a strong influence on him, but it did not take him long to realize that her island nation was not the appropriate site for Moscow's appeal to the hearts of the French and Germans.

Precisely because at that time the West German government correctly tried to advance its policy concerning the two parts of Germany, it could not ignore Soviet interests. To this consideration was added Moscow's massive need for economic relations with us. Given the appropriate signs, the standing of the Soviet general secretary quickly rose among West Germans. The first shouts of "Gorbi, Gorbi" could be heard. Such shouts caused some unease here and there in the West, especially in the United States. Kohl, who made every effort to remove any reason for such worries among the Allies, had that intention when in an interview with *Newsweek* he noted that Gorbachev was working with the propaganda finesse of Joseph Goebbels. Moscow's response was immediate and sharp. The requisite contacts, which of course Kohl also desired, were blocked.

But this situation could not be allowed to stand. An unusual idea began to take shape: a state visit might help. But this time it would not, as usual, be the crowning end of a development toward better relations—it would initiate such a development. My "counterpart" in Moscow, the former foreign minister and then Soviet president, Andrei Gromyko, extended the invitation. The German media called my trip an "ice breaker." The Tass news agency demanded that my visit mark a "return to the track of stability."

It was hard work. Together with Genscher, who participated materially in the preparations, I set out for Moscow. My delegation included special guests, among them to my great delight the writers Siegfried Lenz and Alexander Kluge; Professor Klaus Ritter, West Germany's most knowledgeable and respected political scientist; Prinz zu Sayn-Wittgenstein, president of the German Red Cross; and Wilhelm Christians, head of the Bank of Germany. We were accompanied by 136 members of the media.

During the Wehrmacht's drive on Moscow in the winter of 1941–42, I was one of the infantry troops sent farthest forward and came within sight of the flak fire above the city before Russian resistance and bitter cold forced us to retreat. This time we were greeted at the entrance to the metropolis by the words, bannered in red and white, "Welcome to Moscow, President Weizsäcker." We were quickly swept into the prohibition-free state suite of the Kremlin and there left to ourselves with ever renewed offers of vodka. We were not scheduled to rough it in the manner Gorbachev had just boldly ordered his people to do.

Every topic touched on a sore point. Was disarmament the only way to peace? Wasn't it more likely that disarmament had to follow proven collaboration in other peaceful ways? Would we ever be able to stop worrying about security? I quoted a Russian saying to the effect that no one wanted to be the chicken that the raven kissed down to its last feather. Why did Germans living in Russia who wanted to go abroad still have to fear losing their jobs and apartments merely because they applied for an exit visa? How long were the borders in Europe supposed to retain their divisive, inhuman character?

"The Germans who today are separated into East and West have not ceased, and will not cease, to think of themselves as one nation. The unity of the nation is fulfilled in liberty." Only two and a half years later the Berlin Wall fell. But in the summer of 1987 the walls of the Kremlin chamber where I made a public address seemed simply to swallow up my words. Once again the Communist Party newspaper *Pravda* was untrue to its name, which means "truth." Counter to established Moscow procedure it censored my speech, omitting everything I said about borders, unity, the raven and the chicken, the Soviets' long-overdue retreat from Afghanistan, and even Immanuel Kant, who had lived in Königsberg, today's Kaliningrad. This, then, was my first experience of glasnost. Genscher intervened with his Russian counterpart, Eduard Shevardnadze, and a few days later the full text was published after all, though this time in the Soviet newspaper *Izvestia*.

Almost everything was difficult. A young German amateur aviator, Matthias Rust, had preceded us. Spiritedly and irresponsibly he had flown under the Soviet air-traffic control net and landed his light plane in Red Square. Now he was waiting to be sentenced after his Soviet trial. I intervened on his behalf but had no success for some time.

Recalling the prison in Berlin's Spandau district—the only site in Berlin still maintained by the Four Powers—I made a formal request for the release of the last prisoner there, Rudolf Hess, one time the so-called Deputy Führer. I did not question his sentence, but he had been in custody for forty-six years and was now an old man of ninety-four. Further imposition of the sentence had lost all humane sense. Mercy is the support of justice, says a Russian proverb, which I quoted. But no one in Moscow responded. Six weeks later Hess killed himself, still in prison.

During our parliamentary visit in 1973 to Moscow, then President Podgorny had responded to my intervention with a denial that there were German soldiers' graves on Russian soil. This time I was finally permitted to lay a wreath at our military cemetery in the Lublino district of Moscow. Our trip also took us to Leningrad, where I paid another visit to the Piskarevsoye Cemetery, a reminder of the terrible sacrifices made during the war by the civilian population and Red Army soldiers. For the first time Soviet and German officers jointly carried my wreath.

The patriarch of the Russian Orthodox Church received us in the Danilov Monastery in Moscow. Lidia Gromyko very considerately gave my wife a tour of the church. When the two ladies stopped at a side altar, our hostess pointed my wife toward the candles the faithful lit before an icon of the Virgin Mary.

Encouraging signs of reform were emerging. I was the first visitor from the West to have a lengthy discussion on Soviet television with twenty young Moscow students. Our conversation was emotional but by the end relaxed and almost cheerful. I was delighted that my daughter Beatrice—the only German student who participated—voiced opinions that contributed measurably to the success of the encounter.

Our ambassador, Andreas Meyer-Landrut, hosted a discussion with writers, film makers, and especially leading editors of the Soviet media. Among the participants were Yevtushenko, Akhmatov, Valentin Rasputin, and Elem Klimov. It was fascinating to feel the passion, sense of responsibility, sharpness, and courage this intellectual elite brought to give life to this great moral and political movement emerging from new, still slight opportunities at freedom.

The crowning achievement of the trip was a long discussion that Gorbachev, flanked by Shevardnadze, held with me and with Genscher. It was my first encounter with him. He spoke with a kind of clenched energy, without distortion. His unveiled gaze was clearer than his ears as he radiated not only intelligence but also feeling. However, at this meeting he displayed little evidence of the cordial charm he was able to exert and was not easily accessible at first.

Gorbachev did not waste a minute on ideology and propaganda. Instead he turned to long-term ideas and visions, which he expressed cogently. His convictions were not blurred by doubt. When I brought up the unresolved German question, he flatly denied there was any such problem. I tried a second time, only to have him answer that we should leave the solution to history, since it was impossible to predict what things would look like in a hundred years. When I asked him with a smile if he knew what things would look like in fifty years, he too began to smile. According to his subsequent statements this was Gorbachev's first discussion with a German leader about the German question, only a little less than three years before he gave a binding answer to our chancellor in Moscow and then later in the Caucasus.

Shortly after our talk, Gorbachev told Franz Josef Strauss that my visit had "opened a new page in history." At home Kohl characterized my trip to Moscow as a "milestone of understanding," which he later translated into action with Gorbachev in a personal and impressive manner. German reaction to my trip was serious but relaxed, as fifty-eight different cartoons and a wealth of letters reveal. I was particularly happy to receive a letter from the actor Heinz Rühmann. He knew very well how hard it had been and what was at stake. He was all the more relieved, he wrote, when he saw cheerful faces on the television reports. "If you really mean what you're saying, then say it with a smile," a director used to advise. He had taken the advice as a signpost for his life and was pleased to see it in action during my trip.

Honecker, Bush, and Gorbachev
Visit Bonn

Today many look back on the three years before the fall of
the Wall as if they had pursued a clever plan, a steady will,
and therefore a foreseeable course of events. But such retrospective determinism is deceptive. In spite of Gorbachev's full determination to put in reforms, disarm, and work for peace, in 1987 no
one, probably including himself, could foresee the concessions he
would have to make in 1990. The internal situation of the Warsaw
Pact nations had progressively worsened, yet we still saw no clear
indications that the division of Europe was coming to an end. And to
the extent that a revolutionary situation in Lenin's definition could be
detected—where those below become unwilling and those above become unable—the most imaginative courses of events were now conceivable.

An increasingly conflicting situation arose for the East German
leaders in particular. They were quite unwilling to follow Gorbachev's
call for reform. For domestic consumption East Germany clung to the
traditional hostile images of imperialism, capitalism, and revanchism at
the same time it needed and sought West German financial aid.
Honecker tried to practice détente with the world beyond his borders
and to refuse it domestically. Politically Honecker needed demarcation
from the Federal Republic, but in economic matters he worked to win
West Germany's partnership and grew increasingly dependent on
Bonn. He paid us back with eased travel restrictions. For twelve years,
until 1985, about 40,000 to 60,000 East German citizens below retirement age were allowed to travel to the West. In 1986 the number rose
to 250,000, and the following year to 1.2 million. The hard deutsche

mark became a kind of second currency, with isolated instances of East German employers paying part of workers' wages in Western marks. The sentiment of the East German population grew more and more favorable to reunification.

In fact, all kinds of new and astonishing signs of loosening appeared. In the mid-1980s a major biography of Bismarck, written by the renowned East German historian Ernst Engelberg, was published simultaneously in East and West Berlin. A little while later I was visited by a representative from an East Berlin publisher who wanted to print some of my speeches in East Germany, a project that eventually received the necessary approval from the SED politburo. Late in 1985 the first intra-German sister-city partnership was concluded between Saarlouis in West Germany and Eisenhüttenstadt in East Germany. In May 1986 the first cultural agreement between East and West Germany was signed.

Honecker now urgently requested an official visit to Bonn. Twice Moscow had stopped him from coming. The Soviet Union was still deeply suspicious of intra-German relations, especially as the sizable West German financial grants were deeply suspect to the Soviets. Shortly after my visit to the Soviet Union, Gorbachev gave Honecker the green light for his trip, and in September 1987 Kohl welcomed him to Bonn with full military honors, his national anthem, and his flag.

What would be the consequences of this visit? Honecker himself seemed to feel that all his wishes had been fulfilled by this formal recognition of East Germany's separate status by the other German state. "The division is complete," wrote *Neues Deutschland*, the central organ of the SED. Honecker went so far as to call the demarcation less compulsory than it used to be. In this context he said at his press conference in Bonn that the day would come "when the borders will no longer separate us but will unite us"—but of course not into a single state.

Nevertheless it is hard to imagine that he had no inkling of the ambiguity of events. When he arrived in Bonn, he had not been officially received, as protocol prescribed, by the federal president but by the chancellor. We would not consider East Germany a foreign country. In our speeches and discussions Kohl and I had welcomed Honecker as a German among Germans. Both of us stressed the solidarity of the two parts of Germany, and we clearly stated what we expected from East Germany in the interest of a united Germany. On a long walk we two made alone on the grounds of Villa Hammerschmidt I gave concrete indications of the intra-German requirements and the shared German task to maintain peace in Europe. The federal government concluded several more cooperation agreements with the East Berlin delegation.

Certainly at that time none of us saw a realistic chance of unification in the foreseeable future. Brandt had called it the "survival lie" and Kohl noted later that it was not yet even an item on the agenda of East-West policy. Realistically Honecker's visit, far from promoting the permanence of two states, was a sign of German cohesion. The influence of the Federal Republic on East Germany grew progressively stronger. This increased pressure was exerted on the straitened economic conditions in the SED government and especially on the feelings of the East German people. The Soviet ambassador in Bonn, Yuli Kvitsinsky, characterized the situation by saying, "The GDR is swallowing the golden bait, and once it's done that, it's hooked."

The world was still captivated by the reorganization Gorbachev was instituting in breathtaking fashion: decentralization, encouraging self-determination, rewarding individual achievement, better constitutional protections for citizens, open toleration of criticism, attempting to gain truthfulness about Soviet history, and permission given to all partner nations to freely find their own way. The risks were still as high as the opportunities. These were the longest strides by far as—operating within its own structures—the East incorporated the principles of the West.

The magic phrase now was "New Thinking." For us in the West it was important to vigorously collaborate in this effort within the framework of our tested systems.

The fortieth anniversary of the day our Basic Law took effect came on May 23, 1989. The Federal Assembly met and elected me to a second five-year term as president by 881 out of 1022 ballots cast—a great vote of confidence. The following day, speaking at an official ceremony, I talked about the goals laid down for us in the preamble of the Basic Law, which were now turning into reality: peace, European unity, German unity. In his day Theodor Heuss had called our constitution a deferred item. Now it was time for us to translate its concepts into reality. I also recalled the great Frenchman Jean Monnet, who shortly before the end of the Second World War reminded our opponents that the Allies had won the First World War but lost the peace. This time, he noted, it was crucial to win the peace, not only in the West but in all of Europe.

Peace can be won only in concert, not in conflict. After the difficult decades of the Cold War on a divided Continent, facing European history truthfully was one of the primary ways to secure peace. That objective was a central historical and moral motive of West Germany's Eastern policy in the second half of the 1960s. Gorbachev was now urging it on his own nation.

In the Federal Republic we more or less survived the high point of the so-called historians' quarrel, a controversy that began shortly after my address of May 8, 1985. At the German historians' conference in late 1988 I did what I could to keep the squabble from spreading and if possible end it. I emphatically turned against a historical and ethical relativization of the past. Historical references and comparisons have their place in scholarship, but in the long run scholarship cannot account for the singularity of history. These explanations are supplied by the moral sensibilities of ordinary people. Everything happens in a historical context. At the same time everything that happens in history is unique. It happened this way and not another, differently from elsewhere. What use is it to investigate whether Auschwitz can be compared with the cruel exterminations of other ethnic groups? Auschwitz remains unique. It happened because of Germans. This truth is irrefutable, no one in the world will forget it, and it will go on shadowing us.

Insider discussions and confrontations among experts are inevitable. But their "sainted neutrality" should be helpful to us. When history is examined, that process takes place in the hearts of the whole nation. History belongs not only to historians but to all of us. Our democracy has proven itself viable for forty years now, not least in our undefended openness toward history. The fact that we can accomplish so much and continue to learn allows us to be self-aware in the true meaning of the word. Now our democracy was waiting to use its viability in the job of assuring peace in all of Europe.

At the end of May 1989 we welcomed our good friend President George Bush on a visit to the Federal Republic. He and his outstanding secretary of state, James Baker, had decided to seize the initiative regarding the German question before Gorbachev could do so. Baker vividly recounted how he awakened the President's competitive instinct, remembering full well from tennis games they had played in Texas how strong that drive was in Bush. In Mainz, Bush made an important speech on foreign policy in which he called the United States and the Federal Republic "partners in leadership" and went on to say that very soon borders would have to fall everywhere as they had in Hungary: "Let Berlin be next." This was six months before the collapse of the Wall.

No sooner had Bush left than Gorbachev came on his long-awaited state visit to Bonn. I had not seen him for almost two years. From the first handshake the mood was cordial, quite different from the atmosphere in the Kremlin, which had been correct and fairly severe. On the grounds of the Villa Hammerschmidt he carried on a relaxed and cheerful discussion with Russian and Russian-speaking German students. At a private luncheon of the Gorbachev and Weizsäcker families he told long and vivid stories about his childhood, apprentice period, and political rise. On this warm June day the Villa Hammerschmidt, attractive though in no way ostentatious, with its grounds lovingly and knowledgeably supervised by my wife, completely fulfilled its purpose in both the personal and the political aspects. The history of its construction seemed made for the state visitor from Russia. Albrecht Troost, a businessman from the Rhineland, had built it in the mid-nineteenth century. The next owner, Leopold Koenig, was born in St. Petersburg and made a fortune as a sugar merchant in Russia. He is well known to everyone in Bonn for the museum he built for his son, a zoologist, across from the villa—the same Museum Koenig where in 1949 the parliamentary council, chaired by Adenauer, had enacted the Basic Law. The man who gave the estate its name, Rudolf Hammerschmidt, had also been a merchant in Russia.

Gorbachev was hugely pleased at these close links between his country and the history of the mansion. He became a complete enthusiast when he stood on the terrace with its splendid view of the Rhine, which reminded him of his beloved Volga landscape. All this is not, of course, to say that the politically charged visit was made up only of personal reminiscences and natural scenery. Our discussions were serious and intense. Gorbachev was approaching the apex of his time in office. The whole world was impressed with the magnitude of freedoms he had introduced in his empire, although in the Soviet Union questions were beginning to surface about the consequences. To understand both points of view, evaluate them correctly, and utilize them properly were duties of central importance to us, and therefore every moment of the visit was devoted to building confidence. Our visitor was clearly moved by the warm, spontaneous, enthusiastic welcome the West German people gave him wherever he went.

Confidence building made particular progress in the long, intense, and very personal exchanges of biography and ideas between Gorbachev and Kohl. Their frank, mutual respect and liking for each other allowed the crucial negotiations in 1990 in favor of German unity to succeed.

This state visit was a prime example of how incalculably valuable my wife's help was during my ten-year presidency, going far beyond running the house and grounds. Though the wife of the federal president—or at some future time perhaps the husband of the president—is not mentioned in the constitution, she feels the same responsibility and is willing to share it, less visibly but just as responsibly and at times more selflessly. She was also eager to help those who looked to her as their last and best hope because no one else in the country was able to help them. Whenever we prepared to receive a foreign guest or when we traveled abroad, she informed herself thoroughly and conscientiously about the country and its people, its history and current problems, anything that might come up in discussion.

Furthermore, my wife worked in a specific area that put her in touch with the misery suffered by countless families: drug addiction among the young. She counseled parents of addicted young people and established the foundation that bears her name and sponsors the reintegration into society of former addicts who by their own efforts and great strength freed themselves from the bondage of drugs. The foundation helped them find work, living quarters, ways to repay debt, and in general their place in the world. This nearly universal concern put my wife in touch with similar problems and attempts at solution in other countries whenever we traveled abroad and pretty much filled any gaps in her schedule, often for days and nights. Questions put to her by many in the media might lead one to believe that she cared only about clothes, souvenirs, and similar trifles. In reality she performed highly interesting and equally hard work that contributed considerably to the success of our country's concerns, just as she did once again during the encounter with Gorbachev I have just described.

PART FOUR

Unification

The Wall Crumbles

E xciting events now occurred in East Germany almost daily. The situation was in the hands of the people, while the political leaders had a hard time responding promptly, keeping their wits about them, and holding on to their nerve. Honecker had just affirmed that the Wall would still be standing in fifty or a hundred years, as long as the reasons for its construction remained valid. But in June 1988 the Hungarian foreign minister, Gyula Horn, and his Austrian counterpart, Alois Mock, symbolically cut the barbed-wire fence marking the frontier near Sopron. When the wave of "vacationers" from East Germany crested soon after, West German embassies in Budapest, Prague, and Warsaw were filled with them. The problems of finding enough provisions and maintaining hygiene for these crowds grew beyond anything imaginable in these havens. A flurry of contacts flowed between Bonn and the governments involved. These involved dramatic negotiations, with the active participation of the East German attorney Wolfgang Vogel in Prague and East Berlin. They resulted in Genscher's and Seiters's traveling to Prague in late September to bring their countrymen, crowded into the embassy grounds, the liberating news that their path to the Federal Republic had been cleared. This moment marked the first of the radical changes.

Starting in early September, each Monday saw demonstrations outside the Nikolai Church in Leipzig. The demonstrators' banners were emblazoned "Freedom to Travel, Not Mass Flight." On September 9 the first countrywide opposition movement, called New Forum, was founded at the home of Robert Havemann's widow; Bärbel Bohley and Jens Reich were among the members.

To commemorate the fortieth anniversary of the founding of the German Democratic Republic on October 7, Gorbachev visited East Berlin. Once more his conflict with Honecker over the need for reform led to heated disagreement. Gorbachev did not understand why East Berlin resisted following the example of other socialist countries. He may have underestimated how much more difficult this step was for the SED leadership than it was for Hungary or Poland, because it demanded a perspective that saw Germany as one nation, and this outlook the SED could not want.

At his Berlin press conference Gorbachev, using his vivid vocabulary, casually dropped a phrase that became part of our stock of frequent citations: "If you come too late, life will punish you." Later he told me that his intention was not to provide us with a familiar quotation. What mattered, he said, was the realization that history itself makes all the decisions, and trying to anticipate it was as futile as expecting to profit by missing the moment. He insisted that he had held the same opinion during our meeting in the Kremlin in 1987, when he had deflected my question on German unity by talking about the workings of history. It is crucial for statesmen to understand in good time where history is headed. This was what he meant by his statement in East Berlin; he had mostly been talking to himself.

Immediately after Gorbachev's visit the largest and most dramatic demonstrations were held in numerous East German cities, once again primarily in Leipzig; "We are the People," "No Force," "This Is Where We Stay," the banners read. The strain was unimaginable. All of Germany sat glued to the television screen. All Germans near and far held their breath; but no shots were fired by either side. The Soviets had managed to avoid a bloodbath during this momentous provocation. Unlike the Chinese government, which had shortly before used deadly force against the students in Tiananmen Square in Beijing, the Soviets ordered all troops to remain in their barracks. These marked the decisive hours of Germany's peaceful revolution. It was a success.

On October 17 Honecker was ousted and Egon Krenz became his successor. The demands on the banners immediately changed to

"Unlimited Freedom." On November 4 the largest demonstration, seven hundred thousand people, was staged on Berlin's Alexanderplatz with police approval. A colorful mix of writers, an actress, a clergyman, and two leading SED members spoke. "Flowers, Not Borders," "Legal Security Makes State Security Unnecessary," and "We Are the People—You Are the Ones Who Should Leave" were seen on large banners. German unity was not yet a topic of slogans.

No one knew what would happen next. On November 8 Kohl made an official visit to Poland of several days' duration while I fulfilled obligations in southern Germany. On the evening of November 9, shortly before 7 P.M., Günter Schabowski, a member of the Berlin SED politburo, announced that beginning immediately short-term "travel abroad" would be granted. The barriers dividing Berlin were raised after 11 P.M., and that same night huge crowds thronged past the old, hated obstacles. There was no end to the joyous outbursts. "Last night the German people were the happiest people in the world," Governing Mayor Walter Momper stated on November 10 outside the Schöneberg city hall. Never before and never since in my lifetime have I seen an event on German soil literally gladden the entire world, which shared our joy.

Three moments remain most vivid in my memory from the following days, which I spent in Berlin. The first thing I did was cross the Glienick Bridge, which crosses the Havel and is the only pedestrian connection between West Berlin and Potsdam. This bridge had constricted us into West Berlin for decades, sealing us off even more hermetically than the midtown sector crossings. Only the Four Powers could use the bridge. This was where the now famous exchanges of spies took place between the two sides, among them Francis Gary Powers, the U-2 pilot shot down over the Soviet Union. But the courageous Russian dissident Nathan Sharanski had also walked this path to freedom. Many times I participated in a custom unique to West Berliners. On weekends we would drive along the Potsdamer Chaussee toward the bridge, only to bump our heads, as it were, against the barricade at the center of the bridge, where the barriers and guards forbade us access to Potsdam—a place I came to know well as a boy and where my garrison was based—and the Mark Brandenburg. We felt like animals caged behind bars. And now, strolling across the bridge and back again with big smiles on our faces, we gave in to our feelings. It was as if we all knew each other.

At the city's center I went to the Potsdamer Platz, still a big, empty square controlled by guards on both sides. All alone I crossed from the west, a distance of 200 meters to the other side, where the barracks of the Volkspolizei (People's Police) were located. What would happen? A guard unit watched my approach through a telescope. Then the head of the unit, a lieutenant, peeled off from his men, marched toward me, saluted smartly, and calmly said, "Reporting, Federal President: No uncommon occurrences." We saluted each other as if our encounter were the most ordinary thing in the world, though we were living through an event that could not have been more unusual.

The third day after the Wall was breached I took part in the Sunday service in the Gedächtniskirche, which was overflowing with people from East and West. My bishop, Martin Kruse, with whom I had a very close relationship, asked me to address the congregation at the end of the service. My speech, which turned out to be an awkward mixture of lay devotion and a welcome to Berliners from both parts of the city, was based on St. Paul's words to the Galatians, which I had come to cherish during the Protestant Conferences. The verses read, "Stand fast therefore in the liberty wherewith Christ hath made us free, and be not entangled again with the yoke of bondage. . . . For, brethren, ye have been called unto liberty; only use not liberty for an occasion to the flesh, but by love serve one another." In speaking, I was thinking primarily of residents in the West. Their duty was to be ready with open doors and hearts instead of blundering into other territory and insisting that their opinions and values were the only valid ones. What East Germany needed now was not high-flown words but aid. "None of us knew ahead of time—none of us knows what will happen next." "The people show the way to politics. When politics is a concern of the people, it deals with the liberty humankind longs for and with the responsibility without which liberty leads to license. Responsibility means solidarity one with the other, the solidarity in which liberty is fulfilled—love, as we Christians say. Let us stand fast in this kind of liberty." These words were the first signal of things to come: Those who would unite must learn to share.

A huge crowd gathered outside the church after the service. We could not sort ourselves out by Eastern or Western origin and had no wish to do so. We crushed and cherished each other. No one wanted to go home. Everyone was ready to share.

This was how the first radical change in Germany was completed. The second was still not clearly identifiable. While other nations tapped around in the dark, Kohl discreetly took the initiative on November 28 in the Bundestag by launching his ten-point program, which Horst Teltschik had detailed for me the previous day. Kohl spoke of the stages we must follow to arrive at unity and announced his readiness to take up a proposal by East Germany's prime minister, Hans Modrow, for a "treaty community." Further, he suggested that "confederative structures between the two German states" be developed with the ultimate goal of federation, and he defined the political objective as Germany's national unity. On the road to this goal, he suggested, no one could now give correct and conclusive answers to the many difficult questions that would arise.

Reaction to this program among the neighboring capitals and Four Powers was at first mixed. Paris expressed irritation because three days earlier, during a private dinner with Mitterand, Kohl had given no indication of his plan. Washington too would have preferred being informed ahead of time instead of receiving formal notification immediately after the speech. The following day Secretary of State Baker had a clever explanation for the way the event unfolded: To unite Germany, the road of self-determination was essential; but the legal position and responsibility of the Allies must be properly observed. Unification must come about gradually and peacefully, and the permanent German obligation to NATO and the European Community must

be preserved; therefore unification could not be bought with neutrality. After all, the inviolability of borders had to be observed, a concern
Kohl had not addressed. Baker thus focused on the missing piece in
Kohl's ten points, relating to Poland's western border, an omission
noted everywhere, especially abroad. By verbalizing the problem, the
United States contributed to easing tensions and plainly indicated the
direction negotiations must take in the immediate future.

The East German leadership was in turmoil. With Krenz still
general secretary of the SED, the Volkskammer canceled the party's
leadership set forth in the constitution and openly debated numerous
past abuses of authority and instances of corruption. The situation was
quite unprecedented. On the one hand the GDR's constitution kept it
from even approaching democracy. On the other, new impulses were
sparked by the people far more than in an established democracy as
practiced in the West. Actually, it was as if the authority to set directions for policy lay in the hands of the people. Mainly it was the
people who manifested the radical change and decisive force in the
GDR at the inception of unification.

Immediately before Kohl announced his ten-point program, the
first public demands for national unification were heard in East
Germany. Until that time most popular phrases had called for an independent GDR with such slogans as "Don't sell out the GDR" and "We
won't be Federordered around." Now increasing public demands for
unification replaced these earlier mottoes with sentiments such as "We
Are *One* People" and "Germany One Nation," especially at the Monday
demonstrations in Leipzig. Visitors to East Berlin and East Germany
during the second half of December were greeted by this new sentiment, which Kohl also noticed when he visited the ruins of the
Frauenkirche in Dresden shortly before Christmas. The Rubicon had
been crossed. Radical change carried the day. The majority of the
population was demanding unification.

Foreign-Policy Successes

The major steps taken to restore Germany's national unity have already been described exhaustively. Almost all the principal actors in Germany and other countries have written books or had books written about them on the subject. Of course the narratives do not always agree, and many tend to express a more or less covert international competitiveness concerning the author's personal merit and others' failings. That is only normal in human beings. It is even interesting. But it is inadequate to describe the essentials of this period.

In Europe a landslide washed away the decades-long status quo of the Cold War. There is no precedent for it in history. Its momentum was unstoppable. No one person could have planned what happened. No one could have clearly foreseen where it would come to a standstill. It was therefore all the more important to understand its dynamic, channel it into the framework of the possible, and steer it in a beneficial direction. This is always the heaviest demand on those who bear national responsibilities. What is required of society is to not submit unquestioningly to the masters of history, but to be free of inherited prejudices and fears so this crucial goal can be accomplished: to think and act in light of fundamental movements of progress at their highest point.

The turning point in Europe and Germany was full of formidable uncertainties. No one lacked the imagination to see the potentially immense dangers, the possibilities for violence and bloodletting. At the same time unexpected opportunities arose that might otherwise pass unnoticed.

In this situation it was our great and historically rare good fortune that the most important actors did justice to their responsibilities in this multinational effort.

Gorbachev and Foreign Minister Shevardnadze had to summon up the most courage and bear the heaviest burdens. It was Gorbachev who guaranteed the peaceful course of the upheaval. And when in 1990 a decision was needed on the international status of a united Germany, he quickly found the energy to review his original objectives and change them in accordance with the new realities. He managed these difficult tasks with an awareness, unique to him, that he was not a sovereign lord but an attentive and responsible tool in the inexorable march of history—who of all those involved had done the most to set these changes in motion. With this outlook he communicated with Kohl, whom he trusted.

Gorbachev's unprecedented achievement was to explain to his people why he had handed over the German Democratic Republic, this jewel in the Warsaw Pact and in COMECON (Council for Mutual Economic Assistance), to a unified Germany and thus to the traditional enemy, NATO—for nothing in return, as it seemed to his compatriots, who saw only the continuing decline of Soviet power and could not forgive Gorbachev.

Kohl understood the situation with his sure instinct of pinpointing sentiment among Germans in the GDR. The layers of hopes for unification peeled away more and more rapidly from the shell of an elementary desire for freedom. Kohl measured the speed to the objective and in a quick transition from caution to acceleration, he went to work. It was important to create the necessary foreign-policy preconditions for unification at once and to put the whole force behind this peaceful and irresistible revolution at the service of this purpose; Baker, a Texan, had already compared this revolution to a runaway herd of cattle. While worries and fears were heard all over Germany, and under the auspices of a highly uncertain future for Soviet policy, the question was whom the hour favored. Together with Genscher, Kohl understood the matter of time and used it with energy, caution, and the trust that he and Genscher had created with the powers involved. The foreign-policy mission of reunification was fulfilled brilliantly on Germany's part.

President Bush, highly skilled in foreign relations, and his secretary of state, James Baker were invaluable friends to Germany at this time. For one thing the United States had always supported the concept of German unification provided that the process was peaceable and democratic. For another, as a superpower the United States was not concerned that Germany might use its increased weight as a unified power to pursue an unforeseeable course counter to its interests or those of NATO and Europe. Accordingly Washington assumed the leadership role when the time came to arrange the conference where the resolution on unification was to be considered internationally. To determine qualifications for participation, Baker and his German counterpart, Genscher, developed the Two-Plus-Four formula—that is, the two German states with the Four Powers—and with tenacious energy secured its acceptance in Moscow, Paris, and London. It was important for Germans that the name of the talks not be "four plus two," meaning four decision-making votes to which our two further votes were to be appended—to eat at the children's table, as it were. We did not want unification to resemble a kind of Four Power dictatorship. We could not accept such an agreement on political, democratic, and moral grounds. Until the negotiations' final conclusion time and again Bush and Baker found ways to overcome obstacles, and they acquired lasting credit for laying the foreign-policy foundations of unification.

Among our European partners France and the European Community were the most important. An outstanding role was played by the president of the European Commission, Jacques Delors, a Frenchman. From the beginning he reinforced the indivisible solidarity of German unity by roping us into Europe. He made sure the GDR became a member of the Community from the moment of unification, without the usual negotiations and treaties. For us this was a considerable help; for him it was a crucial requirement to accepting and trusting a united Germany in its further role in Europe. Beyond this, Delors did a fine job of personally tending to domestic conditions in East Germany and promoted its opportunities within the European ensemble. When I rendered Germany's official greeting to him in front of the assembled Bundestag and Bundesrat on the Day of German Unity in 1990 in Berlin, he was welcomed on all sides with almost tempestuous applause.

Among the European national leaders in this great time the role of François Mitterand was especially important to us. To this day it is said that he tried by fair and foul means to oppose German unification. In 1996 a conference was held in the German-French Center in Genshagen near Berlin, which was founded by the clever, conscientious, and generous French linguist Brigitte Sauzay and the German historian Rudolf von Thadden, where the main topic was the situation of France in 1990. Even before I walked in the door I was assaulted by both French and German television news with the question of whether Mitterand was "for or against." A preconceived opinion had been established, palpable everywhere. Based on my personal experiences with Mitterand, I believed the opinions critical of him were mistaken and founded on a lack of that historical judgment and farsightedness displayed by the French leader.

Without a doubt his perspective differed from that of the United States and the Soviet Union. Under recent French governments the relationship with Germany was based on a dual foundation. Each one was serious about overcoming old enmities and furthering European integration, even if not every French president was as devout a European as Mitterand. At the same time Paris was concerned about France's security when it came to Germany. On this point in particular the European Community, with the inclusion of Germany, played a vital role. Even though French rejection of dictatorships in the East and Germany's forced partition appeared genuine, the division of the Continent into two parts provided additional security. Cooperation and control of Germany formed a dialectical relationship for Paris.

Now, with German unification becoming an actuality, Mitterand considered it his mission to proceed with caution. In the interests of his nation he felt responsible for making certain that an appropriate international context existed. For the superpowers, especially the far-distant United States, it made no qualitative difference whether 60 or 80 million Germans lived in national unity at the center of the Continent. But for Germany's European neighbors the outlook was quite different. Until this time France, Great Britain, and Italy had been about the same size as the Federal Republic. Now, through unification, Germany would obtain a unique, measurable quantitative advantage. The sovereignty of the Four Powers over Germany as a whole, long seen by France as a security and an advantage, was ending. This was hard to swallow politically, economically, and psychologically. Though the joyful empathy with the fall of the Wall was entirely free of the notorious French arrière-pensée when the subject was Germany, excitement over the coming unification was kept within bounds. Could anyone be surprised at this state of affairs? No French president would have viewed the situation differently or defended a different view to the French people.

Mitterand had to consider two questions in particular. One concerned the firm linkage of greater Germany with Europe, now all the more necessary, which was the unanimous wish of every political party in Germany. The previously described course of action taken by Commission President Delors had Mitterand's complete approval.

The other question, which briefly led to more serious conflicts between Mitterand and Kohl, concerned the Oder-Neisse Line. Kohl's position that only a united Germany approved by all could make a definitive statement on the question isolated him internationally, and even domestically he was exposed to widespread lack of understanding. Mitterand then tried an unusual method. He invited Poland's President Wojciech Jaruzelski and the democratically elected Prime Minister Tadeusz Mazowiecki to Paris. The three of them, in the presence of the press, called on the West German government and Bundestag to finally make a definitive declaration on Poland's western border. The tone was hostile. Such a joint admonition from the French and Poles to the Germans might earlier have led to precarious conflicts. Kohl had allowed the border question to escalate to an international level, a situation better avoided for reasons of psychological foreign policy. Nevertheless, the outrage voiced in Paris was exaggerated, since in the end Bonn had not the slightest intention of altering the letter or spirit of the Warsaw Treaty concluded earlier by Brandt's government. And so, after thorough discussions between Bonn and Paris, the crisis was averted.

Without a doubt Mitterand approached German unity with circumspection and devoted his energies to achieving a unity tolerable to France and all of Europe. This outcome eventually led to the subsequent Maastricht Treaty. This statesman who was eminently schooled in and shaped by history, however, never made any serious attempt to obstruct unification. His principles of history would not permit such an action. He always saw history as a process. For him it was more than the product of individuals, more than strictly political power and cunning, which he knew how to use masterfully, more than crediting or blaming the actors. Concerning himself intensely with my country, he played a greater part in forming France's new view of Germany than anyone else. Time and again he spoke to me about the "book of history." Therefore, in line with his guiding rule, he said in 1990, "The unification of Germany has been recorded in history." Accordingly he did his part to steer the avalanche in a sensible direction.

In this sense Mitterand took his farewell from Germany during his final days in office when on May 8, 1995, he spoke of the German soldiers he had met when they were prisoners of war during the Second World War. They had fought for an evil cause, he noted, but acted out of love for their homeland. He was aware of the distinction and honored it better than his critics in France.

This left Great Britain, which participated eagerly in all negotiations. The strength Prime Minister Margaret Thatcher showed in bringing about domestic reforms won her worldwide respect, but her distance from continental Europe became notorious. Her lack of enthusiasm at the idea of a united and strengthened Germany is hardly surprising. Her image of Germany had been formed around 1942, during the heart of the war, and as long as she headed her government, it remained unchanged. Of all the Germans in public service she showed the greatest interest in the then president of the Bundesbank, Karl Otto Pöhl. She issued him charming invitations to talks so she could learn more about currencies from him. She behaved with the rest of us as I saw her behave during my state visit in 1988, when she invited me to a private luncheon together with Genscher and her foreign minister, Geoffrey Howe. After two hours, when saying good-bye to us, Howe mentioned to us that he had one complaint—that we Germans had been unable to get the prime minister to at least once listen to the cause of Europe. In the end she had no influence worth mentioning on the course of Germany's unification.

Friendships in Warsaw and Prague

International acceptance of German unification required the votes of the Four Powers, the European Community, and NATO as well as the Czech Republic and especially Poland. The irritation I have already mentioned (caused by Bonn's withheld approval of the Oder-Neisse Line) made this necessity as clear as did Warsaw's strong wish to be invited as a participant to the Two-Plus-Four Talks, eventually satisfied in the form of an auditor's role.

Of all the resistance groups and peaceful revolutionary movements in the Eastern bloc nations, Poland's Solidarnosc was by far the most effective. Under the leadership of Lech Wałęsa it had developed into a strong opposition deeply rooted in society. Its power not only changed conditions decisively in Poland, it also influenced the country's foreign relations, especially as they related to Germany. After difficult negotiations in Helsinki, Chancellor Schmidt worked out an agreement with Poland's party chairman, Edward Giereck, on complex issues. This outcome improved official relations, but because of martial law and other sharply oppressive measures the Polish leadership imposed in response to the Solidarnosc movement, the situation soon worsened again.

A phase of frozen contacts between the governments now set in. Instead, the people began to form more lively connections, and their contacts and exchanges increased in unforeseen ways. For example, many religious congregations in the Federal Republic offered help to their sister congregations in Poland, even to totally unknown recipients. At that time a number of rental trucks filled with supplies and provisions could be seen heading eastward with German clergymen at the wheel.

For me this event showed most persuasively the will of the German people to carry out their intentions and personally contribute to restitution and reconciliation. This grassroots action was détente from the ground up, peace policy in the people's hands. Sometimes the people are ahead of their governments.

At the same time many German politicians, especially on the left, had a hard time correctly interpreting the course of events in Poland. They overestimated the danger of Soviet intervention in a Poland in turmoil and under martial law and underestimated the growing power of Solidarnosc. Therefore they maintained fairly close relations with the government of Poland for too long while at times literally ignoring the Polish opposition. That attitude brought them many reproaches, including even those of Willy Brandt, the inspiration behind the Warsaw Treaty.

Earlier, as a board member on the Robert Bosch Foundation, I had worked hard to create the German-Polish Youth Exchange. An insistent demand for such an organization had existed in both countries. As early as 1987 the German-led Poland Institute in Darmstadt hosted a discussion, made popular on television with Reinhard Appel acting as moderator, between Polish and German young people. It proceeded in heartwarming openness. Why, the Polish participants wanted to know, did German schoolbooks talk about areas "under Polish administration," although we had recognized Poland's current borders since 1970? But speaking of recognition, the counterquestion asked, what was so wrong if in a sister-city relationship with Wiesbaden the Germans talked about Breslau (the older German name of the city) instead of Wroclaw (its current Polish name)? While each side talked about its own people's misdeeds, the young people jointly refused to make moral judgments concerning each other's good and evil aspects. A vital reciprocal interest in culture also emerged. The leader of the Poland Institute, Karl Dedecius, had created the best preconditions for this interest. An editor and translator always looking for people with the same skills, Dedecius had amassed an almost complete library of Polish literature in German translation, a true treasure trove that the Bosch Foundation had funded.

Politically and personally Tadeusz Mazowiecki had long been my confidant in Poland. Our first contact had occurred as early as the late 1960s. As public-relations head and cofounder of the Club of Catholic Intelligence, and later as delegate to the Sejm from the Catholic Znak group, he frequently came to Bonn and told us about the struggle of his friends for liberty and universal intra-Polish solidarity from Solidarnosc to the Communists in questions of national interest, especially concerning the Oder-Neisse Line. Under martial law in Poland his courage and faith helped him live through arrest and torturous interrogation. As a member of the Solidarnosc leadership and adviser to the Pope he had stayed in the background but then grew into a leading political and spiritual role. Mazowiecki contributed measurably to the huge upheaval until Solidarnosc was legitimized again in April 1989, free elections were arranged at the "roundtable," and he was—since late August 1989—the first freely elected non-Communist head of government in the Soviet area.

The day after his inauguration he sent me an invitation to visit Warsaw the following week to help him commemorate the fiftieth anniversary of the start of the Second World War on September 1, 1989. To our mutual regret the trip could not be arranged. The stated reasons were unresolved bilateral negotiations involving both governments. But a rumor was rife that this was only a pretext, that domestic considerations and jealousies were the real reasons behind the cancellation. It was a missed opportunity for both countries. An exchange of personal messages between the Polish president and myself served as a poor substitute.

Nine countries border Germany. I had already visited every one of them except Poland, though along with France it was Germany's most important neighbor. An official visit to Warsaw could not be arranged until May 1990. It was motivated by the impulses Polish resistance groups were exerting on internal liberation movements in the GDR as well. The first initiatives for a trilateral collaboration of Poland, Germany, and France were tested. The Polish president and I visited the memorial site of the former concentration camp of Treblinka north of Warsaw, where the Polish pediatrician Janusz Korczak had accompanied Jewish children from the orphanage he established for them. Offered his freedom, he refused to leave the children and went to his death with them. He saw his sacrifice as a sign calling him to overcome despair in the face of cruelty.

We went to the Westerplatte near Danzig, where the German navy unleashed the Second World War with the first shots fired on the mainland. We drove to the Frischen Haff through blooming fields of golden rape in the southwestern part of East Prussia. Under the church steeple in Frauenburg, which the local canon and astronomer Copernicus made famous with his experiments on the heliocentric system, the Polish bishop of the Ermland region of Prussia spoke bitterly to me about the Soviet policy of strangulation, which blocked Poland from the shipping lanes where the Haff opened into the Baltic near Pillau (Baltijsk). Only a few kilometers from this lookout point I had lived through the last and most difficult battles of the war with my regiment in the spring of 1945. In the old Prussian district capital of Mohrungen (Morag) we visited an exhibit honoring Johann Gottfried Herder, the philosopher who investigated and gave new life to the determining characteristics of different European nations and cultures.

Every stop on this journey was heartwarming, full of memories of happy and harsh events of the past and filled with confident hope for Europe's future.

In his personal, modest, forthright manner Mazowiecki gave a human dimension and focus to the visit. He made his arguments without either subtlety or populism, and he cared less about winning out over other statesmen and politicians by using pressure or tactical evasions than about being easy in his conscience. He would not allow political effectiveness to be played off against adherence to ethical principles, making life harder for himself than others and forcing him to accept defeats. Subsequently he served the United Nations, uncovering inhuman violations of human rights in the former Yugoslavia in order to mitigate the excesses of the horrifying civil war.

Relations with our neighbor Czechoslovakia developed in quite different ways. In that nation Charta 77 embodied a spiritual and moral power without turning into a popular movement. Its central force was Václav Havel, a thinker, writer, and dramatist. His essays and letters from prison demonstrate this intellectual's struggle to achieve inner liberty under a dictatorship. His book entitled *To Live in Truth* is guided by his conscience on his way to live in liberty.

Havel's imagination and philosophy, ethical thinking and brilliant wit unite in him to guide his investigative search for responsibility in politics.

I had not yet met him but often used ideas in his work as our compass bearings in the thaw of East-West relations. However, we began a correspondence in which the central document became his letter to me in which he expressed pleasure at receiving the German publishing industry's Peace Prize and explained why he could not come to Frankfurt to accept it in person. The Prague Communists, who had put him in prison so often and for so long, were willing to have him leave the country but would not let him back in. The heart of his letter was a carefully reasoned reconciliation with us Germans, true to the admonition of the Bohemian Bishop Comenius: "When it comes to improvement, everyone must begin with himself." Havel therefore listed by name the errors committed by his own Bohemia as no one had done before. He wrote, "I myself—as well as many of my friends—condemned the expulsion of the Germans after the war. This deed always seemed to me deeply immoral, damaging not only the Germans but also and perhaps to a greater degree the Czechs themselves."

Then a rush of events occurred in Prague. If at first progress was slow, now the velvet revolution gained the upper hand overnight. On January 1, 1990, four months after writing his letter concerning the Peace Prize, Václav Havel became president of the Czech Soviet Socialist Republic. This great event marked the beginning of a year that would see huge upheavals in Europe.

A few days before his inauguration Havel called and told me about his plans to visit Germany. And literally on the fourth day of his presidency he did travel to East Berlin, where he spent the morning with leading figures in the GDR. He then went to Munich, where he visited me that afternoon during a New Year's vacation I was taking in Upper Bavaria. The effect of his visit in Germany and especially in his country is hard to imagine. Munich was the site where in 1938 the infamous pact that sealed Prague's fate had been struck. In Berlin in the spring of 1939 Hitler had humiliated President Emil Hácha of Czechoslovakia. Yet these were the sites where the new Czech head of state directed his first steps outside his country.

I met Havel on the tarmac at Munich airport, where he arrived in a military plane. A Czech lieutenant saluted. When Havel had taken a few steps, the officer pointed at him and said, loudly enough for me to hear as apparently I was intended to, "There he goes, our new commander-in-chief, our own Good Soldier Schweik." Surely these are a blessed, gifted people!

Havel also met with Kohl and the Bavarian prime minister, Max Streibl, at the Prince Charles Palace in Munich. This assemblage of totally different personalities meeting in a relaxed and hopeful atmosphere is hard to describe.

Very soon thereafter I had another call from Prague. On March 15, 1939, Havel said over the phone, Hitler's troops had forced their way into the Prague Castle. The upcoming March 15, fifty-one years later, he wanted to take the same walk with me, peacefully. How could I say no?

So Genscher and I traveled to the capital of Czechoslovakia, where a ceremony was held in the large gothic hall of the Castle. The old maestro Václav Neumann conducted Dvořák's New World Symphony. As each of us spoke, we had difficulty keeping our emotions in check. After the ceremony Havel hosted a reception surrounded by his "royal household"—artists, critics, and freedom fighters. His office had already taken on the look of a studio of contemporary art, with art-work almost burying the desks and telephones.

Nevertheless Havel was not satisfied with the decor and asked me for two kinds of help. First he needed to acquire appropriate furniture, then locate expert technicians who could disable the hidden listening devices in the office.

After this he hiked with me on foot down from the Castle toward the Moldau River at the center of a cheerful mixture of citizens, members of the press corps, and a few security agents. Abruptly he grabbed me by the sleeve and turned me into a small door facing the street. It led to a bar that had served as a cell for conspirators during the time of the dictatorship. We shared a drink of good Czech beer there, just a few of us.

But this was not the end of the surprises. He confided a worry to me: Before he could have considered becoming president he had agreed to deliver the opening address at Austria's next Salzburg summer festival. Now he was president, and his fellow citizens would no longer understand the ways of the world if they turned on their television sets and saw a huge reception given him by Austria's President Kurt Waldheim, hardly a favorite in Prague. What should he do about his acceptance now? I came up with the suggestion that he had obviously been waiting to hear. I worked out a plan whereby he would first come to Bayreuth as my guest, then we would fly together to Salzburg in a German plane. No sooner said than done. In Salzburg we walked side by side—almost hand in hand, like Hansel and Gretel—through long lines of friendly spectators toward the Felsen Riding School, where Waldheim gave us a hearty welcome. The pushing, shoving, and crowding of photographers was so indescribable that none of them managed to capture on film the welcoming embrace Havel had feared somewhat.

Then came one of his memorable speeches on liberty. To him, Havel said, life without liberty had felt like that of the mythical Sisyphus, who laboriously lugged a rock uphill each day only to have it roll back to the bottom each night. But lo and behold, one day the huge rock suddenly remained at the top of the hill. The disturbed hero asked, "What shall we do now?" Then we heard Havel's ideas on how we would manage this new gift of freedom, with all its diversions and temptations. With his sharp eye for human weakness under conditions of liberty he spoke about political commitment and a bourgeois society, the democratic weight of smaller regional entities, and culture, without which we lack moral standards and a spiritual dimension. Freedom changes everything.

Thus Havel makes his way in a world that is fully aware of his worth but only rarely lives up to his expectations. The Czech prime minister, Václav Klaus, ran under the campaign slogan "Speed Is Better than Caution"—a motto not always unknown in Germany and elsewhere. But of course the reverse applied to the German-Czech declaration on the past; fearing stagnation in this developing climate of good neighborliness, early in 1995 Havel made another forceful beginning. He opened a lecture series at Prague University with an urgent call to let the future be unobstructed by a controversial past and encouraged the draft of that declaration. In agreement and by arrangement with him I closed the lecture series late that same year in the same place. In Germany in 1995 the Chancellor placed the declaration on the agenda as a "chief topic," whatever that New Democratic concept may mean. Yet it took fourteen months before Klaus and Kohl finally met in Prague to sign the document in January 1997.

After the Two-Plus-Four Treaty was signed, international interest shifted very quickly. Member states of the CSCE did meet in November 1990 and issued the significant Charter of Paris for a new Europe. At the end of the Cold War they had their sights set on liberty, human rights, self-determination, and common security. It was a historic moment full of opportunities. Since the sensitive points of international tension seemed to be solved and the Cold War ended, every nation began to concentrate on its own affairs. Not a single one of the assembled heads of state and government called for an expansion of NATO to the western frontiers of the old Soviet Union. Nor did anyone give a thought to the incipient aggressions and horrors in the former

Yugoslavia. The United States was almost entirely occupied with obtaining a mandate from the United Nations to combat, along its own lines, the Iraqi dictator Saddam Hussein after his invasion of Kuwait. Though Germany stood at the center of many new international demands, it was busy implementing internal unification.

I was given greater insight into all this in the fall of 1990, when I met most of the other national leaders at the World Child Summit of UNICEF in New York. This large-scale function at the United Nations was held to call attention to our most urgent responsibility: our concern for generations to come. Topics included infant and childbirth mortality; high birth rates, a cause of poverty and one of its consequences; and ethical and religious authorities who must call for and contribute to better family planning. As a very active patron of the German committee for UNICEF my wife supported the outstanding work my former colleague in the Bundestag, Marie-Elisabeth Klee, performed with UNICEF for many years.

But the attending delegates talked almost exclusively about the imminent war in the Gulf and hardly at all about hunger, development policies, demographics, and children. During the meeting I invited the president of Yugoslavia to a discussion at which I expressed my open dismay and deep concern over the increasing oppression of the Kosovo Albanians by the Serbs. The foreign minister of Yugoslavia, Budimir Loncar, took part in our conversation. He was a Croatian whom I knew well from his time as Belgrade's ambassador in Bonn. After his president had left, he thanked me for my intervention on behalf of Kosovo. But the discussion remained an isolated event. If at that time, the fall of 1990, the West had massively intervened with Slobodan Milošević, perhaps some of the horror that followed might have been prevented. I had the feeling that the Serb dictator was testing the world's reaction to his repressive measures in Kosovo and then, when there was little stirring, let his power plans escalate.

Internal Challenges of Unification

In 1990 foreign affairs brought unlimited amounts of work and enormous challenges as Europe approached a new phase in its history. Nation states had survived, but the age of the balance of power among fully sovereign states was coming to an end, as was external leadership by global superpowers. For the first time people on our continent had an opportunity to coalesce into a shared and peaceful life by their own efforts. Would they find the necessary will and strength? Would they use these to strengthen their influence and stake their potential on their new position in the world while taking action to end overpopulation, hunger, environmental destruction, and spiritual void?

The German government had seized the moment to unify its nation. Under the pressure of time unification was accomplished with energy and openness, leaving Germany more accessible to Europe than ever before. In order to become a useful partner to other nations, however, we first had to perform the domestic duties pertaining to unification. So we began the task of achieving inner unity and went to work in the context of a powerful whirlwind.

The German Democratic Republic was still an entity, but the large majority of its citizens was pressing for unification. Freedom of information and travel were already won. The objective now was the reality of unity. How would it work economically and socially, communally and individually?

Willy Brandt had summed up the situation: "Now those things that belong together will grow together." In mid-December 1989 I followed by saying on East German television: "We are one nation, and that which belongs together will grow into one. But it must grow together. We must not try to make that growth rampant. We need time."

We would have to be patient enough to take the time, since there were no tricks to speed it up. True cohesion occurs on a deeper human level. To grow rampant means to grow unhealthily instead of organically. To this day we are struggling with the unhealthy aspect. I was not being critical of courageous action in the international world, which was necessary and right, but it was my aim to address sentiments within East Germany and most especially the reciprocal perception of the Eastern and Western populaces. Later, Brandt twice confirmed to me that he understood and accepted what I had said. But his instincts had not deceived him: We did not have the time we needed. No one could stop its course.

One of the best outcomes was the prompt democratic election of a free Volkskammer in East Germany. During the months that followed, its members had to work out the most difficult problems almost without preparation and arrive at decisions of unprecedented significance. Occasionally these legislators were called amateurs. Was that supposed to express contempt? As they struggled to find solutions with unequaled devotion, their lack of routine professional parliamentary behavior was actually an advantage because they did not pin themselves or each other down to specifics. They showed how valuable it is "not always to expect the worst in others, or even to hope for it, simply to confirm one's own image of the world" (Richard Schröder). Each legislator was allowed and virtually required to be open-minded and to acquire new knowledge. Amateurs holding their own with professionals—not a bad omen for democracy. The brief period of the freely elected Volkskammer in East Germany is one of the finest chapters in German parliamentary history.

Until this time direct democracy had determined the direction and tempo in East Germany. Now it was rapidly transformed into a representative system on the Western model. The four words "We are

the people" grew into many thousands of words in ever new agreements and decrees. Working with unprecedented efficiency and energy, politicians and officials, under the principal leadership of
Wolfgang Schäuble and Lothar de Maizière, worked out the basic
dates for unification. In May 1990 the Commercial, Credit, and Social
Union was established. On July 1 the GDR restored personal property
after setting graduated upper limits as well as all recurrent payments on
a one-to-one scale. The Treuhandanstalt (trusteeship institution) came
into being. The Volkskammer announced East Germany's submission
to the jurisdiction of the Basic Law. On August 31 the Union Treaty
was signed in East Berlin's Crown Prince Palace.

On the night of October 2–3, 1990, a large crowd gathered
outside the Reichstag in Berlin. Referring to the preamble of the constitution, at the stroke of midnight I expressed our shared task to the
multitude: "We want to perfect union and liberty in free self-
determination, conscious of our responsibility before God and men
and animated by the resolve to serve world peace as an equal partner
in a unified Europe."

Everyone there was thinking of the many German roads leading
to this unforgettable moment. We were united as one nation again, in
harmony and peace with all our neighbors. This time history was kind
to us.

When we met in the Berlin Philharmonia for the official ceremony on the morning of October 3, our ears were still ringing with
the closing chorale of Beethoven's Ninth Symphony. We had heard
it the night before in the center of Berlin at the Gendarmenmarkt
during the ceremony bidding good-bye to the German Democratic
Republic: joy—the divine spark.

But now it was time to get back to work. All the tasks already
accomplished and those still pending were much too complex and the
consequences far too incalculable for us to expect flawless solutions.
However, everything humanly possible was done to achieve success.

Everyone had something to say, and we heard criticism from all sides. But none of us could do everything right, as I was well aware at every phase. But this truth did not free us from an honest, unavoidably critical review of initiatives whose consequences we face to this day.

From the outset it was clear that enormous financial help from the West was essential to unification. How would we raise these funds? Three days after the Wall was opened I had first spoken about the necessity of sharing. Helmut Schmidt asked Germans to make sacrifices of the kind Churchill had in mind in his "Blood, sweat, and tears" speech. In several precursors to my Berlin address to the Bundestag and Bundesrat on October 3, 1990, I appealed to the ruling authorities: "Today it is often said that no one will suffer any deprivation, provided only that the increase in goods is apportioned correctly. This is all well and good in the marketing language of contemporary political communication. But on sober reflection, we will realize that this course will only postpone the need for sharing. No road can bypass the recognition that to unite means learning to share. German unity cannot be financed with high-interest loans alone." Subsequent muttering in the hall came from the groups I had mentally been exhorting.

The early phase of unification saw a great majority of Germans in the West prepared to bear real sacrifices. Every political party made such appeals, and they resonated strongly. Left unspoken, however, was a clear signal from political leaders, given in good time, that unification must be accompanied by financial assistance from the West in amounts comparable to the event's magnitude, and that such aid must not and could not be financed out of growth earnings or a huge budget deficit. The reason for the omission was unfortunately only too obvious: The West German population must not be confronted with depressing news in an election year. Though a sense of community existed, it was never invoked. This omission proved serious on both material and human levels. All Germans are aware of and still feel its consequences.

Later, without a doubt too late, I seized the public initiative once more. I frightened more than one market economist and power politician by suggesting a second equalization of burdens. I'm sure there were opposing viewpoints concerned about possible bad effects on the economy and a long period of extensive administrative expenditures because of the disputes over distribution, which had grown more severe again, and the general Western sentiment. A heated debate followed. Kohl declared that he did not wish to introduce any new assessments and was intent on preserving a stable climate for investments, which domestically had mainly supported rationalization of production at the cost of jobs and for the rest had been sent abroad.

My prevailing concern was the internal connection between social solidarity and material effort. As a result we added only the most modest solidarity surcharge on the income tax.

Soon after the war the old Federal Republic had deployed a great equalization of burdens in favor of the twelve million driven from their homes. This distribution was not to be discharged from income but from capital, and this at a time when affluence in the West was only a small fraction of the height on which it stands today. The allocation ran its course with a great deal of administrative work, but not without a number of injustices. Nevertheless it became West Germany's outstanding achievement in its solidarity with the hard-hit expellees.

Now it was time for chapter two. It would be appropriate, just, and enormously supportive if Germans in the GDR could be made to feel—not in an anonymous governmental way but on a personal level—that we in the West were well aware of the heavy burden borne by East Germany. Without a doubt we West Germans had worked hard to achieve the level of affluence we now enjoyed. We did so in complete freedom under the favorable auspices of our international situation, first with strong support from the Marshall Plan and later with help from an expanding market in the European Community.

These opportunities were never available to the Germans in the East. And what sense would it make for our Basic Law to explicitly declare that we would act—even for those Germans who were denied participation—only if West Germans interpreted this to mean that affluence was meant for them and them alone?

The transfer payments that flowed for many years from the general budget to the Eastern provinces were huge. At first the West German people did not have a clear understanding of where such funds were found. The government had spared the people such information, preferring to lull them into a sense of security rather than prepare them to sacrifice. After all, it was important that they vote the right way. Only after some time and having grown suspicious did they begin to sense that the West would be affected immediately with higher taxes, assessments, payments into social security, and the consequences of the inevitable drastic emptying of the public coffers. All too often they felt that this was not a historically, moral, and humanely appropriate conciliation of all Germans but an increasingly dubious burden that favored ever more ungrateful fellow citizens in the East.

Clearly there was no stinginess in the sums that flowed from West to East to help achieve union. But how this help was mobilized led to a disassociation of the material from the human mission, the anonymous fiscal disposition from personally palpable participation. This phenomenon impeded internal union instead of promoting it. The total public debt of regional governments more than doubled between 1989 and 1996. More than 600 billion marks went to cover the costs of unification alone, and the solidarity surcharge was very far from covering the equalization of burdens. Private holdings in money and property were much higher than the public deficit, and the discrepancy between private wealth and public poverty reached its apex. Almost a doubling of government debt and interest burdens is a hard nut to crack.

During my weekly trips to the Eastern provinces I encountered many encouraging examples of helpfulness. Innumerable West Germans of all ages contributed their expertise and understanding on construction sites. Private as well as nonprofit organizations were at work, and sister-city pacts concluded in the time of partition did superb service. Our daughter Beatrice studied these alliances in the field and devoted her doctoral thesis to them under the title "Sisterhood in the Brother Nation." The West German people also gave spontaneous aid beyond their frontiers. Their willingness to help suffering people in the Soviet Union in particular was extraordinarily impressive.

Those were the good signs. In the majority of the population the enthusiasm over our newly won unification nevertheless gradually gave way to a much more sober mood. While unification had no noticeable effect on the personal lives of most people in the West—nor did they expect such an effect—it was quite a different story in the East, where unification became a daily, immediately perceptible process of read-justment. One woman wrote to me that the people were deeply grate-ful for liberty but had not realized ahead of time how much these changes would strain the nerves. Though they most fervently wanted to be rid of their regime, replacing so many elements of their personal lives from one day to the next with something new, something un-known, almost like saying good-bye to yourself, was more than a body could bear. And yet every life has its meaning and dignity. No slice of life is in vain, especially that of someone in need.

Uncertainty dominated questions of education, "settlement," jobs, property, and care of the elderly and small children. "It used to be that we were all alike, on a low level, and all of us had work," a man from Mecklenburg wrote me, while another declared, "In our souls we have not joined you yet." He join us? Why not the other way around? Was he to go the whole way alone? How far had we gone to meet him?

It probably could not have run any other course. We had known too little about each other's domestic situation; West Germans in par-ticular had been too ignorant about the East. Despite this ignorance the West set the course. It furnished enormous help, but it also caused great irritation. One example was the maxim "Restitution of compensa-tion." My wife and I drove with our youngest son, Fritz, to Potsdam to show him the home of his maternal ancestors. The last thing on our mind was claiming possession. I saw an elderly woman looking out a window and asked her if it would be all right for us to walk around the house. She answered drily, "Go ahead. There's nothing here you can steal."

I had a quite different experience in the company of a young man, a former sergeant in the national people's army, who thanks to his personality and abilities had quickly made his way after 1990 in the united Germany. He and I were stopped at a red light in a car near the Brandenburg Gate under the street sign "June 17 Street." Though this street leads directly to the old sector border to the East, it runs only through the Western part of the city. In reply to my question about his opinion of the street's name, he said, "If it were put to a vote, most West Berliners would want to keep it and most of the East Berliners would want to change it." When I asked why East Berliners would feel this way, he explained, "We don't want you to keep boasting about our heroic deeds. And it wouldn't do you any harm, either, to at least once feel what it means having to change street names all the time because the other side insists on it."

Such events in the previously divided city, while not unusual, are instructive and beneficial. After all, people cannot be expected to give up their beliefs, but they do need to expose themselves to the lives of the other side as often as possible, even daily. That is one of the unavoidable and central challenges facing Berliners today.

This was one reason that motivated me to hurry ahead in the selection of a capital and use the utmost of my authority as president in the process. I had been given the great distinction, first in Bonn and then as the first in the united Berlin, of being made an honorary citizen. Both times I honestly proclaimed my allegiance to the good chapter of German history that bears the name of Bonn in perpetuity. The ceremony was held in the Church of Saint Nicholas in Berlin on June 29, 1990. A debate about the future capital was not yet on the Bundestag agenda. I assured my audience that I would of course do my best to contribute to the parliamentary decision in favor of Berlin or Bonn, whichever way it turned out. But then I added my clear preference for Berlin as the capital. This was what we had promised in the old Federal Republic since the Basic Law went into effect, and so in my opinion the mission of unification demanded even more. "Only in Berlin do we truly come from both parts and yet are one. Politics must witness this daily at first hand, since it bears the responsibility for the permanent success of our unification. . . . In Berlin, as nowhere else, we have learned what partition means. In Berlin, as nowhere else, we recognize what unification demands of us. Here is the site for the politically responsible leadership of Germany."

My words met with both approval and criticism. Some West German politicians who in earlier years had often kept aloof from the old Federal Republic state were now overcome by anxiety about an enervation of the world of Bonn, which had become familiar to them. Most arguments from both sides were serious and went far beyond simple local interests, though there were a few exceptions. The owner of a bar in Bonn-Bad Godesberg hung a sign outside his establishment, "Weizsäcker not welcome here." Of course I had never patronized this bar and did not set foot in it until years later, when we were again of one mind.

Another year passed after my speech advocating Berlin as the capital before June 20, 1991, when the Bundestag, following a heated all-day plenary debate by a narrow majority, adopted a resolution naming Berlin the capital.

One of the most important reasons for promptly enacting economic, currency, and social union was concern that the stream of people emigrating from East to West was raising problems not easily solved. Political battles about the usefulness of the measures taken have long since been fought. Of all the consequences, one emerged quite soon for which the chief responsibility lay not with politics but with the parties to the tariff treaty. After currency reform, which had its share of problems but was a political inevitability, negotiations on adapting wages in the East to approximate those common in the West were taken up. Understandably from the social aspect but devastating economically, wages rose much more quickly than market and competitive conditions could handle. Dilapidated production equipment in the GDR was not the only reason, and not even the primary one, for the economic collapse and massive unemployment in the East. Orders and clients still came in, but with employers paying high wages in hard currency prices had to be raised to the point where customers were unable to afford them. The East's ability to compete in the global marketplace suffered massively from wages that were too high for the Eastern market.

A calamitous side effect was a complete lack of independent East German tariff partners. West German trade unions and employers were the primary negotiators of East German wage rates. In this process quite a few times the ulterior motive was to gain an edge to protect the West German position. It happened according to the motto "Only those who accept our conditions may compete in our markets"—and that meant accepting our wage rates as well. This attitude was a significant reason behind the disastrous course of events in the Eastern labor market.

Other former Eastern bloc companies not granted a warm drizzle of transfer cash from the West remained of necessity on a much lower wage and social scale, but this situation gave them an economic advantage. I vividly recall a function in Dresden in the early 1990s. Prime Minister Kurt Biedenkopf, speaking in the Semper Opera House, gave one of those gripping addresses that marked him as an expert analyst who dug deeper to understand the causes of our situation and draw the necessary long-range conclusions. This time he spoke on the mutually stimulating connection between living culture and economic performance among the people of Saxony. It was an illuminating hour. As an aside Biedenkopf noted that at the present time a high percentage of Saxony's budget still came from financial conveyances from the Federal Republic. At the conclusion of the speech Prime Minister Václav Klaus of Czechoslovakia, a guest at the ceremony, spoke to me on this point. A rigorous and first-rate market economist who took Margaret Thatcher as his model, he told me that Biedenkopf's remark had amused him because the Czech Republic received no transfer payments from abroad. This circumstance gave his country the distinct advantage of keeping currency adaptation, wage rates, social expenditures, and general requirements strictly within the framework of the market and the price range of the export clients. It also helped Czechoslovakia attract investments from large numbers of Western companies at these advantageous rates. We would see, he assured me: by the year 2000 the Czech economy would be doing better than Saxony's. This was vintage Václav Klaus. He never lacked self-confidence. But his prognosis that the blessings of his economic policies will come to pass is already in grave doubt.

Injustice, Justice, Reconciliation

Adaptation to new living conditions was at the foreground. But it alone could not bring about unity. To manage the present, another topic soon arose: How could we make peace with the past? Would this burden separate or unite us? It was one of the questions most difficult to answer.

When partition was imposed after the Second World War, both German states had to answer for the demonic injustices of National Socialism. But this answer was sought by focusing on completely different goals, and this difference resulted in two separate chapters of history in the past few decades.

For the sake of unification the old Federal Republic, which had grown strong, sought to safeguard its history and carry it forward without, if possible, interference from the history of the GDR. But East Germany had burning questions: Would a partitioned history be permanent? Could unification succeed under such conditions? This could hardly be expected. Granted that the West was only indirectly involved with events in the East, reality would not allow it simply to disclaim any responsibility for the heritage of the GDR, to declare itself, as it were, "not affected" by the destiny of others. Both parts make up the whole. We could become one only if we were united in our understanding of the past.

The former Federal Republic's most important answer to the past was its codified and practical constitution of a free, social, and democratic state. It has proven its mettle. Of course there was also a prolonged sleep and a mountain of silence, delay, and repression concerning our past. These revelations were abruptly resurrected once more in the generational conflicts of the late 1960s—with mixed results.

In East Germany the simple answer to the past was summed up in one word: "antifascism." It was essential to ideology and incorporated in the government. A considerable number of German Communist leaders put into office by the Eastern victor were legitimized by their own history of persecution during the Nazi period. For the general population, simple lip service to antifascism was considered a sufficient apology for the past. Then the years passed under increasing totalitarianism.

The SED state was not responsible for any offensive war or Holocaust. Its leaders were put into office and controlled from abroad. To discipline their own population, they created the state security organization (Stasi) and developed it into a system of domination without equal. Its methods included indoctrination and control, spreading fear among the people, coercing citizens, and blackmailing them into collaboration as the only alternative to being offered up themselves. Backbones were bent or broken in subtle ways, and in this manner cores of attempted resistance or self-preservation, of civil courage or guilt emerged.

Unlike the end of the Nazi period, when most victims were no longer alive and foreign powers ruled the land, now Germans were left to themselves with the burden of East Germany's past. Most of these victims live among us. There is a deep human need to reach as deeply as possible for historical, moral, and individual justice. Satisfaction for the victims and understanding among the culprits are sorely needed.

The importation of liberal laws from the West caused deep sighs in the East. "We expected justice and were given the constitutional state," was the response, by now proverbial, given by Bärbel Bohley, the civil-rights advocate. Is there anyone who cannot understand the sentiments these words conceal, who cannot sympathize with this anger when all too many misdeeds—including having people spied on, threatened, impeded in their schooling and professions—remain unpunished?

The constitutional state alone cannot accomplish everything, and yet it is an indispensable asset. Criminal law cannot sentence history or prior politics; the judge can only rule on whether personal behavior is punishable according to the laws prevailing at the time and place where the unlawful deed occurred. This limitation may morally benefit the wrong people as well. It is essential, not to protect the culprit but to protect all of us from our errors as contemporaries, as witnesses, or as lawyers with public opinions and documents. The constitutional state itself rests on the understanding that human beings simply do not have access to absolute justice.

When the law must render verdicts on deadly shootings at the Wall and especially on the ominous ambience of so-called government criminality, it faces complex tasks. It attempts as far as possible on the one hand not to violate the prohibition against retroactivity, the *"nulla poena sine lege"*—a problem difficult to resolve even during the Nuremberg Trials—but on the other to express our clear distinction between good and evil. It does so first by invoking the famous formula of Gustav Radbruch, the legal philosopher from Weimar, who said, "The contradiction between political law and justice must be so intolerable that the law, as an unjust law, must make way for justice." This is an argument from natural law, especially directed against the weaknesses of those statutory offenses that, though defined by law, we consider illegitimate in the real world. To safeguard the precarious balance, the law, in rendering verdicts, must further rely on the fact that even under East German law it can be applied only "in interpretations respecting human rights." The law does what it can.

It is highly unlikely that all attempts to reach fair verdicts will succeed. For example, consider the trials of the East German attorney Wolfgang Vogel. I will not comment on the various verdicts, only on the behavior of the prosecutor in charge of the case. Like every prosecutor he is obliged by law to seek out the truth and to find and evaluate incriminating and exculpating evidence, not to mobilize sentiments for his side. But he declared in public that Vogel was "the biggest slave trader of our century." Did he have any idea what he was

saying? Among the greatest slave traders of the last century were those
who lured and captured native Africans for sale into slavery in the
Americas. But Vogel was the indispensable counterpart to West German authorities in every government, from Erhart through Kiesinger,
Brandt, and Schmidt to Kohl, in opening the road to freedom for
untold numbers. Of course it matters that people were made to pay,
whom they had to pay, and where the large sums sent from Bonn
ended up. We in the West have no reason to regret the funds expended in this effort. Even during the final phase of flight from the
GDR to refuge in West German embassies, cooperation with Vogel
was essential to Genscher, Schäuble, and Seiters. If the prosecutor,
whose duty is to uncover the truth, contends quite generally and
widely repeatedly that there was "slave trade" in the GDR—and of
course he is free to do so—what I find wrong is that he does not talk
about a West-East mafia of the slave trade. Such a glaring lack of
knowledge and understanding of the historical-human facts can only
make the task of passing legal judgment much harder than it would
otherwise be.

But a passionate discussion of good and evil in the Cold War
past, beyond the confines of criminal law, was necessary. It was of
central significance for the individual and for an understanding of how
the East German system worked and the forms of coercion it employed. What freedoms did the system allow? To what extent was it
impossible to evade the willingness to adapt, to what extent was the
system forgivable? What room remained for concealment or resistance? What moral responsibility may be assigned to an individual?
How can such responsibility be seen, described, admitted, overcome?

And with the evidence of deep inner conflict, of an ambiguity
that seems inevitable, who can bring about retrospective clarity? Especially if that judge comes from the West and cannot repress the insight
that, given the conditions prevailing in the SED state, he would have
done the same?

No final reckoning can help us advance in such moral and spiritual questions. Anyone who lived through that time as a victim, cul-

prit, or merely a contemporary who witnessed what happened must gain insight into the course of events. This process must also include opening up Stasi documents. Even if they do not furnish unassailable evidence for every case—we need only read Günter de Bruyn's memoirs, *Vierzig Jahre* (Forty Years)—they are indispensable for investigating facts and modes of behavior. Many give a picture of human weakness while others display extraordinary civil courage.

Our methods of working through and evaluating these documents reflects the Stasi's thoroughness in recording all incidents. No other former Eastern bloc nation had anything like our Gauck Agency (the commission headed by Joachim Gauck to examine Stasi records), though some countries discussed setting up such an organization. This agency is and will remain open-minded. Whatever consequences result from the documents, these actions must be justifiable for public as opposed to private reasons. This is especially true in matters dealing with public agencies and services.

In the area of human relations we would do well to focus on the goal of finding peace among ourselves, united in an understanding of the past. This objective includes making every effort to determine the difficult truth about what really lies in our past. This truth reaches deep into personal relations. To anticipate an unexamined harmony means pretending that such harmony exists, and such an attitude does not result in peace.

Premature leniency is nothing short of an insult to the East Germans says the theological jurist and Saxon minister of justice Steffen Heitmann, who adds, "Prosecuting criminal guilt and identifying moral guilt serve the cause of truth." Who could disagree? In the same context he also writes, "For the process of social integration we require in Germany the concept of reconciliation is not useful." His words make us realize that this complex topic will engage us for a long time to come.

Even if we cannot compare the SED informer state to the apartheid power against the black people of South Africa—the crimes that have come to light in that country are monstrous—there are nevertheless parallels. In South Africa the Nobel Peace Prize laureate Archbishop Desmond Tutu is the spokesperson for an agency dealing with the past. Its spirit is reflected in its name: Truth and Reconciliation Commission. Nelson Mandela was imprisoned for twenty-seven years; he also preaches reconciliation. When a journalist asked Tutu about the possibility of forgiveness, he answered simply, "You forgive by forgiving." In the same discussion Joachim Gauck, the clergyman from Rostock, replied to the Archbishop, "I can forgive only those who know what they did. The culprit must 'arrive' at his deed, his sin." To which Tutu replied, "We are all sinners," and later, ". . . they are human beings. They are capable of change. Without this belief in change there is no hope." Only God knows whether we human beings will ever truly arrive at our guilt.

It is certain that the greatest strength behind real change remains the recognition of one's own failings. It offers the most sincere point of departure for a chance at a new beginning. But as human beings we are open to and need encouragement. We can all learn from our mistakes. What matters is helping others in that effort, not leaving them fixed in the past but guiding them into and trusting them with a new future. This step is vitally important to secure the liberty in which we wish to live together. Reconciliation among a divided people cannot succeed without truth. But truth without confidence in reconciliation is inhuman.

The Churches in East Germany

It is no wonder that we entrust clergymen with such examinations of the past. They offer the best hope of a painful but healing cleansing of wounds. In our case the examining institution was governmental: the Federal Commission for Documents of the State Security Service of the Former GDR. The "Commissioner," Joachim Gauck, was not given specific orders. He is a clergyman, even though he temporarily gave up his office in favor of this new mission. He won my full respect when we worked together on church initiatives during the time of partition. As a longtime member of the EKD executive and head of the Protestant Conference, I came to know many clergymen and lay members of the Protestant church bodies and saw their struggles and conflicts. The churches themselves represent an important and enlightening chapter in the history of the German Democratic Republic.

According to their mission and self-understanding, the churches are independent of the state. This situation is obvious in the Roman Catholic Church; it is the universal church. In German history the relation of the Protestant Church to the state contains some disastrous chapters as well, as the motto "Throne and altar" attests from the nineteenth well into the twentieth century. Under National Socialism there were the unspeakable "German Christians," with their so-called Reich bishop. But the core of Protestant Christians gathered against this aberration in the so-called Confessional Church.

In East Germany atheism was the ideological program of the ruling SED. The churches were openly opposed to its official state ideology from the outset. They were the only nationwide, organized, and internally connected institutions not in the hands and under the open scrutiny of the political rulers. Precisely for this reason they were the most intensely targeted objects of the SED's suspicion, surveillance, and covert attempts at infiltration, sometimes tempting, sometimes threatening.

The churches never had a chance to revolutionize the SED state as such. Their most important task was to preserve the Proper of the Mass—that is, administering the sacrament, preaching the gospel correctly, holding congregations together, and helping and ministering to people in need.

Even these tasks brought the churches into perpetual conflict with the political leadership, for example in education, even beyond the tensions caused by religious instruction and confirmation. The constant confrontations with the minister of popular education, Margot Honecker, tended to be even more vicious than those with her husband, Erich.

The churches protected the rights and promoted the dignity of all people regardless of their strengths or weaknesses. With this in view they did their utmost to help the handicapped. They expended great effort and compelled the SED government to gradually grant a minimum of respect and funds for this group.

The SED used a twofold strategy in its attempt to control the churches. On the one hand it engaged in open harassment and prohibitions as well as massive covert surveillance. Conversely, the longer the GDR was in existence and the more severe its internal problems grew, the more the SED tried to befriend the churches and use them to soften antigovernment feelings among the population. At times this latter tactic gave rise to the supposition, especially in the West, that important segments of the churches had come to an arrangement or possibly even entered into an alliance with the SED state.

The sinister concept of a "church within socialism" was a further cause for Western concern. But that is no reason to misunderstand it. Pastor Gauck and his Mecklenburg bishop, Heinrich Rathke, liked to call it "the church for others," an accurate appellation. The upright and brave Berlin bishop Gottfried Forck never hesitated to quote the ideas of the young Karl Marx from "Contribution to the Critique of Hegel's *Philosophy of Right*: An Introduction" to the effect that there is "a categorical imperative to overthrow all conditions in which man is a degraded, an enslaved, an abandoned, a despised being." In this way Forck harshly countered actual and existing socialism with humanistic concerns.

The large organization that goes by the name of *church* doubtless encompasses the strong and the weak, and in its inevitable contacts with the government employs heads of churches who display extremely varying degrees of intelligence and courage. We also have shocking examples of clerics who made themselves available for spying. People are what they are.

On the whole, however, the churches preserved their independence from the state. They not only did not become its instrument, they could not even be turned into instruments of stabilization. The longer the regime lasted, the more the opposite became true. The churches also publicly embraced freedom of conscience. Under great pressure they advocated draft resistance for reasons of conscience under the slogan "Swords into plowshares." The advocacy for freedom of movement from East to West was started by the churches, and they were the voices appointed to denounce the SED's horribly restrictive frontier policies. Time and again the Eastern clergy sought advice, help, and collaboration from the West in order gradually to attain the human rights detailed in Basket III of the Helsinki Final Act.

One of these men was theological jurist Manfred Stolpe, whose church had assigned him to maintain contact with SED committees and the state, including the Stasi. One of the most difficult and delicate of church mandates, it was carried out by Stolpe on his own responsibility and thought of in his own terms. West Berlin politicians do him a grave injustice when they abuse him as a man once "in the service of the Stasi." Stolpe never acted in the service of the Stasi—he served the church. The reasonable Bishop Johannes Hempel of Saxony and many others have confirmed this, as explicitly as was appropriate to the intraclerical experience of East and West.

The churches in the GDR were not resistance organizations directed against the government. But they did offer sanctuary to government opponents and human rights activists without inquiring into their faith and church membership. Churches were the only organizations with the necessary public space, which they utilized completely, although their efforts often made it more difficult for clergymen to hold their congregations together.

Before November 1989 open demonstrations for liberation started out from these protective church spaces. Then the representatives assumed leadership roles at the roundtables, where the great change was initiated.

On the whole the SED and Erich Mielke's Stasi lost their intense struggle to supervise, infiltrate, instrumentalize, and make puppets of the churches.

Party Strategies

Democracy and market economies are firmly rooted in liberty. In an open society the competition of political ideas, material goods, and spiritual concepts—and their prices—prevails. Democracy and a free market economy allow us to choose, to learn anew, to settle conflicts, and to solve them without violence. They are clever, rational—and comparatively impersonal inventions. They are not concerned with deep feelings, which, according to Ranke, determine the ways we live together. They warm the heart only sparingly.

After the initial unadulterated joy when the Wall fell, democracy and the market economy showed the way to unification. Together with great successes in foreign policy and the admirable help of many in the West, the moment of Western power came—the power of the market, of prices, of politics, of parties. Shops were brought outside the front door, supermarkets sprouted from the sidewalks, and glossy magazines touted their novelties with photos designed to seduce. But most especially on the way to making history, the GDR saw four election campaigns in the single year of 1990.

Their outcomes were not as surprising as many had expected. It was easy to understand that many in the East voted differently from the way their grandparents had during the Weimar Republic. They turned to the parties and people promising the greatest help and profit and which—thanks to their seats at the controlling levers of federal power—seemed to have the greatest influence. The Bonn government had the advantage over its opposition, especially as the latter—with its warnings, not always unjustified—aroused the impression that it was necessary to rethink everything from direction to pace, perhaps even the climax of everything about to happen.

Clear democratic perceptions emerged, which was helpful in itself. However, they also rested on campaign swings along Western lines that resulted in profound aftereffects felt even years later. One example was offered by Konrad Weiss, a fearless human-rights advocate, implacable accuser of the Stasi past, critic of recorder playing, and visionary of liberty in a unified Germany. He complained about his countrymen's unused opportunities, their persistent indolence and lost hopes. Weiss also felt that it was a revolutionary miracle for the East German people to start out into democracy without a charismatic leader. But now abruptly everything was to be just the same as in the West. He called it the "hour of the power-mad." "The West German parties invaded the country and buried everything that had just begun to stir." The "raid of the party strategists," to cite Weiss again, speaking in terms of power politics, may "have been a stroke of genius, but it had a devastating effect on morale in Germany."

These are harsh words. Whether we agree with them or not, the strategy of the campaigners was characteristic of our Western party system. I frequently addressed this topic publicly, even before the great change. Now the experiences learned in the course of unification were added. They motivated me to adopt a detailed position published as a collection of speeches, which created quite a stir.

Criticism of parties has a long tradition, and its motives and effects can be controversial. Political parties certainly do not have a tradition of being popular. During the Weimar Republic defaming the parties was frequently a simple way to express a vague antidemocratic position.

After the Second World War memories of those times remained. Now, however, the situation had changed. In the former Federal Republic, under Allied supervision for many years, the populace was satisfied with a government of representative democracy. A pluralistic party structure was quickly and successfully established to general approbation.

Nevertheless, after several sobering experiences a new discussion of the party system was heard. Many were reminded of Max Weber's statement, according to which the sights of the parties were set on plunder. The strongest resonance and controversy was created by Karl Jaspers in the 1960s with his essay "Where Is the Federal Republic Heading?" He warned against a road "from democracy to party oligarchy." He pointedly noted, "The parties are the state." In clear contrast to the position espoused by Carl Schmitt, with his general stand against parliamentary party rule, Jaspers saw his mission as advancing democracy and freedom by his criticism. He spoke out against an authoritarian state and for an ethical one.

Without a doubt the parties succeeded within the structure of our constitution to enlarge their power far beyond what the framers of the Basic Law could have imagined. In the Weimar constitution, parties were mentioned only in a negative way in the paragraph that noted that officials—but not parties—were servants of the citizenry as a whole. Today's constitution specifies, "The political parties contribute to developing political objectives." This is an almost comically classic example of constitutional understatement. Finally the federal constitutional court gradually began to take the parties as seriously as reality warranted. Given their power, today they practically overshadow our five constitutional organizations without themselves possessing such legal standing. In fact, party leadership and coalition bodies even make the decisions on political guidelines. The way our government really works, this can hardly be otherwise. But our constitution does not provide the controls for the arrangement that it stipulates for the constitutional organizations.

As we all know, the parties also reach deep into the structures and personalities behind the electronic media. The media are protected by the constitution and vitally important to our democratic functioning. The honorary title of "fourth estate" they neither need nor deserve. In their private electronic sector, a steadily growing element of a free economy, a tendency is emerging not only to lessen the critical function of the ruling parties but to transform politics into entertainment. Whenever controversial verbal duels and personal power struggles can be presented as championship games or whodunits, the media give the parties lots of time and space. The difficult, complex, less entertaining, fundamental questions, on the other hand, get short shrift. Politicians play along, since the process gives them more air time.

For different reasons than those prevailing during the Weimar Republic, it is equally important today to be wary when the power of the parties is criticized. In contrast with the first German republic, today we are a people firmly shaped by party democracy, a large society that cannot govern itself directly by periodic meetings on the village green. This situation became clear in East Germany as well after the crucial weeks of change in the winter of 1989–90, when the people took charge. Because political tasks are complicated, a blanket position dictated by emotional consensus is not sufficient for governance. Official controversy is not bad but necessary. Decisions must be justified— that is, represented by individuals, not by anonymous masses. There can be no alternative to a representative system.

As is widely known, the Western democracies accord varying importance to political parties. For example, in the United States they are far weaker than in Great Britain and Germany. In the United States television debates determine the outstanding candidates, who campaign on their personal initiative and spend great amounts of money they have raised themselves. I prefer our financing of parties, in spite of all its problems.

No democracy can get along without a pluralistic party system; it is part of its definition. Parties fight for mandates and power; their struggle for majorities is necessary and legitimate. But precisely because the party system is essential, its weaknesses must always be countered.

The same difficulty emerges over and over again: the strain between problem solving and power struggles. The competition between party proposals is intended to expose the best way to deal with actual tasks; that is the meaning behind the system. Because only those who are elected can bring their proposals to completion, they must fight to gain power.

It should, however, remain clear and understood by the public that power is only a means to arrive at the goal of problem solving. But when the dispute about real tasks degenerates into a mere vehicle for winning power, the system's credibility is at risk. I am not talking here about tilting at windmills in attacking party tactics. I bring up the subject only because it touches on our success in achieving unity. The Federal Republic is dominated by parties steering a Western course. They must also deal with the PDS (Partei des Demokratischen Sozialismus—Party of the Democratic Socialism), which has its roots in the East and is the successor party and heir of the former SED. Dealing with it is not only a question of campaign tactics but also one of a historical-ethical nature. Currently the PDS, though it does not pursue a clearly defined ideological program, is the focal point for feelings of protest and resentment. New and young voters choose it generally not out of nostalgia for Honecker and Mielke but as an expression of ordinary anxiety that—rightly or wrongly—they ascribe to Western self-involvement, while the PDS deals with these Eastern worries primarily by staying active in local politics.

When election campaigns of the Western-directed parties—especially the two large popular parties—pay attention to the PDS, they are primarily concerned with separating themselves from the PDS by defining it as a neo-Communist cadre unwilling to repent the past. If one Western party eases up on its eagerness to combat this red peril, the other party immediately exploits this perceived weakness. Massive power interests are also at work. Meanwhile solutions to problems— that is, everyday anxieties of many PDS voters—go unattended. For them the Western strategy of aloofness has a calamitous effect. It "appears," wrote Konrad Adam in the *Frankfurter Allgemeine Zeitung*, "no longer as dealing with an authoritarian party but as disregard of the people in the East." At present it is the PDS that profits as a party whenever elections are held.

The strain between means and ends in the party struggle, between power struggles and problem solving, will always be with us. It is the job of the voting citizenry to make certain that the party system remains credible. It is therefore important for the process of unification that the East's everyday problems will continue to be visibly taken seriously even in Western election campaigns, though without giving them preference by neglecting the "We Are We" slogans of an Eastern party.

Collaboration Between Chancellor and President

Along with my great respect for Chancellor Kohl's achievement in winning the world over to German unification and his historically significant commitment to a unified Europe, I also felt some anxiety and had cautionary questions concerning the domestic course of events. Together with my critical stances on reconciliation with Prague, financing reunification, the party system, and the problem of the PDS, other divergencies between Kohl and myself began to emerge. However, this did nothing to hinder collaboration between chancellor and president. We followed the constitution to the letter, as the Basic Law stipulated. Our actions reflected the differences in our offices. It is not the head of state's task to interfere with the executive's authority to set guidelines and determine everyday policy. The advisability of extending his sphere of responsibility was widely discussed, but I never thought it crucial. The president's mandates are to ask questions independently and impartially, propose ideas to carry out the voters' desires, and especially to map out long-term social directions. This far-reaching authority makes it difficult enough to do everything it demands.

Kohl and I met regularly and with mutual trust. In Bonn our offices were right next to each other, separated only by a long garden wall. In the language of protocol, the point where one can cross from one property to another is significantly called the "breach in the wall." At this point we met or passed guests of state from one to the other. This is how Bush and Gorbachev, Mandela and the Emperor of Japan, and one day even Honecker made their way through the "breach in the wall" from president to chancellor.

The two offices worked in close collaboration. Important co-workers in the chancellery, especially Horst Teltschik and Eduard Ackermann, called on me from time to time, and sharing information and impressions was useful to both sides.

Of course now and then we were on opposite sides of an issue. Our job then was to turn these differences from occasions for dispute into supplementary insights that enhanced our work. The British writer Timothy Garton Ash, who has given us one of the most important books on Eastern European policies, described the relation between heads of government and state in different countries and came to the conclusion that, compared with the others, Kohl and I were "one of the most effective couples in recent years at the head of a European state." It is not up to me to say whether this is true; it certainly should be.

Development in the Southern Hemisphere

During all my time in office public attention was focused primarily on Atlantic and European questions, on policies affecting East and West Germany. In these efforts it was essential to preserve development aid and collaboration from damage. Though Heinrich Lübke made significant contributions to this end, new efforts were always required to overcome the serious disappointments and obstinate prejudices implicit in north-south policies. To reach my objectives, it was not nearly enough for me to speak on television from time to time on programs devoted to fighting world hunger and similar catastrophes. I needed to go on personal inspection tours and draw my own conclusions in the field; then I could be more effective back home when asking for help.

My first trip in 1985 took me to the Sahel region of West Africa, at that time ravaged by a long-lasting famine. A German army transport plane loaded with supplies flew us to western Sudan near the border with Chad, where large refugee camps were waiting for aid. On the one hand we had to provide immediate help to alleviate the catastrophe and secure basic human survival in extreme want. On the other hand we had to furnish badly needed supplies so that the people could farm self-sufficiently: small wells, seeds, granaries, and tools. Bringing food was not enough; more crucially, we had to help people return to their villages rather than remain in camps, where there might be a meal today but no prospects for tomorrow.

Nor was government help alone enough. We found that German individuals could make perceptible contributions with even the smallest sums. Some heartwarming incidents occurred. In the Black Forest, for example, one class of schoolchildren was persuaded to organize a collection, and in their little town they managed to raise 400,000 DM for wells in Nigeria.

Traveling to Bangladesh, Mali, and Bolivia, I visited the poorest countries on their continents. In Bolivia the sharp decline in prices for raw materials, especially the collapse of the world market for tin, resulted in serious crises for the mountain people. In addition the country faced a burden of debt and a difficult battle against cocaine manufacture. The German and Bolivian governments collaborated effectively on a wide range of aid projects with churches, political foundations, and unions committed in the course of an old and proven friendship between Bolivia and Germany.

In Bangladesh, the most densely populated of the poorest nations on earth, I saw the astonishing activity of the Andheri Help Organization, founded by Rosi Gollmann of Cologne to remedy eye diseases widespread in that country. We visited a village school where a small medical team had set up its meager station to perform cataract operations on over a hundred inhabitants in a very few days. Rosi Gollmann's ophthalmologists and their assistants have gone about this work for years and in countless cases have created a helpful precondition for a new life.

Another project we went to Bangladesh to observe was a bank that made small, unsecured loans to women in the agricultural sector. Women's lives are particularly harsh in that country. Women own no land, have no income, and often have been abandoned by their husbands. As a result they and their children have no protection and are entirely dependent. However, with help from a small bank loan they can start an independent existence. The bank's experience is illuminating: When it loans money to a man, the first thing he does is buy a transistor radio or motorcycle; he thinks only of himself and the present. A woman, on the other hand, spends the loan on her children and housing; she takes care of others and the future. Remarkably, the bank rarely sees defaults on these loans.

We also visited a village lecture where a puppet play was performed to teach family planning. Practical advice was underlined with ethical incentives taken from the Koran.

I came to understand that extreme poverty in the famine zones and overpopulated areas of the world is the greatest social challenge of our day. Time and again I was impressed by the widely scattered private aid organizations in our population, in direct contradiction to the widely heard accusation that Germany thinks of development aid only in terms of financing the golden beds of African dictators. Collaboration in development primarily helps people to help themselves. Often it is in relation to reciprocal giving and taking, a mutual learning. But progress is still impeded by Third World debt, the declining prices of raw materials, the persisting protectionism of wealthy nations, and huge arms exports.

Preserving the Creation

Environmental protection was constantly on my agenda from my first day in office, and not only in the context of north-south relations. Industrial fairs, Berlin's annual Green Week, travels to the Eastern provinces, and almost every state visit abroad brought environmental concerns to the table—with the most disparate responses.

In Malaysia, Nigeria, Latin America, and the United States the tropical rain forest was a central topic. No one denies that it is the most important ecosystem on the planet. Each year wooded areas roughly the size of a Central European country are deforested. However, after just two or three harvests the cleared land is exhausted and not useful for further cultivation. In the countries I visited I was generally told that the governments were helpless and economically dependent on us. I was told that we were the ones who set prices, then demanded increased exports from them so they could pay off their debts to us. But because the prices of all other raw materials had fallen, they had nothing left but wood. Everywhere there was a feeling that the destitute cannot afford to treat nature carefully. Time passed as reproaches bounced back and forth. The destruction of the forests will indeed have foreseeable consequences on water supplies and the global climate.

In the United States, the leading world economic power, there is little evidence of a pioneering role as far as environmentally sound climatic policies are concerned. For example, domestically taxes on fossil fuels and other environmentally detrimental products are not raised. But the European nations are also moving at a snail's pace. All the way to my farewell address on July 1, 1994, I agitated for heavier taxes in Germany and the European Union in view of the carbon dioxide danger.

I occasionally ran into the most contradictory phenomena. During a trip to Malaysia we were shown an area of tropical rain forest covering several square miles, where we could clearly study two different enterprises from Germany. One was a wood trader, who bought trees and had them cut down and shipped abroad. The other, almost within sight of the first, was a reforestation project for the benefit, as it were, of German wood dealers in a hundred years.

Without a doubt many initiatives are along the right lines. Ecologically beneficial building materials are developed, the energy consumption of household appliances and heating installations is lowered, automobiles grow less noisy and use gasoline more sparingly. The environmental industry is a growth sector. But the general population must still bear the cost whenever the private market causes environmental problems not covered by the price. It is a social responsibility and sensible economic goal to make certain that prices tell the ecological truth.

Worldwide energy use is the central concern. Today 20 percent of the world's population consumes 80 percent of its energy. It is hard to believe that people in threshold and developing countries will accept this disparity forever, but global energy use at our high level would be devastating. Power savings and alternate forms of energy with fewer pollutants could make a difference. Humanity will run out of energy sources if we do not find alternatives in time. The question is how seriously we are searching.

The earth is older than humankind and will outlast us. It will shelter us only as long as we claim just that part of its energy we may legitimately appropriate—no more. We will never dominate nature. Instead, we are part of the life-preserving cycle. We will preserve our life if we do not destroy it but respect it.

Culture & Art

Among my tasks in the areas of domestic and foreign policy, development cooperation, and environmental matters, culture always played a central role—culture in the widest sense of the word. As we know, "culture" comes from the Latin word "to cultivate," to till, to deal sensitively with nature and our fellows. The objective of culture is to promote peaceful coexistence.

If we check the newspapers, we gain a different impression. They treat culture primarily as a pleasurable or irritating luxury that contributes little to solving the hard problems of daily life, has hardly any significance for the process of human integration, and tends to be expensive. As a result, readers will not find articles on culture alongside reports on politics. Instead, they are sparingly placed in the local pages or isolated close to the real-estate news at the end of the feature section. Any newspaper reader who lacks time, interest, or practice remains ignorant of cultural topics in the news. This state of affairs not only diminishes culture's importance, it also narrows the value of the principal sections of the newspapers.

Of course culture also includes works of art and music that can be evaluated only by experts, but culture deals with the whole and is not limited to the enjoyment of initiates. It affects the way we live by helping us to coexist humanely—people with their neighbors, one contestant with another, native with foreigner. Daring to be different and therefore keeping the peace—that is the lesson culture can teach us, and it is why culture is part of political guidelines.

Fortunately there are a few exceptions in the German forest of printer's ink where political questions are discussed in the feature section and cultural topics are moved to the front pages. These first pages are therefore often more interesting and reflective of life than in many publications with the standard format.

And yet the customary order remains a different one. It is revealing that lately "culture" can sometimes be found in the first section of our newspapers under a very specific rubric—discussions of the multicultural society. These include heated disputes about asylum, aid for refugees, immigration quotas, and reform of the antiquated right of citizenship. At stake is competition over apartments, jobs, and xenophobia.

These complex problems of competition are among the central questions of our day. On the threshold of the next century one of the most important and difficult tasks of our culture is to deal with the migrations of other nationalities over our new, open borders. How can we learn—under the conditions of an enlarged Europe and the globalization of our economy—not to close ourselves off while preserving our sense of having a homeland of our own? Our nation will benefit immeasurably from understanding other cultures and learning to respect them. By seeing all the differences in other peoples' ways of life and traditions, we recognize the universal kinship of human needs. By learning to understand them, we encounter ourselves. When the papers "open" with such cultural themes, they do not displace politics but take its substance seriously.

During my second term I saw the difficulties and confrontations as well as the growing willingness of Germans to deal better with problems of this sort. In East and West I visited evacuee groups, refugee camps, and temporary homes for people seeking asylum. After serious excesses against foreigners had been perpetrated we met in Rostock, Solingen, and Cologne. On November 8, 1992, the largest demonstration of the last ten years comprising several hundred thousand participants marched from Gethsemane Church at Prenzlauer Berg to rally at the city center on the Berlin Lustgarten. The protest concerned Article I of our constitution, which guarantees the inviolability of the dignity of all men, not only Germans.

Since the collapse of the Wall and the war in the former Yugoslavia, no other European nation has taken in as many foreigners as Germany. This influx repeatedly led to great problems and even clashes. At the same time it revealed the willingness of a broad majority not to leave all the work to the state but to personally and actively protect their neighbors, fellow workers, and schoolmates. The strings of lights in numerous cities during the winter of 1992–93 were only one sign of people's shared responsibility and helpfulness.

Promoting beneficial coexistence and easing tensions between nationalities by using culture requires more than open-mindedness and civil courage. The recognition that culture is an important budget item is also needed. In my farewell address of July 1, 1994, I turned once more to the budget directors, finance officials, and government heads in the nation, provinces, and communities with the request that they follow their hearts and minds. We have an untold number of cultural and artistic centers and cells in our country devoted to coexistence with culture of every type on stage, sports arenas, choirs, and orchestras. For the most part they are also models of the cost-use relation. They require less money than almost all other budget items, yet their effects are far-reaching and benefit all of society. Culture not only makes life more pleasant; in the end promoting culture saves money compared with paying the consequences of social unrest.

Encounters between politicians and artists do not always run smoothly in Germany. Art does not like to compromise; it seeks absoluteness and often feels most comfortable in opposition. But unwillingness to compromise in politics damages democracy.

In Germany art, science, thought, and everything else included under the vague umbrella of intellectual endeavor traditionally keep a conscious distance from political power. A tension carefully nurtured by both sides predominates, to the detriment of both.

Philosophy often interferes in political discussions without a willingness to participate in the struggle for power. Many justify this attitude by invoking Immanuel Kant's skeptical statement against Plato's philosopher-king "because the possession of power inevitably impairs the free judgment of reason." But in Germany we only wish for the works of the mind and imagination to participate critically and support democracy, not to place them on the throne. We coexist in a time of transition, of a shift in our consciousness, of a search for new directions. This effort should include all the creative minds, cosmopolitan citizens, and intellectuals. They are not needed to solve problems, nor are they wiser about what should be done. But it is helpful if they can tell us what not to do. It is more of a hindrance than a help when left-leaning intellectuals challenge the right to philosophical and moral duels and when right-wingers ride roughshod over moral teachings and "the intellectuals," meaning the left. And yet the highly extolled "mainstream" is neither constant in mass nor standing on firm ground. Little tolerance is shown in either direction.

Loners open new perspectives, even if they are too easily assimilated into the mainstream. It is worthwhile to cite as one example Botho Strauss's observations in *Anschwellender Bocksgesang*, in which he considers what is liberal in our society. The liberal person no longer appears liberal in himself but is ever more inconsiderately liberal as the outspoken opponent of antiliberalism. He is cordial to foreigners, not for the sake of the foreigner but out of anger at his xenophobic countrymen. Strauss is not fair to everyone in this judgment; some Germans are certainly friendly to strangers for their own sake. Nevertheless, we should test our understanding of what is liberal against his judgment. We can only learn.

In some countries fruitful reciprocity between mind and power are part of the national tradition. Early in my presidency I encountered a living example of this fact in the Mexican poet Octavio Paz, for whom I gave the address in Saint Paul Church in Frankfurt when he was awarded the Peace Prize by the German book trade long before being awarded the Nobel Prize for literature. Few people have given as much thought to Latin America's social, political, and cultural problems as Paz. As his poems enriched world literature in the second half of our century, he also gave significant aid to his continent in its struggle for identity. His penetrating voice became the conscience of the culture and freedom fight in Latin America. As well as founding a secondary school for campesino children in the Yucatan, he fought on the Republican side in the Spanish Civil War and later served his country as ambassador to France and India.

Other outstanding intellectuals and literary figures held important political posts in South American countries, including Pablo Neruda in Chile, fellow combatant and friend of Salvador Allende; Ernesto Sabato, head of the Argentinean commission to expose the crimes committed by the generals' junta in Argentina; and Mario Vargas Llosa, a presidential candidate in Peru.

Our neighbor France is also blessed with outstanding writers who by word, deed, and office shouldered part of the public responsibility for their nation: Paul Claudel, Jean Giraudoux, Saint-John Perse, and others.

In Germany such efforts are modest. At one time Willy Brandt successfully persuaded intellectuals to actively participate in political initiatives and even election campaigns. But this was an exception in party politics.

However, one institution in Germany, still vital to this day, owes its existence to a recognition of the mind by the state. It is the order of "Pour le Mérite," created in Potsdam by Frederick the Great, whose initial still decorates the medal. The earliest recipients included Voltaire and Jean d'Alembert. Frederick did not yet make a distinction between state and mind. He neither thought of himself as the state personified, on the model of Louis XIV, nor did he have any reason to doubt his membership in the world of the mind. It was in a way his recognition of his own person, in his inner and lone disputes between power and mind, one of the most impressive qualities of this monarch. It is all the more valuable among the treasures of German history because later relapses of mindless power brought this state into great ill repute.

After Frederick Wilhelm III in 1810 limited the order to military achievements during a time of intellectual flowering, Frederick Wilhelm IV established the peace category of the Pour le Mérite in 1842 for science and the arts, as it exists now. The initiator and first chancellor of the order was Alexander von Humboldt.

After the order all but died out during the Hitler period, Theodor Heuss saw to its revival at the beginning of the Federal Republic. He created a new relationship between the state and the "republic of the mind" and made the order independent in the choice of recipients and in all other aspects. By virtue of his office the Federal President became Protector of the Order.

In this way I too came into close yearly contact with this illustrious circle, whose membership includes Carl J. Burckhardt and Sarvepalli Radhakrishnan, Oskar Kokoschka and Thornton Wilder, Elias Canetti and Karl Popper, Adolph Butenandt and Friedrich August von Hayek. Theodor Heuss defined the essence of the order as the "contemporary commentary on intellectual history." But the order remains conspicuously noncommittal. It takes no part in the tensions between mind and power and as an organization takes no position on contemporary problems, not even intellectual history. More than once the wish for an "articulate Pour le Mérite" was publicly uttered. I too appealed repeatedly to the order and urged that in this time of epochal historic change it do its part to contribute perceptibly to the search for direction and shift in consciousness instead of remaining silent, pleased with its uniqueness. Every member voices individual opinions in his way. But as a whole there is silence. This is regrettable though apparently inevitable.

In general one of my most intensive interests as president was to invite intellectually and artistically prominent figures to conversations, introduce them to the public in the sense of politics as I understood the term, and honor them. That most of them responded positively and went along with me are among the best experiences and true privileges of the office.

Of course I had some different outcomes as well. I recall an encounter with Joseph Beuys, who arrived with a motley crew of companions, sat down without taking off his hat, and left the conversation to his friends, who talked fairly wildly, when general political subjects came up. But as soon as he began to speak about education and art, he impressed me with his demands that we not allow ourselves to be divided into artists and nonartists. All people, he said, participated in shaping life and the future and thus did artistic work in their own way. That too is an expression of culture as an essential element of politics.

Heinrich Böll died soon after I became president. I had met him earlier through a mutual friend and had come to value this always alert, often bitter, and at times cheerful polemicist. Internationally he was the most famous German writer of the postwar period. At home he remained much admired as well as controversial, a situation he never shied away from. When I privately attended his funeral with only a few participants, I was loudly criticized without reason by various sides.

We also held a ceremony to celebrate Wolfgang Koeppen, the novelist and critic from the Adenauer period. Thomas Bernhard and Hans Magnus Enzensberger, Jurek Becker and Stephan Hermlin, Ulla Hahn and Marcel Reich-Ranicki, all spoke in praise of him, as did his publisher Siegfried Unseld, to whom Koeppen owed a great deal. Two years later we were visited by the entire "Group 47" to honor its founder, Hans Werner Richter. He had created something extraordinary. For twenty years after the war this radical group was virtually the only one with a really new idea and institution created entirely from scratch, with no ties to anything left over from the Weimar Republic. Its effects went deep and continued even after the group voluntarily disbanded. Under Richter's leadership it contributed significantly to the importance and reputation of German postwar literature, not least by its internal "reading workshop" with its spontaneous, reciprocal, substantial, and skilled criticism. Among our guests at the ceremony for Richter were Ilse Aichinger and Günter Grass, Walter Jens and Hans Mayer, Wolfgang Hildesheimer and Peter Härtling, Alexander Kluge and Günter Kunert.

Albrecht Goes, the musical genius, came to a celebration of his eightieth birthday. His infallible sensibility had a lasting effect in East and West, even if it was his intention "to speak only very sparingly of great and important things." His historical conscience and alert senses always let others deal with what he thought of as important things.

We met in April 1989 to celebrate Golo Mann. I began by praising his *Deutsche Geschichte des 19. und 20. Jahrhunderts* (History of Germany in the Nineteenth and Twentieth Centuries), in which he demonstrated a moving empathy with human destiny. When I mentioned that I wished the work had told us more about his judgment of Prussian reformers and Bismarck, even if at the expense of stories from Vienna, he spontaneously declared his adherence to the house of Habsburg. His inimitable gift of storytelling was an expression of his poetic talent, organized by research. In his work research had humility, and poetry had substance. He ended his letter of thanks by noting that, now close to the end of his life, he could be satisfied with his work: "Not great, but not small either, and sometimes stimulating, even helpful—and subservient to no one. That is enough."

Although our republic is neither patrician like the Villa Hammerschmidt in Bonn nor regal like the Hohenzollern Bellevue Castle in Berlin, these residences of the federal president were both highly suitable for their task. At the beginning of my term Professor Otto Meitinger of Munich started a thorough renovation. Thanks to his rich historical and practical experience, sure sense of style, and devoted commitment, his work turned out splendidly. He found a harmony among the architectural triad of utility, permanence, and beauty, and eventually won over everyone involved, from preservationists to technicians. My wife and I took great pleasure in working with him.

The leading supervision from the official side for this and all subsequent construction, including the new office building in Berlin next to the Bellevue Castle, was in the hands of Walter Karschies. The office of the federal presidency had wooed him away from the chancellery in the friendliest fashion. His grasp, energy, and never-failing helpfulness created indispensable preconditions for work and life in the residences.

The Bundestag budget committee had collaborated pertinently and constructively in these projects. In order to regulate expenses with the necessary scrutiny, it held an extraordinary session in Bellevue Castle solely for this purpose.

Museums and private collectors generously loaned works of art for the residences. German impressionism and classical modernism prevailed in the Villa Hammerschmidt, with works by Max Liebermann and Max Slevogt, Lovis Corinth and Wassily Kandinsky, Paul Klee and Max Ernst, Emil Nolde and Ernst Ludwig Kirchner. A portrait of Brahms by Willy von Beckerath hung in one room, and many visitors mistook it for Karl Marx, much to our amusement. In the reception room a priceless large painting by Ernst Ludwig Kirchner depicting in predominantly violet colors a lightly clothed girl playing the mandolin hung diagonally behind the principal guest's seat. The British Queen and Gorbachev, Mandela and Pope John Paul II, all were reproduced in press photographs with the extraordinary musician behind them.

In Berlin's Bellevue Castle pictures from Prussia's history hung alongside contemporary works from East and West Germany, among them works by Jörg Immendorff and Bernhard Heisig, Wolfgang Mattheuer and Werner Tübke. Gerhard Graubner created two oversized painted pillows following the color palettes of Turner and Monet for the large hall where concerts, readings, performances, and receptions were held. During functions when the lights were dimmed these invited meditation. In the castle's reception hall I gave President Roman Herzog an exhibition of mythical-symbolic works by Markus Lüpertz.

The huge grounds surrounding the residences flourished under my wife's special care and were used—along with official welcomes to guests of state—annually for large outdoor functions, especially for youth groups including older and younger scholarship and fellowship holders of the Alexander von Humboldt Foundations. They came with their families from every corner of the world and spent a year in Germany pursuing their studies. Under the impulsive and ingenious care of Heinrich Pfeiffer, head of the foundation, a large global Humboldt family grew into the most fervent friends of Germany around the globe. One of my greatest pleasures was to encounter the gratitude and loyalty of these fellowship holders in almost every country we visited.

My duties as host in the two residences had two distinct focuses. Because I cultivated foreign relations in my work, one central task concerned visitors from abroad. My other focus was on cultural evenings and honoring achievements of our compatriots in all spheres of activity. In the presidential office Erich Milleker was primarily responsible for conceiving the ceremonies. Milleker, whom I had "inherited" from Helmut Schmidt's chancellery, had a sure artistic overview and extensive network of personal connections. Together with the proven protocol chief of the office, Horst Arnold, he made sure that planning and organization were as creative as they were efficient. A number of unforgettable events resulted, thanks to young and unknown artists along with world-famous ones.

Regularly in December the youthful prize winners of the German Music Councils performed one of their first public concerts in Bellevue Castle. The violinists Gidon Kremer and Pinchas Zukerman, the violist Juri Baschmet, the cellist Yo Yo Ma, and the pianist Anatol Ugorski, all played for us. Lady Gwyneth Jones, the British soprano, joined with the countertenor Jochen Kowalski, a Berliner, to perform "O Fortuna," a piece of chamber music inspired by musicologist and critic Klaus Geitel. Dietrich Fischer-Dieskau performed "The Human Voice" one afternoon. The harpsichordist Edith Picht-Axenfeld worked with the Anglicist Wolfgang Clemen to present a program on "Shakespeare and Music." In Salzburg the Vienna Philharmonic and Berlin Philharmonic are rivals, but in Bellevue Castle soloists from both symphonies play happily together, conducted by James Levine. The wealth and quality of the performances are as difficult to describe as is the pleasure of the audiences we invited.

I developed close and amicable ties with the Berlin Philharmonic Orchestra while serving as governing mayor. Now the orchestra earned my gratitude with its willingness to give an annual "Federal President's benefit concert." For no more than an eventual reward in heaven, some significant musical events came into being. Even before the fall of 1989 one of these concerts was planned featuring Beethoven's *Missa Solemnis*. The performance took place immediately after government unification in October 1990. Daniel Barenboim was the conductor, and the concert was a benefit for the preservation of Jewish graves in Berlin. Barenboim is an old, dear friend who for many years was one of the instigators of Berlin musical life. He helped determine its nature and became a generous, responsible partner in the capital; his very life inspires goodness in others. When the Wall collapsed, he arrived at once and made music among us. Then I shared in the successful conspiracy that persuaded him to become the director of the Berlin State Opera Unter den Linden, where he raised the state orchestra to new heights in spite of overwhelming material difficulties. Julia Varady, Waltraud Meyer, Siegfried Jerusalem, and Dietrich Fischer-Dieskau accepted his invitation to participate in "my" benefit concert. The success was overwhelming.

Once I even took part in a Barenboim performance. To celebrate his fiftieth birthday, I was allowed to sing in a small choir conducted by Zubin Mehta. It was a new composition involving sight reading, and my only baritone colleague, a world-famous operatic star, sounded far better than I did, but twice I had to poke him so that he would not miss his cue.

Fortunately for me, I also had an opportunity to do a good deed for the orchestra. With Milleker's active help I succeeded in winning over two of the outstanding conductors of our day for benefit concerts. The older of the two was Sergiu Celibidache. Originally from Romania, he had become a genuine Berliner. Because of his close collaboration with Wilhelm Furtwängler, he had taken over leadership of the Berlin Philharmonic Orchestra in the postwar years and kept it until 1952. Then their ways diverged in painful ways. Since then he had had no further contact with the orchestra until now, after thirty-eight years, he declared himself willing to come, to the great pleasure of the orchestra and very expert Berlin audiences. Two splendid performances of Anton Bruckner's Seventh Symphony thus came about.

The other conductor was Carlos Kleiber. At times it seems that he exists only in dreams, because his shyness dictates that he remain as invisible and inaudible as possible. But when he does arrive for a concert, the dream becomes reality. He was cordially willing to conduct the first of these benefit concerts. Then his and the orchestra's generosity toward me culminated with their farewell concert for me in the Berlin Philharmonia on the third-to-last day of my second term in office. They were playing to benefit the "neighbor in need," Bosnia. And they played in a way no one in the audience will ever forget. Before they struck up, the trustees made me an honorary member of the orchestra, an invaluable honor. Nevertheless, in my old age I will forbear returning to the instruments of my childhood—the violin, the trumpet, and the trombone. The honor will last as long as I live, in spite of my skills, without my forcing the orchestra to submit to my musical interference.

Instead I was happy expecting to follow the motto of the old orchestra manager Wolfgang Stresemann, son of onetime Reich Chancellor Gustav Stresemann, whose book is titled *And at Night in the Philharmonia*. Our concert hall is a haven where music lovers feel at home surrounded by a knowledgeable and sensitive audience, especially thanks to Claudio Abbado, another friend, who since 1989 has served as artistic head and permanent conductor of the Berlin Philharmonic. We should also thank him for his intensive promotion of future generations of musicians, for example in the European Gustav Mahler Youth Orchestra, which he founded. We are further connected through Cambridge University in Great Britain, where in June 1994 I was awarded the last academic honorary degree of my presidency along with Abbado.

In both residences evenings of music were supplemented with evenings of literature and science. The actor Martin Benrath performed his production *Die Fülle des Wohllauts* (The Wealth of Melody), adapted from Thomas Mann. Martin Walser—who said we must unite with the course of history, letting the historical process work for us, to adapt to it even as we infused it with our own interests, as it were—

read from his work *Breakers*. Maria Wimmer read from Marcel Proust's *Remembrance of Things Past*, and actors Bruno Ganz and Otto Sander transformed themselves into Ivan Turgenev and Gustave Flaubert to read from these writers' correspondence. Günter de Bruyn and Günter Grass joined in discussion one evening in Bellevue Castle, leading to a dispute on the response of the federal army to Picasso's gigantic work *Guernica*.

What began with Wolfgang Koeppen and Golo Mann grew during the course of my presidency into a planned series of invitations for outstanding figures on the occasions of their birthdays. We celebrated the eightieth birthday of Cardinal Joseph Höffner of Cologne, a leading Christian social teacher whose contributions to basic values and the image of man sharpened political consciences. Among the guests were Cardinals Franz König from Vienna, Franciszek Macharski from Cracow, and Jean Marie Lustiger from Paris.

To our great pleasure Karl Carstens came to celebrate his seventy-fifth birthday in his former residence, the Villa Hammerschmidt. Together with Chancellor Kohl, several provincial prime ministers, and Roman Herzog, the president of the federal constitutional court, we honored his personal humaneness, practical intelligence, and prudent adherence to the constitution.

Other birthday parties were held to honor Hans Georg Gadamer, the Nestor of German philosophy who was as old as our century; Theodor Eschenburg, with his inimitable gift of grasping history and telling its story; Otto von Simson, the researcher and teacher of European history of art and culture who was forced to emigrate during the Nazi period and returned shortly after the war to fill young people with new courage.

As if to turn the dreams of my childhood into reality, one day I found myself between Heinz Rühmann and Max Schmeling, who had been kind enough to accept our invitation.

To celebrate Bernhard Minetti's eighty-fifth birthday, the leading lights of the theater appeared, among them Marianne Hope and Jutta Lampe, Martin Held and Klaus Maria Brandauer, Claus Peymann and

Dieter Dorn, George Tabori and Klaus Michael Grüber, Elisabeth Trissennaar and Hans Neuenfels.

On the occasion of Countess Marion Dönhoff's eightieth birthday we held a party, a family get-together, and a modest official ceremony. We learn from Kleist and Fontane that it is women above all who preserve the stature, dignity, and inner strength of Prussia. In this sense Marion Dönhoff is the century's outstanding Prussian.

We also honored Hermann Josef Abs on his ninetieth birthday. With intelligent and confident independence he not only headed his house but brought honor to his country and won respect for it. The high number and sterling quality of his acts to benefit German culture and art can hardly be counted. These include his initiative for the Beethoven archive and the chamber-music hall in Bonn, for which the city of his birth thanked him only inadequately. Many jokes and witticisms have been noted by him and about him, which he enjoyed. Thus he took part in our celebration by exhibiting his unique self-confidence, as he said that he would graciously let others share in the pleasure he took in himself.

The celebration of Willy Brandt's seventy-fifth birthday caused the biggest stir among these functions, which had become public knowledge. Friends and statesmen from all over the world attended, including Presidents Mitterand of France, Mario Soares of Portugal, and Carlos Perez of Venezuela, the heads of government Helmut Kohl, Franz Vranitzki, Gro Harlem Brundtland, Ingrar Carlsson, Shimon Peres, and Mieczyslaw Rakowsky, as well as Jacques Delors, Bruno Kreisky, Walter Scheel, Rainer Barzel, Hans-Dietrich Genscher, and other close friends of Brandt. We spoke about "birthday politics"—and why not? Participants from Germany and abroad were as one in honoring Willy Brandt for his courageous and firm will to find a peace free of illusions. One of the leading figures in the postwar world, he was a singular and thoughtful loner who never played at heroic decision making. Often the butt of abusive attacks, he was not thick-skinned. He grew into power but never uttered authoritarian words. And his public apology at the Warsaw Ghetto was like the signal sent by a stranger to the powerful. His person removed any contradictions between power and morality.

When he declared during his first speech as chancellor that now democracy would come into its own, the opposition party, which had just concluded twenty years of democratic government and into whose ranks I had been voted, of course did not accept this statement without objecting. But when he used Adenauer's anchoring in the West for his Eastern policy, both parts grew into a cohesive whole, a policy never seriously debated—a valuable common property. The ceremony honored gratitude and the objective of living in a world where breaches can be healed. That is how we celebrants felt, and that was the sense of public reaction during this extraordinary event.

Final Month in Office

During the final months of my presidency I took a number of trips abroad. Before then I had met with Pope John Paul II three times in the Vatican and twice in Germany. My farewell visit was to Rome as a regular state visit at the suggestion of the Holy See, which was a rarity. When it comes to pomp and regulations, papal protocol put everything I had seen in my forty-nine official state visits in the shade. Let me describe it briefly.

The papal chamberlain calls for the guest in his quarters. Saint Peter's Square is closed off. After the drive into the Vatican, the Swiss Guard, with plumes and halberds, pays tribute and plays the visitor's national anthem. The prefect of the papal household and—of supreme importance for the Curia—the special delegate for the Vatican state, together with the papal chamberlains and commandant of the Swiss Guard, lead the guest to the second loggia, where a procession forms on the way to the papal chambers. The gentlemen of the antechamber and the deacons lead the way. In the first chamber the excellencies, the almoner, and the pope's throne assistant await the guest. The march continues through the Sala Clementina, then the Sala Ambrogio, and finally to the Sala del Angelo, each room more sumptuous than the last. In each chamber some members of the procession remain behind. Only then do we enter the Sala del trono, where the Pope welcomes his visitor. While the almoner and the throne assistant remain in the adjacent Sala del tronetto, the pope invites his guest to a personal interview in the library, the most modest of all the chambers crossed until then, where a painting of the resurrection by Perugino, Raphael's teacher, hangs on the far wall.

Later the reception and guest delegations are invited to join us and stand at their places. The Pope and the guests give speeches. Modest presents are exchanged. The Pope then leads the visitor back through several rooms and takes his leave. The processional arrives at the chambers of Cardinal Angelo Sodano, the Papal Secretary of State, who heads the Vatican government. After a personal interview he delivers a political address in the large Sala Regia, according to Vasari the "most handsome and richest chamber in the world," and introduces the heads of the numerous diplomatic missions at the Holy See to the guest. Thereupon the whole procession returns to the Damascus Court. The band plays the papal anthem. The guest leaves to return to his embassy because the Papal Secretary of State along with German Cardinals Razinger and Meyer will be arriving shortly for the return visit.

This description is merely a pale reflection of reality, because the historical uniqueness and wealth of the palace and its chambers are as impossible to fully picture as the perfectly measured solemnity of each movement. No current monarchy has preserved even a fraction of the protocol ceremonial that the Vatican offers state visitors. The whole is a vivid record emphasizing the consciousness of one's own solitary rank, combined with respect for the visitor.

Despite the undiminished protocol, the personal talks ran off as directly and easily as one could wish. The Pope prepared an altogether warm reception for us. The Vatican had never recognized the partition of Germany. The Pope had helped bring about the collapse of the Wall, for which I thanked him. Conversely, he was impressed by our nation's willingness to help great numbers of war victims, refugees, and asylum seekers. He thanked me especially for my commitment to further German-Polish relations.

A few months before my visit the Vatican had issued the encyclical "Veritatis splendor" expressing the Pope's anxieties, which he discussed clearly and explicitly with me: Those in the East were not the only ones struggling with the political and economic changes to the system. The West too suffered increasingly from a subjectivist misunderstanding of freedom. Its growing ethical laxness brought with it a danger of damaging democracy.

In this as in all earlier conversations with the Pope, one topic was the relationship between denominations. Germany is the country of the Reformation, where Catholic and Protestant Christians exist in roughly equal numbers. The theological rapprochement between Catholics and Lutherans in our country has advanced to the point where both agree on Luther's exculpation teachings, the most controversial religious topic during and since the Reformation. There are still differences, however, in the ecclesiastical understanding of offices and practice of church services. I had repeatedly and personally submitted to Pope John Paul II the same request I made in 1986 at the closing session of the Aachen Catholic Conference before fifty thousand participants: Millions of marriages and families in Germany are "denominationally mixed." It would be an encouragement and a gift to them and to us all if we could be fully admitted as guests to services and celebrations of each other's Eucharist. The feast we celebrate represents Christ's love. Can't this help in bringing all churchgoers closer together? Being forbidden to worship at each other's houses contributes more to de-Christianizing the family than to strengthening its faith. The Pope in his paternally benevolent manner listened in silence.

On my visit to Rome I called on my counterpart, President Oscar Luigi Scalfaro, whose courage and trustworthiness decisively help Italian democracy deal with the country's multiparty system. I also had a reunion with his predecessor and my friend of many years, Francesco Cossiga, who never minced words when it was important to guard against grievances. I also had a fruitful exchange of ideas about Europe with the intelligent Prime Minister Carlo Ciampi.

Václav Havel thought up an extraordinary way to mark the end of my time in office. He invited seven heads of state from Central European nations to Litomyšl, a city in eastern Bohemia, the birthplace of Bedřich Smetana, one of the leading composers of Czech music.

The Czech Republic, Poland, Slovakia, Slovenia, Hungary, Austria, and Germany were represented.

We met in the city's large renaissance castle to hold a discussion about Europe. Each of us added his own note to this concept that, though shaped by history, was not unencumbered. The other six agreed that their fears faced Eastward while their hopes turned to the West. This made it easy for me to allay concerns articulated in the French and British media even before this meeting, according to which Germany might once again loosen its ties to the West in order to become a leading power in Central Europe. For this two-hour discussion among the seven of us, I had been cleverly seated under a large painting glorifying the victory of Prince Eugene against the French near Höchstedt on the Danube during the Wars of Spanish Succession. But it was and remains quite evident that Germany's current close relationship with France is absolute and irreversible and that our role in Central Europe is focused on helping the reform democracies of Eastern Central Europe enter the European Union. At the same time I expressed more clearly than my colleagues an urgent message to the Russians to refrain from any striving for hegemony along their western borders.

At the end, along with the others, Havel handed me a seventeenth-century etching of a map of Europe designed more to reflect the artist's wishes than historical reality. Each of us looked for our own country on the print, and President Thomas Klestil of Austria was forced to note that the artist had distributed all the lands of the Habsburg monarchy among its neighbors so that it disappeared entirely. It seems that the idea of Central Europe has always been an occasion for dispute.

There followed final calls to our closest neighbors: Queen Beatrix and Prince Claus in The Hague, François Mitterand in Paris, and Queen Elizabeth II in Great Britain.

My last official trip, four days before I left office, was to the country whose fate and relations with Germany were the first to concern

me. It was also my introduction to international politics—our neighbor Poland. I enjoyed a cordial reunion with President Lech Wałęsa
and old friend Tadeusz Mazowiecki. The central event of the trip was
a conference devoted to the German objective of bringing Poland
closer to Western Europe and including France in this work as much as
possible. This trilateralism was our primary aim.

My final month in office was busy with visits and visitors. My
wife and I hosted a large garden party in Berlin's Bellevue Castle to
honor volunteers from East and West. These indescribably varied nonprofit arrangements and private initiatives had leaders and workers
committed to benefiting others without compensation. They expended
time and energy but did not lose them as they regenerated their own
beings. By assisting their fellows in need, they see society differently
and much more realistically than do those who think only of their own
professions and pleasures. Many also aid the handicapped, who can
teach us to understand disabilities simply as a difference. Granted,
society sees disabilities as a kind of difference, but a difference that is a
disadvantage, almost a punishment. It is difficult but necessary for us
all to overcome such prejudices as much as possible. There is no standard of what it means to be human. It is normal to be different. Those
who assist the handicapped help themselves and are not looking for
thanks. The intention of our party was to thank them and to publicize
their good work.

As it had done for my predecessors, the federal armed forces bade
me good-bye with a ceremonial playing of taps in Bonn. Familiar with
this solemn tune for many years, I had often visited the army, observed
its exercises, spoken at conferences of commanding officers, taken part
in contentious debates with soldiers at Protestant Conferences, and
exchanged ideas with commanders in the circle of NATO partners.

The playing of taps in the dark grounds of the Villa Hammerschmidt, lit only with torches, was something quite different. In the
military service, where I spent some years, taps means the end of the
soldier's free time At one time a piper and drummer marched through
the inns and beat on the kegs' taps to indicate that no more beer was

to be drawn. Here, on June 27, 1994, it symbolized the end of my
service to the state to which I had dedicated myself ten years earlier.
At the same time it was our final function in the Villa Hammerschmidt
and in Bonn, a function resonant with gratitude for the memorable
history of the Bonn republic. One of its achievements was transforming the old special role of the military into a normal democratic element of our civilian society.

Members of my president's office were invited to celebrate with
gratitude and cheerfulness, but also with sadness over our imminent
separation. Working with the men and women in my office made me
feel good to a degree I had never before thought possible. The office
of federal president is a relatively small one, with about 150 employees, making it possible to strike up personal contacts and relationships.
In the course of my ten years this circumstance made working together
a pleasure—at least for me. Of course the head of the president's
office, Meyer-Landrut, made it very clear in his jocular speech how far
I was from being an ideal boss. An ideal boss, he said, should not know
too much and certainly never question, while I—horribile *dictu*—had
been a semi-Socrates, constantly and persistently questioning, aware
that I knew nothing. I prepared my speeches as if they were word
games without an ending, without winners or losers. No one could
understand the adventurous creation of the final draft.

A burlesque television report later claimed that Siedler Verlag of
Berlin would publish the departing president's memoirs within three
months, in time for the Frankfurt Book Fair. Because time was so short,
a ghost writer had been engaged. A Hamburg magazine, the joke went
on, had even printed that the choice was well-known journalist Konrad Kujau.

A few close coworkers during my years as president who had
earned my special thanks left the office with me. Along with the head
of the office, Undersecretary of State Meyer-Landrut, who had
reached retirement age, his far younger deputy, Undersecretary Mein-
hard Ade also resigned. We had met in the early 1970s when we all
had worked on the Basic Program. During my time as governing

mayor of Berlin, Ade was speaker of the senate. He ran his office in a manner appropriate to his nature: he rarely spoke, but when he had something to say, it was intelligent and reliable. Neither he nor I liked public-relations campaigns. Later he assumed leadership of the domestic department in the president's office. His strategic thinking was indispensable to the office, and he was noted for the good atmosphere he created among his coworkers.

Henning Horstmann, the speaker of the office; Jürgen Heimsoeth, my personal consultant; and Barbara Minkmar, head of my secretarial division were friends with whom I had worked almost every day. My sadness about our coming separation grew steadily. All three had come from the foreign office, which had loaned them to me with a heavy heart and to which they returned. It was a personal and professional blessing, demonstrated anew each time, to recognize challenges, withstand crises, and share emotional moments with them in the daily course of events and on numerous trips.

Horstmann personified trustworthiness. The media took him seriously because he was always well informed, unconditionally reliable in the information he imparted, warmhearted, and yet quite willing—to the point of physical action—to observe the rules of the office. Heimsoeth was known as The Director by our staff. His unerring intelligence and critically loyal spirit proved themselves invaluable in all of our numerous discussions. Barbara Minkmar retained her confident overview in every situation. For anyone who ever had to deal with the secretariat of the federal president, starting with myself, she became the incarnation of competence and understanding, helpfulness, tact, and charm.

It would give me great pleasure to mention many other coworkers. After my departure they continued in their positions—to the satisfaction of my successor, I am certain.

Literally in the final hours of my ten years we hosted the constitutional agencies in Berlin—the presidium of the Bundestag and Bundesrat, the chancellor and vice chancellor, the new president of the federal constitutional court, named the previous day, the prime ministers of the provinces, and the chairmen of the party parliamentary groups. It was both a serious and cheerful gathering. I took temporary leave from all my colleagues of many years with a saying from the Talmud: It is not possible to complete the work; it is not allowed to abandon the work.

The following day, July 1, 1994, we met in the Reichstag in Berlin for my successor's swearing in. I was given the floor one last time. My first thoughts and heartfelt wishes were for the new federal president, Roman Herzog, and his wife. We were all certain he would set about his work with experience and intelligence, a sober mind, wit, heart, and courage.

In connection with the process of unification the talk returned to the German nation. Together with our partner countries we are on the road to consolidation in Europe, our historical and overarching task. There is no other plane than Europe on which to stake our claim in the world, but there is no other plane than the nation on which to safeguard our democracy.

A nation is not an abstract concept fixed for all time. It is constantly re-created in the intellectual-political awareness of its citizens. As Ranke noted, it is determined not by rational prudence alone but also by strong emotion. It is related not only to ethnic roots and geography, to language and culture, but also to great events and tasks. After our long partition the joy at unification in Germany ran deep. Though the change was not brought about by awakening a constitutional act ratified by the total population and a sharing of burdens that affected all citizens but was felt to be just, we are united by our shared history and our will for a common future. This is the defining concept for our nation.

After partition we must accept jointly the whole heritage of our past, its good and difficult chapters or, to use the words of the French historian of religion Ernest Renan, share the responsibility for its renown and its repentance. The nation of the Germans did not come into being with Bismarck, nor did it die out with Hitler. Even the postwar period is part of our joint heritage.

We also have our will to a shared future, our task-oriented patriotism. We want to exist in freedom, from one person to the next, from generation to generation, from native to immigrant, from German to neighbor, from man to nature. If we are confident—confident in ourselves—we can build confidence.

At the end of my farewell address I thanked everyone for the time we had shared and said, "Ladies and gentlemen, Madame President, I have ended my time in office. The baton is passed. Fortunately you have survived me."

At this point the official minutes note, "Laughter."

To Live in Freedom

The secret of happiness is freedom, said the ancient historian Thucydides, and the secret of freedom is courage. Until recently oppression was tolerated and sacrifice was common. Courage marked the struggle for liberty. Today we Germans live united in a free democracy. Especially in the light of the past, we all have reason to be grateful.

As long as the irreconcilable systems of West and East confronted each other in the Cold War, freedom derived its validity and power from the need to contend with the opposite side and defend against its dangers. But triumph over serfdom was not enough. Less than ten years since the dictatorships of the East have passed away, anxious voices are already pointing out that it is easier to topple an authoritarian regime than preserve a liberal system from its own internal collapse. Our job is to overcome the weaknesses of freedom.

The happiness resulting from the collapse of the Wall and the joy over unification did not, fortunately, lead to national excesses. But there are fewer signs of a wave of inspiration than of sobering.

The Germans in East Germany bore incomparably more difficult burdens that resulted from the war, including living under foreign rule and the brutal control of the Stasi. Most led decent lives under the most difficult conditions. When the system of actual socialism collapsed, not least from its own massive economic weaknesses, it nevertheless left behind deep spoors in human attitudes.

The West experienced few changes. Its free political and economic systems proved to be superior—not least because of their numerical superiority. More than three-quarters of citizens eligible to vote live in the former West German provinces. The leadership of nearly all associations, organizations, and parties has remained Western to this day. The effort to preserve the West German reality as well as West German possessions is evident.

In the meantime open borders and increasing global influences permanently altered the situation. Dramatically increased unemployment is its most severe human and material sign. On the basis of economic and social problems, even deeper questions address the internal strength of freedom itself. On the one hand these questions are about the structures of our freedom and on the other, about our personal attitudes as free beings.

Our structures are democracy and the market economy, free systems in an open society committed to competition. Special interests and government programs must be measurable against alternatives. The market of opinions and offers decides the level of success. But how does this sober efficiency distinguish us from the merciless principle of natural selection predicated in Charles Darwin's research? Where and how does our freedom demonstrate its power to civilize, its ethics?

To begin with, freedom protects us from a calamitous claim to absolute truths, which humans do not command. The open society, according to Karl Popper, can expose slips and errors. Instead of demanding the greatest happiness for the greatest number, we should somewhat more modestly look for the smallest degree of avoidable pain for all. This is, at heart, a humane, ethical postulate of honesty.

The founder of the market economy we espouse, Adam Smith, stressed the necessity of this civilizing influence. Coordination of the many participants in the market, each with private interests, is aimed at achieving an optimum in supply. Selfishness, allowed to choose freely, brings far greater success for all than any state-run planning and control of the market. But, according to Smith, this free market can function only within the context of a community that protects itself against outside incursions, maintains a domestic legal system, and provides the services people require but which do not promise material gains: education, infrastructure, and not last social justice—in other words, Popper's minimum of avoidable pain for all. Today we must add environmental protection to this list.

No market can long survive in freedom without a society that perceives the interests of the totality. Economic success in the former Federal Republic depended on taking seriously Adam Smith's postulate of a free market in a state of social justice. Understanding and reason on all sides will continue to be necessary in the future, and a reciprocal understanding between economy and politics will remain indispensable. A policy lessening competition and questioning the striving for success in the markets would in the long run merely undermine public efficiency and supply for the citizens. An economy indifferent to its underlying social structure for the sake of prices and gains eventually endangers its own success. The businessman acts intelligently on his own behalf if he also considers questions of the common weal. The honorable merchant is not an ethical anomaly but someone who has a reasonable understanding of his own and society's interests. Our civilization cannot be slimmed down to social Darwinism. The structures of freedom must prove themselves in this undertaking since the human face of freedom is at stake.

In the last resort, however, our personal attitudes make the difference. Plato has already described the dangers of insatiably free men unwilling to endure the least submissiveness. The unspeakable phrase "the politics of indifference" can be misused as a curtain behind which people retreat into privacy without concern for communal life. Some make policy; others are content with indifference. But indifference about what or whom? About politics? Why not about oneself? If freedom is the secret of democracy, then it is the freedom to participate and share in responsibility.

When oppression ruled the country, the members of the White Rose, whose courage allowed them to face death, broadcast their appeal: "Tear the cloak of indifference that you have wrapped around your heart. Decide before it is too late." Their leaflets advocated, not a particular form of government, but the necessity of an ethical attitude in social participation. Today the situation is no different. To live in freedom is not a question of life and death as we stand at the threshold of the next century, but it is the crucial challenge to our future civilization and to the courage of the next generation.

Sophie Scholl, a member of the White Rose, wrote a motto in her diary as her own guideline: *"Il faut avoir l'esprit dur et le coeur doux"* (Jacques Maritain)—"an indomitable spirit and a caring heart." Even the Psalmist pleads for a pure heart and a new, sure spirit.

This is of prime importance at all times. We cannot control history, but we are part of it. We are not only affected by it, we also bear joint responsibility for it. We are reminded of this truth by a Spanish proverb in its ancient wording: God is a good worker, but he likes a little help.

Appendix

"FORTY YEARS AFTER THE WAR"
Speech in the Bundestag, Bonn, May 8, *1985*

I

Many nations are today commemorating the date on which World War II ended in Europe. Every nation is doing so with different feelings, depending on its fate. Be it victory or defeat, liberation from injustice and alien rule or transition to new dependence, division, and alliances—May 8, 1945 is a date of decisive historical importance for Europe.

We Germans are commemorating that date amongst ourselves, as is indeed necessary. We must find our own standards. We are not assisted in this task if we or others spare our feelings. We need and we can look truth straight in the eye—without embellishment and without distortion.

For us, the 8th of May is above all a date to remember what people had to suffer. It is also a date to reflect on the course taken by our history. The greater honesty we show in commemorating this day, the freer we will be to face the consequences with due responsibility.

For us Germans, May 8 is not a day of celebration. Those who actually witnessed that day in 1945 think back on highly personal and hence very different experiences. Some returned home, others lost their homes. Some were liberated, while for others it was the beginning of captivity. Many were simply grateful that the nightly bombings had passed and that they had survived. Others felt, first and foremost, grief at the complete defeat suffered by their country. Some Germans harbored bitterness about their shattered illusions, while others were thankful for the gift of a new start.

It was difficult to find one's bearings straightaway. Uncertainty prevailed throughout the country. The military capitulation was unconditional, placing our destiny in the hands of our enemies, for whom the past had also been terrible. Would they not make us pay many times over for what we had done to them? Most Germans had believed that they were fighting and suffering for the good of their country. Yet now it turned out that their efforts were not only in vain and futile, but had served the inhuman goals of a criminal regime. Most people felt exhaustion, despair, and renewed anxiety. Had one's next of kin survived? Did a new start amid these ruins have any sense? Looking back, people saw a dark abyss of the past, looking ahead, an uncertain, dark future.

Yet day by day something became clearer that must be said on behalf of all of us today: the 8th of May was a day of liberation. It liberated all of us from the cynical system of National Socialist tyranny.

Nobody will, because of that liberation, forget the grave suffering that was just beginning for many people on May 8. But we should not regard the end of the war as the cause of the massive flight, expulsion, and loss of freedom that followed. The cause goes back to its outbreak and to the advent of the tyranny that brought about the war. We should not separate May 8, 1945 from January 30, 1933.

We truly have no reason today to participate in victory celebrations. But there is every reason for us to perceive May 8, 1945 as the end of a false path in German history, an end bearing seeds of hope for a better future.

II

May 8 is a day of remembrance. Remembering means recalling an occurrence honestly and purely so that it becomes a part of our very being. This places high demands on our truthfulness.

Today we mourn all the war dead and those deaths caused by National Socialist tyranny. In particular we commemorate the six million Jews who were murdered in German concentration camps.

We remember all nations who suffered in the war, especially the countless citizens of the Soviet Union and Poland who lost their lives. As Germans, we mourn our own compatriots who perished as soldiers, during air raids at home, in captivity, or during expulsion. We remember the Sinti and Romany gypsies, the homosexuals, and the mentally ill who were killed, as well as those who had to die for their religious or political beliefs. We commemorate the hostages who were executed. We recall the victims in the resistance movements in all the countries which we occupied. As Germans, we pay homage to the victims in the German resistance—among the public, the military, the churches, the workers and trade unions, and the communists. We commemorate those who did not actively resist, but who preferred to die than to violate their conscience.

Alongside the endless army of the dead arises a mountain of human suffering—suffering for those who perished; suffering from wounds or encripplement or barbarous, compulsory sterilization; suffering because of air raids, flight, and expulsion; suffering due to rape, pillage, injustice, forced labor, torture, hunger, and hardship; suffering because of fear of arrest and death; suffering because of the loss of everything which one had falsely believed in and worked for. Today we sorrowfully recall all this human suffering.

Perhaps the greatest burden was borne by the women of all nations. Their pain, renunciation, and silent strength are all too easily forgotten by history. Filled with fear, they worked, bore human life, and protected it. They mourned their fallen fathers and sons, husbands, brothers, and friends. In the years of darkness, they ensured that the light of humanity was not extinguished. After the war, with no prospect of a secure future, women everywhere were the first to lend a helping hand to set stone upon stone. They were the "rubble women" in Berlin and everywhere. When the men who had survived the war returned, women again had to step back. Owing to the war many women remained alone and had to spend their lives in solitude. It was thanks first of all to women that nations did not disintegrate spiritually in the wake of the destruction, devastation, cruelties, and inhumanity, and that they were able slowly to pull themselves together after the war.

III

At the root of Nazi tyranny was Hitler's immeasurable hatred of our Jewish compatriots. Hitler had never concealed this hatred from the public, but made the entire nation a tool to implement it. Only a day before his death on April 30, 1945, he concluded his so-called last testament with the words: "Above all, I call upon the leaders of the nation and their followers to observe painstakingly the race laws and to oppose ruthlessly the poisoners of all peoples: International Jewry." Hardly any country has in its history always remained free of blame for war or violence. The genocide of the Jews is, however, unparalleled in history.

Perpetration of this crime was carried out by a few people. It was concealed from the eyes of the public, but every German was able to experience what his Jewish compatriots had to suffer, ranging from simple indifference through hidden intolerance to outright hatred. Who could remain unsuspecting after the burning of synagogues, the plundering of Jewish shops, the stigmatization of Jewish citizens with the Star of David, the deprivation of rights, and ceaseless violations of human dignity? Whoever opened his eyes and ears and sought information could not fail to notice that Jews were being deported. The nature and scope of the destruction may have exceeded human imagination, but, in addition to the crime itself, too many people, including many of my own generation, who were young and uninvolved in planning the persecution or in carrying it out, tried not to take note of what was happening.

There were many ways of not burdening one's conscience, of shunning responsibility, looking away, keeping silent. When the unspeakable truth of the Holocaust then became known at the end of the war, all too many of us claimed that they had known nothing about it and had not even suspected anything.

There is no such thing as the guilt or innocence of an entire nation. Like innocence, guilt is not collective, but personal. There is acknowledged or concealed individual guilt which people proclaim or deny. Everyone who directly and consciously experienced that era should today quietly ask himself about his involvement in these awful events.

The vast majority of today's population were either children then or had not been born. They cannot confess guilt of their own for crimes that they did not commit. No discerning person can expect them to wear a hair shirt simply because they are Germans. But their forefathers have left them a grave legacy. All of us, whether guilty or not, whether old or young, must accept the past. We are all affected by its consequences and liable for it. The young and older generations must and can help each other to understand why it is vital to keep memory alive. It is not really a case of "coming to terms" with the past. That is not possible. It cannot be subsequently modified or undone. However, anyone who closes his eyes to the past is blind to the present. Whoever refuses to remember this historical inhumanity is prone to new risks of infection.

The Jewish nation remembers and will always remember. As human beings we seek reconciliation. Precisely for this reason, we must understand that there can be no reconciliation without remembrance. The experience of millionfold death is part of the very being of every Jew in the world, not only because people cannot forget such atrocities, but also because remembrance is part of the Jewish faith.

"Seeking to forget makes exile all the longer; the secret of re-demption lies in remembrance."

This oft-quoted Jewish adage surely expresses the idea that faith in God is faith in the work of God in history. Remembrance is experi-ence of the work of God in history. Remembrance is the source of faith in redemption. The experience creates hope, creates faith in re-demption, in reunification of the divided, in reconciliation. Whoever forgets this experience loses his faith. If we for our part would forget what has occurred, this would be not only inhuman, but would under-cut the faith of the Jews who survived, and destroy the basis for recon-ciliation. We must erect within ourselves a memorial of thinking and feeling.

IV

The 8th of May marks a deep caesura not only in German history but in the history of Europe as a whole. The European civil war had come to an end, the old world of Europe lay in ruins. "Europe had battled itself out," as the German historian Michael Stürmer put it. The meet-ing of American and Soviet Russian soldiers on the Elbe became a symbol for the temporary end of a European era.

Certainly all this was deeply rooted in history. For a century Europe had suffered under the clash of extreme nationalistic aspira-tions. The Europeans had great, even decisive influence in the world, but they were increasingly incapable of arranging their life with one another on their own continent. At the end of the First World War, peace treaties were signed but they lacked the power to foster peace. Once more nationalistic passions flared up and became linked with the distress of society at that time.

Along the road to disaster Hitler became the driving force. He created and exploited mass hysteria. A weak democracy was incapable of stopping him. And even the powers of Western Europe—in Chur-chill's judgment naive but not without guilt—contributed through their weakness to this fateful trend. After the First World War America had withdrawn and in the thirties had little influence on Europe.

Hitler wanted to dominate Europe—and by war. He looked for and found a pretext for war in Poland. On May 23, 1939—a few months before war broke out—he told the German generals: "No further successes can be gained without bloodshed . . . Danzig is not the objective. Our aim is to extend our *Lebensraum* in the East and secure food supplies . . . So there is no question of sparing Poland, [and the decision remains to attack Poland] at the first suitable opportunity . . . In this, justice or injustice or treaties play no role."

On August 23, 1939, Germany and the Soviet Union signed a nonaggression pact. The secret supplementary protocol made provision for the impending partition of Poland. That pact was made in order to give Hitler an opportunity to invade Poland. The Soviet leaders at the time were fully aware of this. All at that time who understood politics realized that the German-Soviet pact meant Hitler's invasion of Poland and hence the Second World War.

This does not diminish Germany's responsibility for the outbreak of the Second World War. The Soviet Union was prepared to allow other nations to fight one another so that it could share in the spoils. The initiative for the war, however, came from Germany, not from the Soviet Union. It was Hitler who resorted to the use of force. The outbreak of the Second World War remains linked with the name of Germany.

In the course of that war the Nazi regime tormented and defiled many peoples. At the end of it all only one *Volk* remained to be tormented, enslaved, and defiled: the German people itself. Time and again Hitler had declared that if the German nation was not capable of winning the war it should be left to perish. Many nations became victims of a war started by Germany before we ourselves became victims of our own war.

There followed the division of Germany into zones of occupation agreed upon by the victorious powers. In the meantime, the

Soviet Union had marched into all countries of eastern and southeastern Europe that had been occupied by Germany during the war. All of
them, with the exception of Greece, became communist states.

The division of Europe into two different political systems took
its course. True, it was the postwar development which cemented that
division. But without the war started by Hitler it would not have
happened. That is what first comes to the minds of the nations concerned when they recall the war unleashed by the German leaders.
And we must think of that, too, when we ponder the division of our
own country and the loss of large parts of German territory. In a sermon in East Berlin commemorating the 8th of May, Cardinal Meissner
said: "The bleak result of sin is always division."

V

The arbitrariness of destruction continued to be felt in the arbitrary
distribution of burdens. There were innocent people who were persecuted and guilty ones who got away. Some were lucky to be able to
begin life all over again at home in familiar surroundings. Others were
expelled from the lands of their fathers. We, in what was to become
the Federal Republic of Germany, were given the priceless opportunity
to live in freedom. Many millions of our countrymen have been denied
that opportunity to this day.

Learning to bear the arbitrary allocation of varying fates was the
first psychological task, alongside the material one of rebuilding the
country. Inevitably, this presented a test of our human strength to
recognize the burdens of others, to help bear them over time, not to
forget them. It involved a test of our ability to work for peace, of our
readiness for reconciliation, both at home and abroad, an ability and a
readiness which not only others expected of us but which we, most of
all, demanded of ourselves.

We cannot commemorate the 8th of May without being conscious of the great effort required of our former enemies to set out on
the road of reconciliation with us. Can we really put ourselves in the

place of the relatives of the victims of the Warsaw ghetto or of the Lidice massacre? And how hard must it have been for a citizen of Rotterdam or London to support the rebuilding of our country, which had so recently bombed his own city. For that support assurance had gradually to grow that the Germans would not again try to use force to avenge a defeat.

In our country, the biggest sacrifice was demanded of those who had been driven out of their homeland. They were to experience bitter suffering and grave injustice long after the 8th of May. Those of us born here in the West often lack the imagination or the heart necessary to grasp the meaning of their harsh fate.

But soon there were great signs of readiness to help. Many millions of refugees and expellees were taken in. Over the years they were able to strike new roots. Their children and grandchildren have, in many different ways, formed an attachment to the culture and to the love of homeland of their ancestors. That is good, since it is a great treasure in their lives. But they themselves have found a new homeland, where they are growing up with youth of their own age and growing together with them, speaking their dialects and sharing their customs. Their young lives constitute proof of their ability to be at peace with themselves. Their grandparents or parents were once driven out; they themselves, however, are now at home.

Very early, and in exemplary fashion, the expellees identified themselves with the renunciation of force. This was no transitory declaration in the early stages of powerlessness but a commitment which has retained its validity. Renouncing the use of force means allowing trust to grow on all sides, trust that a Germany which has regained its strength remains bound by this commitment.

The expellees' own former homeland has, meanwhile, become a new homeland for others. In many of the old cemeteries in Eastern Europe you will today find more Polish than German graves. The compulsory migration of millions of Germans to the West was followed by the migration of millions of Poles and, in their wake, millions of Russians. These are all people who were not asked if they wished to move, people who also suffered injustice, who became defenseless objects of political events and to whom no balancing off of injustices and no comparing of claims can make up for what was done to them.

Renunciation of force today means giving these peoples a lasting, politically uncontested security for their future in the place where fate drove them after the 8th of May, and where they have been living in the decades since. It means placing the precept of understanding above conflicting legal claims. That is the real, the human, contribution to a peaceful order in Europe which we can provide.

The new beginning in Europe after 1945 has brought both victory and defeat for the ideals of freedom and self-determination. It is up to us to seize the opportunity to have done with a long period of European history in which peace seemed conceivable and sure only as a result of each country's own supremacy, and in which peace meant a period of preparation for the next war.

The peoples of Europe love their homelands. The Germans are no different. Who could trust a people's love of peace if it were capable of forgetting its homeland? No, love of peace manifests itself precisely in one's not forgetting one's homeland and for that very reason being resolved to do everything in one's power to live together with others in peace forever. An expellee's love for his homeland is no revanchism.

VI

The last war aroused a desire for peace in the hearts of men more strongly than in times past. The work of the churches in promoting reconciliation met with a tremendous response. There are many examples of how young people are working for understanding. I think of *"Aktion Sühnezeichen,"* a campaign in which young people are active for atonement in Auschwitz and in Israel. Recently, the town of Kleve, on the lower Rhine, received loaves of bread from Polish towns as a token of reconciliation and fellowship. The town council sent one of those loaves to a teacher in England because he had discarded his anonymity and written to say that as a member of a bomber crew during the war he had destroyed churches and homes in Kleve and wanted a sign of reconciliation. In seeking peace it is a tremendous help if, instead of waiting for the other to come to us, we go to him, as this man did.

VII

In its consequences, the war brought old enemies closer together, on a human basis and also politically. As early as 1946, the American Secretary of State, James F. Byrnes, appealed in his memorable Stuttgart address for understanding in Europe and for assistance to the German nation on its path to a free and peaceable future. Innumerable Americans assisted us Germans, the conquered, with their own private funds to heal the wounds of war. Thanks to the vision of the Frenchman Jean Monnet and Robert Schuman and of Germans such as Konrad Adenauer, the traditional enmity between French and Germans was buried forever.

A new will and energy to reconstruct Germany surged through the country. Many an old trench was filled in, religious differences and social tensions were defused. People set to work in a spirit of partnership.

There was no "zero hour," but we had the opportunity to make a fresh start. We have used this opportunity as well as we could.

We have replaced servitude with democratic freedom.

Four years after the end of the war, on May 8, 1949, the Parliamentary Council adopted our Basic Law. Transcending party differences, the democrats who were members of the Council gave their answer to war and tyranny in Article 1 of our Constitution: "The German people acknowledge inviolable and inalienable human rights as the foundation of every community, of peace, and of justice in the world." This further significance of the 8th of May should also be remembered today.

The Federal Republic of Germany has become a state that is respected worldwide. It is one of the highly developed industrial countries in the world. It knows that its economic strength commits it to share responsiblity in the struggle against hunger and need in the world and for social accommodation among nations. For forty years we have been living in peace and freedom, a condition to which we, through our policy among the free nations of the Atlantic Alliance and the European Community, have contributed greatly.

Never have the liberties of the citizen enjoyed better protection on German soil than they do today. A comprehensive social welfare net which can stand comparison with that of any other nation ensures the people's fundamentals of life. Whereas at the end of the war many Germans tried to hide their passport or to exchange it for another, German citizenship today is a highly valued right.

We certainly have no reason to be arrogant and self-righteous. But we may look back with gratitude on the development of these forty years, when we make use of our historical memory as a guideline for our conduct in the present and for the unsolved tasks that await us.

- If we remember that the deranged were put to death in the Third Reich, we will regard the care of people with psychiatric disorders as our own responsibility.
- If we remember how people who were persecuted on grounds of race, religion, and politics and threatened with certain death often stood before the closed frontiers of other countries, we will not close our doors today on those who are really persecuted and seek protection with us.
- If we reflect on the persecution of free thought during the dictatorship, we will protect the freedom of every thought and every criticism, however much they may be directed against us ourselves.
- Whoever renders a judgment on the conditions in the Middle East should think of the fate to which Germans condemned their fellow human beings who were Jewish, a fate that led to

the establishment of the state of Israel under conditions which still continue to burden people in that region today.

· If we think of what our eastern neighbors had to suffer during the war, we will find it easier to understand that accommodation and peaceful neighborly relations with these countries remain central tasks of German foreign policy. It is important that both sides remain mindful of the past and that both respect each other. They have every reason to do so—for reasons of humanity, of culture, and finally also for reasons of history.

Mikhail Gorbachev, general secretary of the Soviet Communist Party, has declared that it is not the intention of the Soviet leaders to stir up anti-German feelings on the occasion of the fortieth anniversary of the end of the war. The Soviet Union, he said, is committed to friendship between nations. Even if we have doubts about the Soviets' contribution to understanding between East and West, and about their respect for human rights in all parts of Europe, we must not ignore this signal from Moscow. We wish friendship with the peoples of the Soviet Union.

VIII

Forty years after the end of the war, the German nation remains divided.

At a commemorative service in the Church of the Holy Cross in Dresden in February this year, Bishop Hempel said: "It is a burden and a scourge that two German states have emerged with their harsh border. The very multitude of borders is a burden and a curse. Weapons are a burden."

Recently, in Baltimore, in the United States, an exhibition on "Jews in Germany" was opened. The ambassadors of both German states accepted the invitation to attend. The host, the president of the Johns Hopkins University, welcomed them. He pointed out that all

Germans stand on the ground of the same historical development. A common past is a bond that links them. Such a bond, he said, could be a joy or a problem, but it was always a source of hope.

We Germans are one people and one nation. We feel that we belong together because we have lived through the same past.

We also experienced the 8th of May, 1945 as part of the common fate of our people, a fate which unites us. We feel bound together in our will for peace. Peace and good-neighborly relations with all countries should radiate from the soil of both German states. And others too should not let this soil become a source of danger to peace.

The people of Germany in common want a peace that encompasses justice and human rights for all peoples, including our own. No Europe of walls can make peace with itself across its frontiers but only a continent which removes from those frontiers that which divides. That indeed is precisely what the end of World War II recalls to our minds. We are confident that the 8th of May will not remain the last date in our history that is binding upon all Germans.

IX

Many young people have in recent months asked themselves and us too why such lively discussions about the past have arisen forty years after the end of the war. Why are such discussions livelier now than they were twenty-five or thirty years ago? What is the inner necessity for this?

It is not easy to answer such questions. But we should not seek the reasons primarily in external influences, although there have doubtless also been such influences.

In the life span of men and destiny of nations, forty years play a great role. Permit me at this point to return again to the Old Testament, which contains deep insights for everyone, irrespective of his faith. There, forty years frequently play a recurring and essential role. The Israelites were to remain in the desert for forty years before a new stage in their history began with their arrival in the Promised Land. Forty years were required for complete transfer of responsibility from one generation to another. Elsewhere too (in the Book of Judges), it is described how often the memory of assistance received and rescue experienced lasted only for forty years. When that memory faded, tranquility was at an end.

Forty years always constitutes a significant time span. That passage of time has an effect on human consciousness, whether in the form of an end to a dark period that brings confidence in a new and good future or in the form of a danger that the past might be forgotten and of a warning of the consequences should that happen.

In our country, a new generation has grown into political responsibility. Our young people are not responsible for what happened then. But they are responsible for what comes of it in our history.

We, of the older generation, owe to young people not the fulfillment of dreams but honesty. We must help younger people understand why it is vital to keep the memory alive. We want to help them to accept historical truth soberly, without one-sidedness, without taking refuge in utopian doctrines of salvation, but also without moral arrogance.

From our own history we learn what man is capable of. That is why we must not imagine that we have become different and better. There does not exist a moral perfection that is achieved once and for all—neither in the case of an individual nor of a country! We have learned as human beings, and as human beings we remain endangered. But we also have the strength to overcome danger again and yet again.

Hitler's habitual tendency was to foment prejudices, enmities, and hatred.

What is asked of young people today is this: do not let yourselves be driven into enmity and hatred of others, of Russians or Americans, of Jews or Turks, of those who call themselves "alternatives" or of conservatives, of blacks or whites.

Learn to live with one another, not against one another.

Let us democratically elected politicians take this to heart and constitute an example.

Let us honor freedom.

Let us work for peace.

Let us cleave to the rule of law.

Let us be true to our own standards of justice.

"THE MARSHALL PLAN"
Speech at Harvard University Commencement
Cambridge, Massachusetts, June 11, 1987

I

Being invited to speak at Harvard's commencement, and in honor of George Marshall, is an accolade I would never have dreamed of attaining.

Harvard is unrivaled in the world as a magnet for the best talents from all continents, and George Marshall has become a symbol of the virtues that have taught us to admire, and indeed to love, the United States.

Thus, to address you as a voice from Europe is a high distinction and a welcome challenge in these critical times.

This unique university has already inspired many a European. For instance, the Prince of Wales delivered a very impressive speech here last year. On behalf of his own university in Britain, he greeted Cambridge from Cambridge. Three cheers for the little difference between the two, if I may say so. Since I studied not only in Germany but also at Oxford, I hardly need to explain why Cambridge on the Charles River is the only university city bearing this name which my self-esteem should allow me to set foot in.

Generations of young people have left Harvard for all corners of the globe. Through their high standards, sense of responsibility, and dedicaton, they have helped people throughout the world to cope with the challenges they faced. With all my heart I wish everyone who is graduating today and thus stepping over a major threshold in his or her life happiness and fulfillment, with the memory of the Harvard experience serving as a challenge and an encouragement. You have every reason to be proud and to have a sense of commitment because you come from this great university.

II

Here, on commencement day in June 1947, George Marshall addressed Harvard graduates and alumni, America, and the world. His speech has gone down in the history of the modern world. How did it come about? Let us try to picture the situation then.

Two disastrous world wars lay behind us. America had been decisive in both of them.

At the end of the Second World War, Europe lay in ruins. Unimaginable human pain, injustice, and death had left their imprint. Millions of Jews had become the victims of an unprecedented crime. The Poles, the Russians—and the Germans too—were deeply suffering, as were other nations. Though there were winners and losers at the end of the war, they all shared a terrible burden. Europe was devastated and exhausted.

In this situation, we young people who had experienced the war and miraculously survived it set about building a new life. This was a bitter and difficult challenge. What we sought most of all were ethical fundamentals. We had witnessed what happens when racist madness, terror, and violence disfigure the human countenance. We had learned that freedom and human dignity are jeopardized whenever we fail to stand up for these ideals.

We had discovered that man cannot live by bread alone. But that was just one side of the coin; for without bread man also cannot survive. "First food, then morals," as Brecht said in "The Threepenny Opera."

Misery prevailed in Europe: expulsion, homelessness, hunger, no heating, no power, no production, no material resources, no prospects, little hope.

It was in this situation that George Marshall announced his program. He proclaimed it without solemnity, rather dryly and soberly. His plan is unparalleled in the history of world powers in generosity, selflessness, and vision.

Outstanding Americans helped to shape it: Dean Acheson, William Clayton, George Kennan, Charles Bohlen, to name but a few. It was the work of a farsighted, highly responsible American administration. It called upon Europe to revive its political and social life and regain its share of political responsibility—with the decisive material assistance being provided by the Americans.

The plan was generous: it included everyone, among them the enemies defeated in the recent war, not least of all us Germans. It was addressed to the whole of Europe, including the East. As Marshall put it, it was "directed not against any country or any doctrine."

The plan was selfless: the assistance was provided with no political strings. The recipients themselves were free to decide on the distribution and utilization.

The plan was visionary, as the plans of great victors seldom are. Victors tend to carry on with their war objectives even in peacetime. They seek to ensure that defeated adversaries or weakened partners remain dependent. The happiest times in history, however, have occurred whenever victors assisted all former belligerents to recover and helped the conquered to regain their self-esteem. In this respect, the Marshall Plan was a standard that has never been matched.

America was at that time materially far superior to all other nations. But it did not misuse its superiority by moral arrogance or political coercion. It did not seek to maintain dependence. Instead, the aim of the United States was to restore the confidence of the Europeans in their own strength, in their own political future.

The Marshall Plan bears testimony to the ability of a great and free nation to define its own legitimate interests in the light of a truly historical perspective and to act in accordance with basic, ethical principles. America gave expression to its own dignity by respecting the dignity of other people.

III

George Marshall added to his printed speech a handwritten statement to which he attached special importance: "The whole world of the future hangs on a proper judgment."

How true this is, and how difficult it is to act accordingly day after day!

Marshall was not an ideologist, but a realist. He was all too familiar with the temptation of nations to adhere to mutual prejudices, instead of seriously trying to understand others. He knew that prejudices generate violent emotions. The outcome is fear, confrontation or crusades. In history, this has proved dangerous time and again. We are facing similar dangers today. Can George Marshall's guidelines help us to cope with them?

First of all, we must soberly anaylze our situation. What has become of the Marshall Plan in these forty years? What has been achieved? What is still unfinished? What is our task today?

The first answer is quite clear: The Marshall Plan produced great, decisive developments. It laid foundations for new life in Europe. The nations that benefited from it are free and sovereign. They experienced an unprecedented recovery.

As intended by Marshall, this recovery was due no less to their own hard work than to the enormous material assistance provided by America. The Marshall Plan is the most successful example to date of a policy of help to self-help.

The plan simultaneously acted as a trigger for cooperation and growing unity. It gave rise to the Organization for Economic Cooperation and Development (OECD). The European Community would be inconceivable without it. It focused attention on global tasks; worldwide forms of cooperation, such as the International Monetary Fund, are the product of its economic momentum. The Marshall Plan is, and will remain, the most fundamental achievement of the Western world in postwar history.

The plan also gave decisive impetus to transatlantic partnership. George Marshall was not only concerned with practical cooperation between America and Europe. His thoughts were deeply rooted in the common stock of ideas of Europeans and Americans. These include universal human rights, cultural openness among nations, free world trade. Such common values and goals, not missiles, have given the North Atlantic Alliance its identity and permanence.

IV

The "proper judgment" that Marshall demands of us also involves tackling many unresolved or new problems.

Though the alliance has worked well over the last four decades, there are mutual misgivings between Americans and Europeans. Many Americans regard us Europeans, not only as strong economic rivals, but as affluent egotists who constantly criticize America without being able or willing to think in global dimensions or to bear our fair share of our burdens of political responsibility. They view us as wavering partners with a provincial outlook.

Seen from the other direction, Europeans believe that their American partners are subject to erratic confusion: Americans on the one hand claim an often rather unilateral leadership role in the world, while at the same time maintaining an inward-looking mentality. Many feel that the Americans are living beyond their means. They regard the huge deficits in the United States budget and trade balance as imposing a burden on the United States and on others as well. They point out that the Americans produce less than they consume and save less than most other peoples, but as the world's richest nation draws on a disproportionately large share of the world's savings to offset this deficit.

I am neither able nor willing to render judgment on the merits of such allegations. More important, in my view, is the perception that our societies have fairly similar weaknesses. Our democracies function well, but they do not educate us to pay attention to the problems of other countries, although our own destiny depends on their destiny. On the contrary, people here and in Europe have learned primarily to organize their own interests, to strengthen their domestic position and to increase their personal prosperity. We all try to safeguard our own claims and rights. Our societies are marked by tight networks of expectations and entitlements. Politics becomes more dependent, its scope narrower.

To be sure, politicians—my own guild—often reinforce this trend instead of opposing it. They are not a club of selfless saints to say the least. Their performance in resolving problems rarely matches their skill in fighting for power. Moreover, all too often they are captives of local and regional interests, tied down like Swift's Gulliver by countless little ropes and chains.

Thus, it seems as though provincialism has taken charge everywhere, as though all of us are dominated by a shrinking horizon and parochial view of the world.

V

Is this trend irreversible? Must we accept that democracy trains us better to exercise our rights than to recognize our duties? Have we really divorced freedom from responsibility? Has the ability to adopt an historical perspective died away? Do young graduates from Harvard or Heidelberg really want to enter a society of indifferent affluence which has difficulty specifying what its goals are, what it believes in, and what it is inspired by?

I think not. A new generation will follow its own path. It will select its involvement itself. It will recognize its own tasks and new opportunities.

Two challenges stand out today. The first concerns the Third World. George Marshall spoke out against "hunger, poverty, desperation, and chaos." His plan helped the recipient countries in Europe to overcome their need. But in large parts of the world there is a completely different situation. Much of his speech has relevance today, if one replaces the word "Europe" by "Third World." America's thoughts and deeds for the benefit of Europe were immensely generous. However, many developing countries see precisely in the prosperity and current practices of America and Europe one of the main causes of their own poverty.

Do we really understand the impact of our trading and financial system on those countries? Are we, the rich countries, ready to stop damaging their export opportunities by forcing our agricultural surpluses upon their export markets at subsidized prices? Have we not all too often misinterpreted the social struggle of those nations primarily as a danger for our own security? How long will we continue to seek and support military solutions there? When will the East and the West put an end to the wretched "zero-sum game" of their proxy wars on the territory of third countries?

This brings me to the second challenge of our time, a matter particularly close to our hearts as Europeans and Germans: to East-West relations.

The purpose of the Marshall Plan was to assist and unite all of Europe. At the time, Poland, Hungary, and Czechoslovakia in particular wanted to participate. Soviet Foreign Minister Molotov had already started negotiations with his Western European counterparts. But they failed. Stalin distrusted the American offer, expecting a weak Europe to be more useful for his own designs. As a result, the division of Europe grew worse. Today, the continent is divided into two seemingly irreconcilable systems, into two blocs which still maintain the world's largest arsenals.

Must the Marshall Plan, which was never intended to create such opposing blocs, remain a torso? Are we satisfied that fate has been kind to us Westerners alone? Do the Europeans accept the division as an immutable destiny?

No, the situation is quite different. Europe is politically divided, but is not and will never be divided in spirit. We have not only a common history based on closely related national cultures: what links us is the common fate of a future on a small continent. After a period of resignation, there is again a growing awareness among Europeans in East and West that they belong together. The people in the Warsaw Pact countries have a more difficult path to travel than we. An entire generation has had to live in forced isolation. But they have never ceased to be Europeans. Theirs is the greater contribution towards keeping the spirit of a united Europe alive.

Among Western Europeans there is a growing perception that we harm ourselves if we try to convince ourselves that the East does not concern us. We know, as Václav Havel put it, "how ambivalent our Western happiness would be if it were obtained permanently at the expense of Eastern misery."

For you here in America it may be difficult to appreciate such European feelings. Many of you may perhaps even regard this as a source of estrangement between America and Europe. You may feel that one can only opt either for transatlantic partnership or for the whole, undivided Europe.

Yet what is the essence of our partnership? It is the concept of freedom. We protect it as our right. We can succeed in that only if we understand freedom as inseparable from responsibility. We would not only be disloyal to our own ideals, but would in fact destroy them, if we were to claim freedom only for ourselves and not champion it for others.

Anyone of you who visits Berlin will appreciate what I mean. For twenty-six years now, a Wall has sliced through the middle of the city. It separates people who belong to the same family, are of the same spirit, have the same hopes, breathe the same air, face the same future. But it has failed in its true purpose: it has not made people become resigned to division. On the contrary, this dead structure is a vital and daily reminder of what it was intended to make us forget: our feeling of belonging together. Intended to be a symbol of the division between the political systems, Berlin has increasingly become a symbol of unity, a manifestation of people's determination not to be separated.

Many neighbors and friends of Germany are not overly pleased when the unsettled German question is broached. But anyone who looks at the walled-off Brandenburg Gate in the heart of Berlin, as I shall do with your president tomorrow, will feel in his own heart what we mean: as long as that gate remains closed, the German question remains open.

This is not tantamount to any neutralistic yearning or nationalistic nostalgia. It is a very simple human feeling of all Europeans. We do not want new conflicts about frontiers. We have learned painful lessons from history. But frontiers should lose their divisive nature for people. This is the crux of the open question for all Europeans, a question of human rights and human dignity for everyone, not just for one nation or solely for the West.

VI

It will not serve to be bull-headed. Grand declarations and ideological crusades do not help either. What we need is a consistent policy of East-West understanding.

Of course understanding does not mean approval of the other system. Faith healing is no policy. Opposing convictions and divergent interests will persist. Nor must we neglect our security. Those who can no longer defend themselves will invariably fail politically.

But, politics does not serve defense, defense serves politics. For all too long, East-West relations were dominated by mere security concepts. It seemed as though deterrence was the only language in which East and West could communicate with one another.

In actual fact, security itself necessitates a policy of confidence-building interdependence. It was the policy of a Harvard professor, Henry Kissinger, whose SALT negotiations first drew the inescapable conclusion that in an era of nuclear, biological, and chemical weapons, security could no longer be ensured against each other but only with each other.

That was the first necessary step toward a cooperation that opens the systems up. Further steps have to follow. We must find "currencies" other than just military power for dealing with one another.

At present, the Soviet Union is making great effort to reform its economic and political structure. To this end, it seeks to widen cooperation with other countries. Of course, the Soviet Union is proceeding this way for its own advantage and not to do us a favor. At the same time, Moscow may very well have a genuine interest in finding new "currencies" in communication with us.

Is this a disadvantage for us? The deficiencies that the Soviet Union is trying to correct arise from a closed system providing no incentives, no participation in decision-making, no free flow of information. The people are the losers, not only in material terms. If there is a chance now for further opening steps, is this a risk for us? Should we respond with mistrust and rejection, renewed containment, and confrontation?

The Soviet Union is neither a mere public relations system founded exclusively on ideology nor a blindly obsessed world revolutionary. At the top of the East-West agenda is not a final apocalyptic struggle between good and evil, but a growing number of problems which neither East nor West can solve on its own: the population explosion and hunger in the world, the progressive destruction of nature, ensuring energy supplies, coping with the ethical aspects of scientific and technological progress, and above all ensuring peaceful relations between neighbors.

In the East-West context today we do not have to provide loans and grants as in Marshall's time, but cooperation of a new quality. We should recall Senator Fulbright, who decisively advanced the concept of international, educational exchange. This is the way to replace prejudice with knowledge. Science requires openness. Business requires vocational and management training. Telecommunication promotes technology and widens people's horizons. The greatest friend of mutual understanding is culture, the greatest enemy is isolation.

It is in these areas that we need an East-West transfer in both directions. The concept of coexistence as class struggle is antiquated and reactionary. Coexistence must imply the capacity to settle conflicts by political means without either side claiming to possess the absolute truth.

Disarmament is important. But history teaches us that usually it is not disarmament that leads to peace, but peaceful cooperation that leads to less mistrust, less fear, and then to disarmament.

Today, we have a truly historic opportunity to engage in cooperation that leads to greater openness and responsibility between the two political systems. We must make vigorous and responsible use of this opportunity. It is mainly the mandate for us, the Europeans. But we want to and must do it together with you, with our American friends.

VII

It is not sufficient to wait and see in which direction the "new thinking" in Moscow moves. New thinking is, first and foremost, a challenge to ourselves. In this George Marshall set us an example.

We should complete what he was prevented from finishing. Fifteen years ago my country set up the German Marshall Fund of the United States as a token of gratitude for the American assistance given to us. This fund is intended as a transatlantic institution serving to meet the challenges of our time. Would it not be in line with the spirit of George Marshall to include prominently in the foundation's projects those countries which were once prevented from participation in the Marshall Plan?

Fresh thinking has always been a characteristic of Harvard. Here, there is freedom and openness in research, interdisciplinary horizons, the concept of teamwork, stimuli for talent, and the vital force of curiosity.

To be sure, Harvard is not an ideal world, but I know hardly any other place on earth where there is more tolerance, where diversity is so strongly encouraged, where talent is not suppressed for fear of competition but is fostered, and where foreigners are not just tolerated but perceived as enrichments to the community.

The Harvard student is encouraged to make intelligent use of freedom, to practice "mature citizenship," as Harvard's president in George Marshall's time, James B. Conant, put it. We in Germany remember him with great respect because he, as America's representative to our country, practiced in exemplary fashion what he had been teaching at his university.

Harvard's motto, "Veritas," is not a claim to a monopoly on truth. It means seeking truth together with other people who are seeking it also, even if they set out from entirely different points of departure. "Veritas" in Harvard has a different meaning than truth in Moscow, the *Pravda*. It is all the more necessary to strive for communication and exchange. This is one of the great tasks for the young generation of our time.

For that we need above all the strength to have historical perspective. In the end, if we resist prejudice and emotion it is not systems and doctrines that will prevail, but people with their human aspirations.

What I would welcome from the bottom of my heart is a new thinking from the "global village" on the Charles River. You have been educated and qualified for this purpose. You owe that to the world. Let me couch my request in the words of Senator Fulbright: "We must learn to conduct international relations with patience, tolerance, openness of mind, and, most of all, with a sense of history. These are qualities of educated men. The cultivation of these qualities is the ultimate challenge to international education."

Harvard itself is part of the message which George Marshall gave the world forty years ago. We are, all of us, called upon to live up to his legacy, and, by meeting the challenges of our time, to fulfill it anew.

Index